Sustainable Sport Management

RUNNING AN ENVIRONMENTALLY, SOCIALLY AND ECONOMICALLY RESPONSIBLE ORGANIZATION

UNEP

David Chernushenko
with Anna van der Kamp and David Stubbs

Chernushenko, David
    Sustainable sport management: running an environmentally, socially and economically
    responsible organization.

Includes bibliographical references and index.
ISBN 92-807-2072-4

David Chernushenko
Green & Gold Inc.
99 Seneca Street,
Ottawa, Ontario K1S 4X8 Canada
www.greengold.on.ca

United Nations Environment Programme
P.O. Box 30552
Nairobi, Kenya
www.unep.org

Every effort has been made to reduce the environmental impact of this book in its research, production and distribution. This book is printed in Canada using vegetable-based inks on acid-free recycled paper.

Notice:

Neither the authors, the publishers or the sponsors of this publication assume any liability with respect to the use of any information, apparatus, method or process described in this book. It remains the responsibility of the user to ensure that all regulatory and statutory requirements are met.

Good-faith efforts have been made to obtain permission to quote from all publications cited in this book.

Book and cover design by Kate Missen, Viriditas design

Foreword

Klaus Töpfer
Executive Director,
United Nations Environment Programme

I am very pleased to give UNEP's support to this publication as it so aptly follows in the footsteps of *Greening Our Games* and because it provides such relevant information on the relationship between sport and the environment.

Environmental impact and lifecycle assessment is becoming a major component of the development of facilities for major sports events and the manufacturing of sport goods globally. The 1994 Winter Olympic Games in Lillehammer, Norway transformed the basis on which mega-sport events are assessed. It ensured that future sports events would be required to include environmental measures as part of their basic mandate. This was followed by the signing of a Cooperative Agreement between the United Nations Environment Programme (UNEP) and the International Olympic Committee (IOC). Many worthwhile and progressive steps have been achieved since then.

First, the Olympic Movement included the environment as a third dimension to Olympism, in addition to sport and culture. A Sport and Environment Commission was created within the IOC to advise the IOC Executive Board on policies necessary for environmental protection and for the constant monitoring of progress in implementing environmental commitments by host cities of Olympic Games.

Second, in 1999, an Agenda 21 for Sport and Environment was developed and adopted by the IOC with the help of UNEP. A UNEP/IOC Working Group was established to promote implementation of the Agenda, which will have a strong bearing on the way future Games of the IOC are organized.

Third, the Sydney Olympic Games ushered in a new era in green Games. Sydney's extensive environmental goals achieved new standards in the organization of mega-sporting events and demonstrated that we can be environmentally responsible while undertaking such huge projects.

Both Lillehammer and Sydney have been awarded the UNEP Global 500 Award for their outstanding environmental achievements.

What is the connection between sport and environment?

Like any individual or corporation, the action of an athlete or sport association or a sports equipment manufacturer has an effect on the surrounding environment. While the nature of these activities, when considered separately may not be harmful, their cumulative impact on the environment is both significant and wide-ranging. Each time a stadium is constructed, every time a golf course is developed, an Olympic venue constructed, a sizeable footprint is left on the planet, from soil erosion to species displacement, loss of wetlands, waste generation or, in some circumstances, atmospheric pollution.

Sport requires the actors to be healthy. Only a healthy environment can ensure the health of our athletes and ensure that we continue to enjoy the sport events that most of us are so passionate about.

By the very nature of their activities, athletes are closer to nature. Many sport activities are carried out outdoors and expose the athletes to a multiplicity of environmental risks. What impact will the thinning of the ozone layer have on athletes' performance? Will it mean wearing hats and the repeated application of sunblocks? Or will it lead to higher incidences of skin cancer and cataracts? What will become of the millions of children in developing countries who start their sport careers in the streets of their communities but have the potential of becoming leading sportsmen and women? As much as the focus for sportsmen and women is on their activities, knowledge of environmental problems can encourage them to promote environmental issues.

The sporting goods industry is growing extensively and is a leading industry in the world. Both athletes and non-athletes drive the increasing demand for sporting goods. These goods are developed using resources from the already fragile ecosystem. The need for alternative ways of meeting the increasing demand for sporting goods is critical. Recycling and reusing of sporting goods and other materials could help reduce the impact on the environment. The development of less resource intensive goods for athletes could also contribute to relieving the burden on the environment.

Sport, on the other hand, is the ultimate spectacle. Billions of people are passionate about one form of sport or another and the opportunity for promoting environmental awareness and inspiring people to take action is nearly unlimited. Millions of people look up to successful sportsmen and women as their role models. The environmental attitudes of young people can be shaped by these role models. We in UNEP see sport as a fundamental outreach tool to the masses.

UNEP, within the context of its good cooperation with the IOC, values the potential of the Olympic Games to attract the masses but UNEP's interest goes beyond to all kinds of sports, such as golf and football. We would like to work with athletes and federations of all sporting disciplines to promote environmental issues.

The underlying message in *Sustainable Sport Management* is that by organizing sports events, operating facilities, making products and providing sports services in a manner that is less harmful to the environment, sports organizations not only stand to save money, but also to conserve the environment for future generations and for the good of sport which we are all so passionate about.

Acknowledgments

We would like to express our gratitude to the many people and organizations that have contributed their ideas, time and resources to this book. It is a pleasure to be involved in a "movement" that has engendered such a stimulating and rewarding atmosphere of sharing.

We wish to acknowledge and thank the book's principal sponsor, the United Nations Environment Programme, an organization whose dedicated members continue to perform so much valuable work, often in anonymity and with limited budgets.

We also wish to thank the Committed to Green Foundation for its important contribution of material and funding to this project.

Preface

In the first book to fully address the relationship between sport and the environment — *Greening Our Games: Running Sports Events and Facilities that Won't Cost the Earth* (Chernushenko, 1994) — the sporting world was introduced to concepts such as "sustainable development", "eco-efficiency", a "green games" ethic, and principles of "sustainable sport". These ideas and terms were at the time foreign to most sports people — and still are to many.

But times are changing, and the scope of sports management is growing. We now hear regularly from decision-makers who have come to understand why they should adopt more sustainable practices. And more and more organizations are taking steps, some tentative and others ambitious, toward greater responsibility and sustainability.

A growing number of sport governing bodies have been introducing environmental guidelines, codes of conduct and criteria for prospective event hosts. Most major golf bodies such as the USGA and in Europe the Royal and Ancient Golf Club of St. Andrews, European Golf Association and PGA European Tour, have been particularly active. Ski resort operators, mountain biking groups, sports facility architects, parks and recreation departments and major sporting goods manufacturers like Nike, Mizuno and Patagonia are among the multitude of longstanding or recent proponents of greater sustainability.

These are just some examples of the steady groundswell of sports and recreation organizations that have begun to understand why environmental leadership is important, and are busy grappling with how to do it. While each may have a different primary motivation for doing so — some in response to public pressure or regulatory requirements, some in pursuit of economic savings, and still others working to capture new customers, sponsors or business opportunities — they have all understood that there is important work to be done. They are all dealing with substantial issues and pursuing real and substantial benefits. Most are also aware that they must do so in a credible way and be seen to be doing it for more than just public relations.

Clearly the context for a sequel to *Greening Our Games* has shifted enormously since 1994. While there is still a great deal of work to be done in setting out the case for "sustainable sport" and in encouraging sports leaders to take up the challenge, the greater demand is now for resources that walk them through the "how" more than the "why."

A few organizations have progressed so far that they now serve as role models, some even as teachers. They are the exception, however. Most readers of this book will be sports and recreation managers and decision-makers seeking additional guidance and resource materials. This book is geared towards that audience.

But there is much that we can learn from the role models and pioneers. By far the strongest such "role model" can be found in the environmental initiatives of the Sydney 2000 Olympic Games. The Sydney Olympics were widely acclaimed for the sporting excellence of the competitors, for planning that resulted in superb facilities and near-flawless logistics and operations, and for the passion and dedication exhibited by the host city and its tens of thousands of helpful volunteers. Another aspect of the Games less publicized by the world's media, was equally worthy of praise: the remarkable accomplishments of Sydney 2000 in fulfilling its commitment to staging a more environmentally responsible – a more sustainable – Summer Olympics.

In bidding to host the 2000 Olympics, the Sydney bid organization made a commitment that was considered at the time to be both daring and forward-looking. The Sydney team included in its bid a document that constituted a formal undertaking to deliver to the world not only a first-class sporting event, but one that would set a new global standard for environmental and social leadership, without breaking the bank. *The Environmental Guidelines for the Summer Olympic Games* was a far-reaching set of commitments covering every major environmental concern and touching every aspect of staging the Games. The Environmental Guidelines sought to integrate the approach of "sustainable development" into all planning and decision-making; to make good environmental management a foundation of all Sydney 2000 preparations, not just an after-thought.

Over the seven years of preparations, Sydney organizers set about meeting those commitments, under the watchful eyes of the public, the media, the International Olympic Committee (IOC), various interest groups in Australia and overseas, a number of regulatory agencies, and even an official environmental reviewer – the Earth Council -- contracted to evaluate progress towards environmental commitments.

And how did Sydney 2000 do? Most observers agree that Sydney 2000 performed admirably, achieving much of what had been promised while falling noticeably short in only a handful of areas. The Earth Council, in its January 2001 Final Review of the Olympic Co-ordination Authority (OCA), awarded an average score of 8.6 out of 10, in comparing the OCA's performance with its public commitments. Even Greenpeace, perhaps Sydney 2000's harshest critic, gave a 6 out of 10, worthy of a "bronze medal". With no standardised baseline against which to compare Sydney 2000, any such scores should be seen as subjective and somewhat arbitrary. However, Sydney will now serve as a valuable baseline for evaluating the sustainability of future such projects.

More importantly, in the long run, than scores and words of praise, however, Sydney 2000 appears to have generated a legacy of greater sustainability. A legacy not just for sports events and facilities, and not just for Sydney and Australia; Sydney 2000 has shown that any facility, event, development project or organization, in any country, can adopt the concept and guiding principles of sustainable development, and integrate them into planning, designs and operations to achieve superior results. Sydney 2000 has effectively demonstrated to the world that the organization that pursues sustainability as a key mission can go beyond conventional expectations. It can build better buildings and infrastructure; reduce resource consumption and the need for waste disposal (cutting costs in the process); and protect employee and client health — better morale, higher staff retention and client loyalty. It can do all of this, and more, while becoming a more environmentally, socially and economically responsible organization.

Though the implications of Sydney's accomplishments extend into most sectors of society and the economy, our focus in this book is restricted to examining why and how the sports organization should and can aim to be more responsible — by becoming more sustainable. This book is for the most part a guide to managing sports organizations more sustainably. But it's a guidebook with a bias. That bias is proudly declared here, and is hopefully evident throughout the book:

We believe that sport and recreation organizations should be run more sustainably. We believe that sustainably-managed organizations will benefit enormously from taking this approach, all the while benefiting the community and the environment upon which they are in many ways dependent for their ongoing success.

The first section of this book sets out our basic thesis, that the sports "industry" — sports and recreation organizations, events, facilities, programs and equipment makers — can be managed more sustainably, for its own good, and for that of its community and indeed the planet.

Sport, while not the greatest environmental sinner on the planet, can cause environmental harm, ranging from the minor to the quite significant. At the same time, however, the practice of sport can be restricted or reduced in quality as a result of poor environmental conditions, whether caused by sport or more often by non-sport factors.

But harm caused by sport or to sport need not be inevitable. The tables can in fact be turned if sport managers and participants recognize and accept that their "duty" to act more responsibly is accompanied by an opportunity to positively influence the environmental conditions under which sport may be practised. Furthermore, the very high profile of sport and its icons might be used to positive effect by helping to improve environmental awareness and the daily practices of the hundreds of millions who are a part of this industry.

The focus of this book is on you the sports manager or decision maker. You may need several things: to be persuaded that adopting more sustainable practices is worth the effort; to be provided with the arguments that will help to persuade senior managers of this need; to have an understanding of the principal issues; and to be furnished with the elements of a game plan for introducing sustainable sport to your organization and situation.

This book aims to:

1. briefly describe the realities and the new pressures and demands on sports managers, with a particular focus on the environment, a growing area that is so closely linked to social and fiscal pressures, and one that has received inadequate attention to date;

2. define broadly a new approach to respond to these demands: sustainability;

3. introduce some specific tools and techniques for managing more sustainably; and

4. provide real examples and case studies of those organizations that have already set off down the path to sustainability.

Thankfully, unlike seven years ago, there is a host of resources to draw upon now. There are books, articles, videos and websites to assist you and experts to consult. We have tried to list as many as possible in the appropriate sections and in the appendices.

A book that advocates sustainability must by definition focus on its three elements: economic, social and environmental. One could approach sustainability from a social or economic perspective, demonstrating how by adopting more socially responsible or economically responsible practices, greater sustainability might be achieved. We, however, take the third approach: helping organizations to achieve sustainability through the pursuit of environmental responsibility, but always in parallel with economic and social objectives. Thus, a book that advocates and steers the reader toward good environmental management should ultimately help that reader to go beyond environmental benefit.

In this new field, we are all pioneers. But sport is about teamwork, and there are many invisible members of this sustainable sport team who have graciously shared their insight and experiences. We hope that you will catch this spirit. We also hope that you will perpetuate it by sharing what you learn with us, and the many others you may encounter.

David Chernushenko
Anna van der Kamp
David Stubbs

Contents

Part II — Building the Team: Inspiring and Involving Staff, Volunteers and Stakeholders

Part III — Facilities for Sport and Recreation: Designing, Building and Operating More Sustainably

Part IV — Planning and Operations: Major Operational and Service Issues for Events and Facilities

Part I
Making the Connection

Sport and the Triple Bottom Line

Sports exerts a growing influence on major areas of human activity, including the political, economic, social and cultural arenas. Its presence can also be felt in the realm of education and health. Sport has infiltrated the great social institutions of family, school, municipality and private enterprise, and it has also encroached upon all the major media to become one of the greatest social phenomena of the twentieth century.

—**Gaston Marcotte** and **Rene Larouche**

There is no more room on Earth to destroy nature for the sake of a mere game.

—**Gen Morita**, Global Anti-Golf Movement

Chapter

1

Why a New Approach to Sport Management?

The 21st Century sport organization is being faced with a host of new demands and restrictions: The owners/shareholders of private sport clubs and companies want to make money; Politicians and taxpayers don't want public sport and recreation facilities and organizations to lose money, and are steadily reducing any subsidies. Environmental harm is tolerated less and less by the public, and the regulators who act on its behalf. Good health and safety practices are expected, and the related cost of insurance and worker compensation schemes are rising. A sport organization's labor practices, including those of sub-contractors and suppliers, are under closer scrutiny.

The manager of the 21st Century must not only have an understanding of these pressures and demands and where they are coming from, he/she must have the tools to deal with them.

How does the manager respond to this wide range of demands? With a new approach — an approach that recognizes that the well-managed organization will be responsible and sustainably operated. Sustainable sport management will consist of responsible economic, social and environmental practices. The sustainable sport organization will integrate these three imperatives, not trade them off against each other. In doing so, it may be surprised to find a "virtuous loop" created, where one wise decision generates one or a series of other unintended, but positive consequences.

Sport is at a turning point. At the competitive level it is losing the few remaining vestiges of amateurism and becoming more and more an entertainment business, dominated by money and politics. Profit and prestige are the name of the game for athletes, coaches, governing bodies, professional franchises, facilities owners and host communities. In such a culture, the traditional ethic of sport — embodied by such guiding principles as fair play, teamwork, respect for others and humility — is of less and less relevance. As Lois Bryson (1990) argues, such an ethic may now be "antithetical" to sport's commercial and national interests.

At the non-competitive or at least less-competitive recreational level, an equally profound transformation is occurring. Opportunities for low-cost, participatory recreation, which flourished throughout most of this century, are now being curtailed. Budget cuts to many levels of government have been passed on to parks and recreation departments. Even where economies remain strong, the mantras of "small government" and "user pay" have often led to reduced public recreation opportunities. Yet while fewer people can afford to use facilities and participate in programs and events, spending on sport and leisure continues to grow and major new facilities are being built or refurbished at an unheard of rate.

In the allocation of funds for sport and recreation, both public and private, a dichotomy has emerged. The proportion of financial support available for smaller, participatory events and simple public facilities is dropping, whereas the percentage that goes to major events and larger, more sophisticated facilities has gone up. Municipalities seem to have little trouble finding money for new stadiums and arenas, used primarily by elite and professional athletes — almost all male — while at the same time pleading poverty when it comes to repairing bicycle paths or keeping open public parks and pools. Similarly, corporate sponsorship has shifted dramatically in favor of major events most likely to receive strong media coverage, to the detriment of local and regional events.

In many countries government officials are also being forced to re-evaluate how they fund the wide variety of sport disciplines. Realizing that they cannot provide adequate funding to between 50 and 100 sports and sport associations, they face the fundamental question of whether to fund sport according to performance or participation. Should the sports that win Olympic medals get the biggest share, or should the emphasis be on sports that have mass participation? Which is more important: public health and fitness or national prestige?

The environmental and social consequences of sport can vary significantly, according to the priorities set by those bodies, public or private, which provide funds. Will the emphasis be on profit and medals or on accessibility and participation? On large, modern, sophisticated facilities or on venues that stress affordability, functionality and appropriate scale? On uniformity and predictability or on diversity and respect for existing natural systems? Will we bring our economic and social models into synchronization with the natural systems that govern the planet and achieve some form of sustainability? Or will we continue to follow the unfettered growth model that denies the existence of limits to what we can take from nature and dump back into it? Today's sport industry must grapple with many such issues as other industries and public institutions have been forced to.

The point is not to spread ecological guilt but to draw the attention of those in the sporting community to the fact that their activities do have an environmental impact and that they have choices regarding the severity of that impact. They can choose to carry on as usual, or they can choose to understand the nature and degree of their impact on the environment as a prelude to taking responsibility for it.

Like society at large, the sport community finds itself at a turning point. With the benefit of hindsight, we can see increasingly clearly just how destructive certain practices, events and decisions have been for the natural environment and for sport itself. Sport is not conducted in a bubble, immune to the goings-on of the real world. Like any individual, organization or corporation, the actions of the athlete, sport association, professional team or equipment manufacturer have repercussions. For the natural environment, those repercussions have been more often negative and destructive than positive or restorative, even though sporting organizations are rarely major corporate polluters.

When you take a hard look at the institutions of sport you can hardly help but recognize a number of features that are not sustainable. To continue management per status quo, denying that sport has an environmental and social impact and ignoring the negative impact of "external" factors on sport practices, will incur two undesirable consequences. First, the bigger sport gets, the less healthy and rewarding the experience will be for future participants. Second, the image portrayed by sport and the example it sets will only encourage individuals, groups and other sectors to carry on with the old unsustainable ways, resulting in sport being forced to make do with an even more polluted and degraded environment.

That a better way exists is becoming abundantly clear. This new direction has been called sustainable sport, and it makes all sides winners, including communities, athletes, and the environment. Sport can be at the same time popular, profitable and socially and environmentally responsible. For this to be possible requires several elements:

◆ an understanding of and commitment to the goal of "sustainable sport;"

◆ guiding principles that lead to sport being more sustainable;

◆ working with people at all levels to promote sport that is good for the world community; and

◆ appropriate tools to assist with planning and the knowledgeable use of materials and technologies.

This book is intended to provide a foundation for all four of these elements. The first two are explored in part I; working with people is the subject of part II; finding the tools to help manage facilities and materials is the broad subject of part III; and part IV devotes special attention to sustainable management of events.

The Impact of Sport on the Environment

From the moment an athlete begins to use equipment, apparel or facilities, there is an "ecological footprint" — an impact on the natural environment.

The impact of a recreational runner may seem insignificant. As she is joined by others on the same footpaths, or begins to train on a running track, compete in neighborhood races, drive to participate in or watch remote events, purchase a greater variety of footwear and clothing, however, her footprint grows. Her choice to participate in sport is accompanied by a series of repercussions: from soil erosion to facilities construction, air pollution and waste generation.

Some Common Ways in which Sport Affects the Environment

Facilities:

- Development of fragile or scarce land types
- Soil erosion during construction
- Construction waste sent to landfill or incinerator
- Pollution from liquid spills (fuels, cleaners, solvents, etc.)
- Noise and light pollution
- Air and noise pollution from increased vehicle traffic
- Consumption of non-renewable resources (fuel, metals, etc.)
- Consumption of natural resources (water, wood, paper, etc.)
- Creation of greenhouse gases (electrical, fuel consumption)
- Ozone layer depletion (from refrigerants)
- Soil and water pollution from pesticide use

Events:

- Impacts from facility construction/ operation (see above)
- Consumption of non-renewable resources (fuel, metals, etc.)
- Consumption of natural resources (water, wood, etc.)
- Creation of greenhouse gases (electrical, transportation)
- Air and noise pollution from movement of people/goods
- Soil erosion and compaction by spectators
- Spectator waste sent to landfill, incinerator and sewage plant
- Paper consumption by media
- Waste generated from signs, banners, temporary booths, etc.

At the other end of the spectrum are sport's "big guns". Huge is the only one way to describe manufacturers like Adidas and Fischer; event organizers and promoters like Ogden; professional sport franchises like the Dallas Cowboys and Juventus; and events like the Olympics and the Tour de France. These organizations employ thousands, purchase and consume resources (some hazardous), produce millions of consumer products, use energy and water, generate solid and liquid waste, develop land and operate fleets of vehicles. Their ecological footprint is often big and deep.

But they are not the only ones. While it may not be immediately clear what Nike or the World Series has in common with a community half-marathon or a high school ski team, they have more in common than their participation in sport activities.

The evolution of sport, its commercialization and globalization means that these people and institutions have more in common than we might have thought — not least environmentally. In all but the poorest and most remote communities, sport participants, activities and facilities tend to have remarkable similarities. The young Taiwanese baseball player may use the same type of bat and ball as his major league hero. He wears a similar type of uniform, catches with the same make of glove, drinks the same drink and plays on the same type of field. Spectators at both levels drive to the game, drink their soft drinks in disposable cups and use the washrooms.

Principal Environmental Issues

Any sport facility or event will contribute in some way to the principal global and local environmental concerns. Standard facility and event management practices contribute regularly to energy consumption, air pollution, greenhouse gas emissions and waste disposal (both toxic and non-toxic), as well as to ozone layer depletion, habitat and biodiversity loss, soil erosion and water pollution. For example:

- Britain's national sport centres consume close to $1 million of energy per year, adding around five hundred thousand tons of carbon dioxide to the atmosphere.

- The typical American professional football/baseball game adds between 30,000 and 50,000 disposable cups to the local landfill.

- Canada's 2,300 ice arenas and 1,300 curling rinks consume more than one million MWh of electricity annually and leak ammonia and ozone-depleting coolants to the atmosphere.

- Community playing fields spread pesticides and herbicides and consume millions of litres of water each year.

- Most swimming pools use dangerous chlorine gas to treat bacteria and algae.

A Sample of Potential Environmental Impacts of Specific Sports

Golf:
- Development of valuable land (agricultural, rare habitat, etc.)
- Introduction of non-native species
- High water consumption
- Soil and water pollution from inappropriate use of pesticides and fertilizers
- Soil and water pollution from fuel and chemical spillages
- Noise from grounds-maintenance equipment

Alpine Skiing:
- Destruction of natural vegetation
- Disintegration and thinning of protective forests
- Soil compression
- Chemical pollution of soils from fuel spills
- Growing landslide, soil erosion and avalanche hazards
- Land clearing for infrastructure (parking, roads, hotels, etc.)
- Solid waste generation
- Noise disturbance
- Disruption of wildlife

Swimming:
- High water consumption
- Use of hazardous chemicals
- High energy consumption for water heating

Ice Hockey:
- High energy consumption for ice refrigeration and heating
- Use of ozone-depleting refrigerants

Soccer/Football:
- High water consumption
- Soil and water pollution from pesticide use
- Soil and water pollution from fuel and chemicals
- Noise from grounds maintenance equipment
- Energy consumption for field lighting

Our recreational practices consume natural resources and generate waste. In this way costs are incurred to the participant, facility or organization as well as to the planet. Sometimes these costs are direct and quantifiable. Other times they are indirect and non-quantifiable. While the direct costs are most easily identified and consequently reduced, it is the indirect financial costs, not to mention the less tangible social, cultural and ecological costs, which are most challenging to address; all the more so since the rewards for doing so, though significant, are less concrete and immediate.

The Longer-term and Global Threats to Sport

Any list of serious global environmental problems is certain to include climate change, overpopulation, deforestation, desertification, ozone-layer depletion, and species and habitat loss. Of these, three are already having an impact on the way we conduct sport: Climate change, habitat loss and ozone-layer depletion. We discuss the first two here; the impact of ultraviolet-B radiation exposure (as a result of ozone-layer depletion) is dealt with as a health impact in Chapter 2.

Climate Change

A global environmental issue certain to affect sport as we know it is climate change. While few scientists will venture to predict either the extent of climate change or the ways in which it will manifest itself in a given region, there is near-universal consensus that we can expect warming of anywhere from two to seven degrees Celsius, rising coastal water levels as a result of polar ice cap melting, and more frequent and severe storms. Though people in colder regions have quipped that a few degrees of warming wouldn't hurt them, recent studies have shown that if you are a ski resort or golf course operator, those few extra degrees might spell doom to your business.

The period since 1980 has been a particularly bad one for the ski industry in eastern North America and in Europe. Unusually warm winters have often meant not only that little snow fell on the resort areas, but temperatures were often not low enough to make snow artificially. Several studies of the anticipated impact of climate change on downhill and cross-country ski resorts paint a far-from-rosy future for these sports. In the case of golf and field sports played primarily on green turf, the droughts which are expected to accompany climate change will make even more intensive irrigation necessary at the same time as water tables are dropping. In the competition for scarce water resources, sport facilities may find themselves well down on any list of priority recipients. Golf resorts in the semi-arid and arid western U.S. are feeling this pressure or likely will soon, but even states like Massachusetts, some parts of Canada and Mediterranean countries grapple with water shortages and irate neighbors in the summer months.

Golf authorities have recently become concerned about the impacts of coastal erosion, one of the most visible consequences of climate changes. In February 2000, a special conference was held at St. Andrews on environmental topics, and the headline debate was on the subject of climate change (Royal and Ancient Golf Club, 2000).

Loss of Natural Habitat

The increasing development of the planet's remaining natural areas — forests, wetlands, prairie, coastlines and other green spaces — means that habitat in its original state is diminishing in size and quality. In addition, what little remains of these natural spaces tends to be in the more remote and uninviting corners of the planet. "Paving paradise to put up a parking lot" has several consequences for sport. First, those sports that rely on natural terrain for their authenticity, appeal, or challenge are running out of options for locales. How many untamed rivers are available for whitewater kayaking in Germany? Where in the more densely populated parts of Europe, North America or Japan can one go for a hike without running into structured facilities and crowds of other hikers? Where is the forest in Bulgaria whose air is unpolluted?

Second, the remoteness of most natural areas, since few have been preserved in the more populated regions of the planet, puts a de facto limitation on their availability for sport and recreational purposes. Third, the pressures on these remaining wild spaces, especially ones that are reasonably close to urban centers, has become so intense it is often inappropriate to subject them to further stress from humans seeking recreational enjoyment. And, fourth, the important function of natural spaces as a purifier of air and water has been vanishing along with habitat. For the athlete, that means the likelihood of finding idyllic conditions of clean air and water is getting progressively slimmer.

A New Management Approach

Changes to the sport industry create new challenges for sport managers at all levels. While sport management has traditionally required a knowledge of business, technical and some social issues, new trends generate new demands. A grasp of key environmental issues is just the tip of the manager's iceberg. Other issues, to name just a few, include: equality and fair treatment for people of all income levels, genders, ages and various disabilities; preventing sexual harassment by staff and coaches; finding a balance between elite sport and recreation; buying equipment (i.e. soccer balls and shoes) that have been manufactured under acceptable conditions.

The sport manager, who has not received training in all of these issues, may be inadequately equipped to deal with this full and ever-shifting agenda. As we chart a new course in this 21st century, some form of guidance will be critical. Such guidance will have to take several forms: a fairly comprehensive approach, based on some manner of agreed ethic that has been widely accepted; some compatible principles and/or codes of conduct; and a "toolkit" of practical resources that can be constantly supplemented and tinkered with as times and experience dictate.

In the absence of all of these for the moment, the sport manager could do well to turn to an approach that has been widely discussed and increasingly adopted in other industries, but is only recently being applied in the sport industry. That concept is sustainability.

The Triple Bottom Line of Sustainability

What is so different about the concept of sustainability is that it acknowledges the need to address economic, social and environmental issues in an integrated fashion. While prevailing myths hold that pursuing environmental and social goals will inevitably involve additional expenses, careful study shows that more often than not this is false. The organization that commits itself to the "triple bottom line" usually finds that meeting business, social and environmental goals can be mutually reinforcing. That is, an organization is more likely to be financially stable over the long term if it is socially and environmentally progressive.

According to Stuart Hart, director of the Corporate Environmental Management Program at the University of Michigan: "The more we learn about the challenges of sustainability, the clearer it is that we are poised on the threshold of an historic moment in which many of the world's industries may be transformed." (1997)

> ## What is Sustainability?
>
> The concept of sustainability has origins in the 1986 report *Our Common Future*, published by the World Commission on Environment and Development. It identified sustainability as the prerequisite for the survival of any organism or society. It called on human society to find ways to "meet the needs of the present without compromising the ability of future generations to meet their own needs." To achieve this state, we must re-evaluate all of our institutions and practices, in the hope of creating and implementing alternatives which do not detract from the long-term ability of our species, all other species and indeed the ecosystem to survive.
>
> *Our Common Future* coined the now-popular term "sustainable development" to describe the form that economic activity would have to take if we were to be able to meet the material needs of human society without further harming the planet. This term has come under frequent criticism from all sides. It has been called vague, an oxymoron, and even an excuse for business as usual. Many attempts have been made to better define the term. Some groups have used the term to legitimize just about every imaginable vision of the future, from unrestricted economic growth to a return to ways of the past. Since the term "development" seems to carry so much unacceptable baggage with it, more and more people are settling on the term "sustainability" to describe the necessary preconditions for simultaneous human and planetary survival.

The beauty of the concept of sustainability (though some would argue its flaw as well) is its adaptability and flexibility. Since there is no final end point that we can call "sustainable", there can only be a continuing quest or commitment to becoming more sustainable. It is an approach or objective rather than an object.

For the sport decision-maker, this means making a commitment to "sustainable sport" at best (or at least "more sustainable sport") .

Building on the 1986 definition of sustainable development (see box above), we can define "sustainable sport" as follows:

> *Sport is sustainable when it meets the needs of today's sporting community while contributing to the improvement of future sport opportunities for all and the improvement of the integrity of the natural and social environment on which it depends.*

Because sustainable sport is an approach and a concept, and one with sufficient scope and flexibility to cover all issues and challenges encountered by the sport manager, it may provide the much-needed guidance for today's and tomorrow's challenges.

On its own, this definition amounts to little more than a statement of intent. It will have to be, of course, fleshed out and supported by additional principles, objectives, codes of conduct and a growing literature of resources and case studies based on practical experiences. Many groups have begun the processing of developing and sharing these elements, some of which are described in this book. More should follow in the coming years.

Some Key Principles

Any actions in support of more sustainable sport will derive strength, direction and a common sense of purpose from a shared ethic that is supported by a common set of principles. Though these may take the form of common assumptions rather than some written code, it is nevertheless helpful to describe some of those most likely to be on the menu.

Stewardship

Stewardship is the belief that all individuals, organizations, companies and countries are "stewards" of the planet's resources, and must be responsible managers of those resources, the regions and the ecosystems on which our activities have an impact. Stewardship is fundamentally good management. A number of subsidiary concepts fall under this rubric: wise use of resources, restoration of resources and ecosystems that have been despoiled, and the conservation of significant resources for posterity.

Pollution Prevention

It is always cheaper to find a way not to pollute than to deal with the by-products of polluting activities and systems or respond to and clean up after accidents. Perhaps the most eloquent rephrasing of this approach came from twelve-year old Severn Suzuki in an address to world leaders at the 1992 Earth Summit: "If you don't know how to fix it, please stop breaking it!" The key to pollution prevention lies in the design of our systems and processes. By stepping back and asking ourselves and our colleagues why it is we do things in the way we do, we can frequently come up with an approach which is more effective, has few harmful effects and costs less.

Eco-efficiency

A term that is popular in corporate circles, eco-efficiency is the idea that the most economically efficient and environmentally benign way to carry out any task or produce any product is to develop a system which minimizes the amount of materials required as input, the amount of processing required of these materials, and the amount of non-productive output beyond the desired end product. The ultimate eco-efficient system buys only what it needs, reuses materials as many times as possible and recycles or sells whatever may go unused. Eco-efficiency can be applied to any activity or field, from office management to facilities operation. This concept does not, however, include social issues in the equation. Eco-efficiency may be part of the solution, or perhaps a check-point along the route to greater sustainability.

Partnership

Greater sustainability can rarely be achieved without working closely with other interested parties. Partnerships involving all stakeholders with a vested interest in improving the sustainability of a sport organization or operation will attempt to make the maximum use of the resources (physical and intellectual) brought by all parties. Examples of powerful partnerships described in this book fall into several categories:

- ◆ involving host communities in the design and planning for a sport facility or event that will involve and affect them, seeking input that will lead to events/facilities that are better for the community and the environment;

- ◆ working with regulatory authorities and various government planning agencies to develop plans that meet legal/regulatory requirements and the needs of the public in a way that is attractive and efficient for the sport organization;

- ◆ inviting respected environmental groups to play a positive role in all aspects of running an event or facility, whether as members of a committee or as designated "watchdogs"; and

- ◆ working with sponsors/donors/suppliers to ensure that issues such as packaging waste and recyclability are considered from the earliest stage, and that these partners are given the opportunity to take a positive role in environmental projects.

Leadership

Members of the sport industry can be leaders not only to other sport organizations, but to groups and individuals outside of sport. They can be innovators, educators, motivators and guides. The prominence of sport provides it with an opportunity and even an obligation to adopt and promote sustainability.

Quality

Improvements in sport need not always involve growth and consumption. As baseball stadium developers are discovering, a smaller, more intimate ballpark may actually provide a superior experience for participants and spectators, who will want to return more often. As society discovers that the capacity of the planet to handle many human activities is finite, we can expect a shift to quality, away from quantity. For sport, that may translate as more durable sport equipment and apparel, fewer but more interesting events, and facilities which through better design cost less to operate and maintain while delivering better service.

Diversity

One thing that any vibrant culture has in common with a healthy ecosystem is diversity. In human society, diversity ensures that the needs and interests of most people can be satisfied, whether in language, career, education or recreation. Biological diversity ensures that individual species are provided with the conditions they need for survival, thus preserving the ecosystem as a whole. Remove diversity from the natural world and you risk starting a domino effect leading to partial or total collapse. Remove diversity from human society and you risk alienation, boredom and tunnel vision. Promoting diversity in sport involves making available the greatest array of opportunities. A visible trend among the youth is toward non-traditional and so-called extreme sports, whereas all ages continue to flock in large numbers to outdoor-based adventure. Preserving these opportunities is thus inextricably linked to the availability of built facility types and healthy habitats with physical attributes that offer a wide range of sport experiences. It follows then that just as habitat loss is the leading cause of species extinction, it may also be "the greatest threat to maintaining a diversity of recreation experiences." (Cable and Udd 1990)

Putting Sustainable Sport Management to the Test

Of course we can go on forever trying to define and refine an idea. The real test of its value is in its application. To have real value, the approach of sustainable sport must actually help you the sport manager to accomplish your goals and do your job in a way that is economically, socially and environmentally acceptable.

What the triple bottom line of sustainability means for sport is that by pursuing sustainable sport you may be able to turn today's problems into challenges and opportunities.

The sport manager aiming to introduce greater sustainability will need additional training and resources to effectively grapple with these issues. While there are many resources on the economics and business of sport, and plenty on key social issues, there are still very few on environmental issues relevant to sport and fewer yet which attempt to integrate all of these. Chapters 2 and 3 look at how a sustainable management approach can help to integrate environmental with social and economic goals, and examine many ways to turn opportunities into benefits.

Chapter

A Prescription for Healthy People and Communities

If we spend so much time playing sport, watching sport or emulating the people and the behavior that are so much a part of contemporary sport, it is understandable that we — our youth in particular — will absorb some of sport's dominant values. Canada's Minister's Task Force on Federal Sport Policy (1992) observed that "the physical activities we engage in, how we integrate them into our community life, the values we express through them... help define us as individuals and as a nation."

The traditional image of sport as a teacher highlights its positive potential. Sport can teach us values, fair play, teamwork and cooperation, self-respect and respect for others. The Task Force concluded that sport can be a means "to develop healthy lifestyles that may translate into improved health, well-being and self-esteem." This is certainly the sporting ideal we have traditionally striven for, but how honest and accurate a portrayal of contemporary sporting culture is it?

Sport as Agent for Change

If it is indeed true that sport values reflect those of society at large, can those values be altered in any substantial way without first altering those of the society in which we are operating? Though environmental awareness may not take hold within sport before it has done so in society at large, sport does have a special role to play in accelerating the process. It may not be the birthplace or breeding ground for such a movement, but sport has an opportunity — a responsibility, even — to take a prominent role in any push toward a more sustainable society.

The role to which the sport community is admirably suited is that of spokesperson and publicist. By virtue of its prominence and influence, sport can become a powerful agent for change, leading society at large. It can lead by example, showing other sectors and the general public the road to and benefits of sustainability. Then, by publicizing its commitment and successes, it can reach the unconverted. Mike Bossy, a respected former professional ice hockey player, feels that athletes are important messengers, especially for children: "I've always been very conscious of the fact that kids look up to professional athletes. If you're going to have that kind of influence on kids, you have to act and speak responsibly." (Minister's Task Force on Federal Sport Policy 1992)

A. Hall and D. Richardson (1982) agree: "Many of the values we admire in our sportswomen and sportsmen — honesty, fair play, hard work, discipline and dedication — are the very societal values we wish to see inculcated in everyone. Sport, therefore, is highly significant in the socialization of young people."

By virtue of the number of participants in sport at all levels, there is an enormous audience for messages either from instructors or imparted through a sport activity itself. At least one organization has recognized and acted on its opportunity to influence environmental values: at a 1991 world congress of ski instructors, "a resolution was passed emphasizing that ski instruction is a means of increasing ... awareness and love of nature." (Skiing 1991) With over 300,000 instructors teaching more than ten million skiers each year, the resolution could bear great fruit.

Sigmund Haugsjaa, environmental coordinator for the Lillehammer Olympics believes that sport organizations have a special responsibility to deliver environmental messages, through events, facilities and training and education. Children, he feels, are especially open to education through sport, since nearly 100 percent participate in sport. Between 70 and 90 percent of North Americans and Europeans of all ages participate in sport in some form.

Furthermore, sports organizations can act as catalysts to protect and enhance the environment. They can work with government and industry to encourage them to bolster their attempts to improve environmental conditions. In Sydney, Homebush Bay, which was for decades an environmental liability as a toxic waste dump, was remediated into a safe recreational site because it was chosen as the main site of the Olympic Games. The 2008 Olympic Bid in Beijing has been the impetus for a massive air quality campaign that has seen a significant reduction in air pollution due to the pressure from the bidding committee to provide a safe environment for competition.

Can an approach to sport that accords highest importance to safeguarding the natural environment also help meet social and economic goals? The benefits for people who organize sport events, design and operate sport facilities and participate in sport, and for communities in which sport takes place fall into four principal

---

Cleaner Air During Olympics in Atlanta

A study by the US Center for Disease Control and Prevention was released in the Journal of the American Medical Association showing that the decrease in use of cars in Atlanta during the 1996 Olympic Games led to an improvement in air quality. Furthermore, there was a 42% reduction in asthma related emergency room visits by children in Atlanta's inner city during that time. The study noted that dramatic increases in public transportation use and widespread implementation of alternative downtown commuting schedules promoted by Games organizers resulted in this observed decrease in automobile use. The study statistically linked the prolonged improvements in ozone and particulate matter pollution to a drop in emergency visits for asthma and also found that traffic pattern changes seemed to account for most of the improved air quality in Atlanta during the Games (Friedman M.S. et al. 2001)

categories: human health, environmental health, community awareness and improvement, and economic savings and opportunities. The first three, and the connections between them, are examined in this chapter.

Environmental Stewardship Improves Human Health

The personal health of athletes, spectators, officials and the ordinary citizen is closely connected to the state of their environment. Environmental improvements, therefore, generally bring human health benefits. Environmental improvements as a result of sustainable sport management can be expected to have positive spin-offs on human health. Health will benefit, for example, when managers make a point of:

♦ limiting the exposure of athletes in practice or in competition to dangerous conditions such as water pollution, air pollution, poor indoor air quality, tobacco smoke, and hazardous chemicals such as pesticides;

♦ taking into account the dangers of Ultraviolet-B radiation when setting the times and location of training and competition, and providing adequate warnings and shelter for all participants and spectators; and

♦ placing a high priority on the health of the athlete when selecting venues and designing facilities.

The entire sport community has the opportunity to become an effective public educator on sport-related health issues. Furthermore, the sport community could start deliberately promoting policies at a national and international level that would address environmental problems placing not just practitioners but entire sport disciplines at risk.

Health is so central to an athlete's performance, whether amateur or professional, recreational or competitive, that you would expect all athletes to be keenly interested in the relationship between human and environmental health.

But are athletes in fact aware of this connection? Finnish sport sociologist Pauli Vuolle notes that in many countries the national physical culture grew out of a close connection with nature. In these cultures, "nature is not met as an enemy, but as an opponent that is to be appreciated and honored," states Vuolle (1991).

It is this intimacy with nature that motivates and inspires many athletes. The activity is a way of getting out into the fresh air or the wilderness where they can feel the exhilaration: the heart racing and the body surging unrestricted. To quote freestyle skier Bronwen Thomas: "As a skier I am in close contact with the environment and a part of my pleasure of this sport is that connection with nature."

But not all modern athletes have or foster that connection with nature. As a result, they may be hardly aware of the important role environmental health plays in determining the conditions in which they train and compete. Nor are they likely to be in tune with the impact the state of the environment has on their own health and their freedom to participate in certain activities, and with their role in the equation.

Understanding the Impact of a Degraded Environment on Sport

How the sport industry and our sport culture contribute to the degradation of environmental health is only one part of the story. For sport is not only a culprit, it is equally often a victim. In an ecologically degraded area it may be hard, if not impossible, to pursue certain sports. And where it is possible, it may often be unwise. There are several ways in which an unhealthy environment not only hurts the athlete but also hinders the motivation of individuals to pursue sport in the first place.

Water pollution, air pollution, stratospheric ozone deterioration, habitat loss, toxic waste, pesticide residues, noise, traffic emissions, climate change, indoor air quality and even cigarette smoke are among the environmental threats to safe and enjoyable sport. Effects of these threats can be short-term and local, hindering only the athletes present in a certain place or participating in a certain event, or long-term and widespread, jeopardizing the very viability of a location, event or sport.

Examples of short-term threats include nitrogen dioxide buildup in ice arenas or cigarette smoke in indoor gymnasia. Though these conditions may cause discomfort and nausea and even hamper the ability of the athlete to practice or perform, the threat ends with the removal of the source of the problem or with the removal of the athlete from that location. Should no attempt be made to address these sources, the athlete who is repeatedly exposed may suffer longer-term consequences. The sport or indeed the facility only becomes threatened if athletes are made sufficiently aware of the threat to their health and decide to quit, switch to some other sport or move to a different facility.

Longer-term threats are typified by environmental degradation whose source cannot easily be identified and/or whose consequences may take years if not decades to fully materialize, and even longer to ameliorate. Falling into this category is everything from localized toxic contamination and high atmospheric pollution, to global phenomena such as the depletion of the stratospheric ozone layer and climate change.

Environmental Threats to Sport Participants

A polluted or otherwise degraded environment would seem not to discriminate between the athletic and non-athletic members of society. However, the athlete's vulnerability increases dramatically through (a) the frequency of exposure to a particular threat, and (b) the intensity of effort exerted in that degraded environment.

Air Pollution

Air pollution is one of the most obvious and frequently named "environmental" threats to sport. It can take a number of forms. Indoor air quality can be affected by environmental tobacco smoke (ETS), poor ventilation, chemical "off-gassing" from carpets, furniture, paint and cleaning products. Outdoor air pollution has both local and long-range sources: vehicles, power plant and factory emissions, ground level ozone and smoke stacks as far as 5,000 kilometers away. Of these sources of air pollution, the most immediately harmful tend to be the most local, whereas long-range sources of pollution will have longer-term consequences. A runner in Hungary may feel the immediate effects of the smog produced by that day's traffic, whereas the heavy metals carried by winds from Romania may not accumulate to dangerous levels in her body for 10 or 20 years.

While all residents of polluted regions are subjected to similar air conditions, athletes may be among the most vulnerable, given their exercise patterns and needs. Reasons for this are several:

Common Environmental Threats to Sports and Athletes

Localized/short-term threats

- airborne smog
- indoor air quality
- toxic chemicals
- pesticides
- water-borne pollutants/bacteria
- noise
- cigarette smoke

Long-term/global threats

- ozone layer depletion
- climate change
- habitat/biodiversity loss
- radioactive contamination
- accumulation of toxins
- soil and water contamination
- acid rain

1) The "quantity of air inhaled during exercise is significantly greater and the depth of inhalation into the lungs — into the sensitive and generally less used tissues — is also greater" (Scherff 1993). When exercising, our consumption of air can increase by as much as ten times. For the endurance athlete, that figure may be closer to 20 times.

2) Not only are we increasing respiration, we are not filtering the air we breathe as efficiently. By breathing predominantly through the mouth, we lose our "usually efficient nasal

filtering mechanism" (Gong and Krishnareddy 1995). The result can be a greater intake of particulates, which can cause shrinking of the air passage, fluid secretion and possibly even lung cancer. The American Lung Association equates running in a typically polluted urban area for 30 minutes with smoking a pack of cigarettes.

3) Although the general public and those with asthmatic conditions will usually avoid outdoor exercise during pollution alerts, competitive athletes may not have the option of not training or competing during high-risk periods or in heavily polluted areas (Atkinson 1997).

Outdoor Air Pollution

An extensive medical literature exists chronicling the effects on exercise and athletic performance of sulfur and nitrogen oxides, carbon monoxide, ozone and other particulates — all of which are common outdoor pollutants in urban and industrialized areas.

Ground Level Ozone (a major component of traffic smog) has its most obvious effects on the respiratory tract. In any active individual high ozone levels can cause restrictive lung function as it limits the ability of the lungs to take in and expire. An athlete who is exercising with exposure to unsafe levels of ozone will experience wheezing, shortness of breath and chest tightness and as a result will have decreased exercise performance (Gong and Krishnareddy 1995). High exposure to various air pollutants can have a particularly dramatic effect on asthmatic athletes, forcing those with moderate to severe cases to stop exercise altogether and exacerbating the conditions of only mild sufferers. According to an article in The Physician and Sport Medicine, 11% of Olympic caliber athletes have exercise-induced asthma (Storm and Joyner 1997).

Though air pollution does not affect all athletes to the same extent, some will lose their competitive edge as a result of airway conditions. Meryl Sheard and Dr. David Martin (Scherff 1993) of Georgia State University's Department of Cardiopulmonary Care have studied the effect of air pollution on athletes. They have found that more and more athletes are hypersensitive in airway function. A number of studies (Atkinson 1997, Bascom et al. 1996, McDonnel et al. 1995), have similarly concluded that the respiratory function of healthy, trained athletes decreases with exposure to ambient air pollutants. In sports where mere millimeters can make the difference between victory and second best, air pollution should be considered an important factor.

Emily Haymes and Christine Wells (1986) note the effect a range of air pollutants can have on both the performance and long-term health of the athlete. They recommend that athletic events and training

Forced to Compete at All Costs

Renn Crichlow, Canada's 1992 World Champion kayaker advised organizers of the 1994 World Championships in Mexico City (possibly the most polluted city on the planet) that he would not compete unless the event was relocated. An asthmatic, Crichlow noted how athletes in many sports are frequently called upon to train and compete in highly unsuitable places. Out of fear of sanctions by national and international governing bodies, or concern that they may slip in rankings, most athletes will nevertheless go ahead and compete at their personal risk, he stated. In Crichlow's case, he finally decided to compete in only one race, the shortest, and to fly in to Mexico City just before it and leave immediately afterward.

sessions be scheduled to avoid the seasons and times of day when levels of such pollutants as ozone and carbon monoxide are highest. In addition, heavily traveled streets and highways should be avoided and all training or competition cancelled when air pollution episodes reach emergency levels.

Worth noting is the fact that the impact of air pollution is not necessarily restricted to either endurance sports or urban locations. Olympian biathlete Myriam Bedard, upon completion of a race in the forests of Borovets, Bulgaria, commented that "the pollution level here is incredible. It's worse than downtown Montreal." Studies on hikers in wilderness areas in the northwest USA have detected high enough levels of pollution to cause a noticeable decline in lung capacity (Korrick et al. 1998). Tennis players at the 1994 Australian Open similarly complained about the combination of heat and pollution, which made conditions unacceptably dangerous to the health of competitors. The astonishing middle-distance runner Haile Gebreselassie in 1997 threatened to skip the World Championships in Athens because of air pollution. In the end, however, he was pressured to compete (for a similar example see box on page 19).

Even in regions where the threat may be less extreme, air pollution in its several forms can pose a threat to sport and recreation Dangerous levels of smog are not only recorded in urban settings, but are common in rural regions where industrial sites are located or prevailing winds blow in heavily polluted air from up to several hundred kilometers away. Needless to say, a city like Los Angeles, Mexico City or Beijing does not produce many long-distance runners. Nor is outdoor sport a common sight in Upper Silesia where male life expectancy is a mere 52 years or parts of Hungary where one in seventeen people dies from pollution-related causes (UNEP 1990).

Indoor Air Pollution

Indoor air quality issues have begun to receive considerable attention, driven primarily by the increasing incidences and recognition of "sick building syndrome" and "environmental sensitivities." Indoor air, in addition to being poorly circulated and exchanged with the outside, can contain emissions from the thousands of plastics and petroleum products now present in a typical indoor setting. Added to that are off-gassing volatile organic compounds (VOCs) from paint, cleaners, photocopiers and laser printers as well as perfumes, and scents from soaps, shampoos, fabric softeners and "deodorizer" products. On their own or in combination, these products are being increasingly recognized as the source of a number of "environmental" allergies and sensitivities. What is harmful in the office or home is equally or even more so in the indoor sport facility, where the rate of respiration and exertion can multiply negative effects. The danger of

Key Indoor Air Pollutants
◆ passive smoking (ETS)
◆ sulphur dioxide
◆ nitrogen dioxide
◆ ground level ozone
◆ carbon monoxide
◆ particulate matter
◆ carbon dioxide
◆ asbestos
◆ formaldehyde
◆ radon gas

exposure to indoor air pollutants led the World Health Organization (WHO) and the American Society for Heating, Refrigeration and Air-Conditioning Engineers (ASHRAE) to produce comprehensive recommendations on maximum contaminant levels for nitrogen dioxide, carbon monoxide, carbon dioxide, formaldehyde, sulphur dioxide, ozone, asbestos and radon gas.

The quality of air in indoor sport facilities is site specific. Whereas a well-ventilated facility which has taken care to limit the amount of off-gassing from paints, varnishes, insulation, cleaners and furnishing, as well as the presence of ETS within the building, may present no health hazard to users, a similar facility may leave athletes with headaches, asthmatic problems, nausea, dizziness or any number of other symptoms.

Environmental Tobacco Smoke (ETS)

Canadian physician Dr. John Read was one of the first to sound the warning regarding the harmful effects of cigarette smoking for athletes. His message was that cigarette smoking has no place in the sport "arena." Dr. Read argued that it was exposure to environmental tobacco smoke (ETS), often referred to as "second-hand smoke," at athletic venues, both indoor and outdoor, that presented the greatest environmental threat to the health of athletes, officials and spectators.

In his study "Smoke-Free Policies and Programs for Athletic Events," Dr. Read notes that athletes can have both their training and performance compromised significantly by exposure to ETS. Burning tobacco produces more than 4,000 chemicals, of which at least 50 are known carcinogens. ETS exposure can trigger immediate symptoms in up to 70 per cent of non-smokers. These include eye and throat irritation.

When 40 elite Canadian athletes were surveyed on a range of environmental issues in October 1993, air quality — cigarette smoke in particular — was often mentioned as an environmental health concern. This was true for those who train and compete outdoors as well as indoors. Nordic combined skier Mark Rolseth described how, at a World Cup competition in Germany, "the course was lined with cigarette smokers, making me feel nauseous during the race." Even cyclists competing in outdoor races have complained about the clouds of spectators' cigarette smoke they must sometimes ride through.

A growing movement toward Smoke Free sport now actively encourages sports organizations, events and athletes to adopt smoke free policies and behavior. SmokeFree Soccer (www.smokefree.gov) is an innovative American program that promotes a healthy smoke free lifestyle, using the U.S. women's national soccer team as a lifestyle model for adolescent girls and boys, who are encouraged to be physically active and resist the pressure to smoke. The program includes a video and a SmokeFree Soccer coach's kit.

Pesticides, Herbicides and More

One of the more significant threats to both athletes and the public at large is the growing accumulation of pesticides in our communities. Rachel Carson's 1962 book *Silent Spring*, which first shone the public spotlight on the risks of using persistent pesticides, herbicides and fungicides, was a rallying cry for the nascent environmental movement. By covering our crops and lawns with chemical compounds that are unable to biodegrade naturally, we are gradually saturating our soil, our water, our plants, our meat, our pets, our children and ultimately ourselves with

Is Golf Good for You?

It is widely held among the medical profession that a round of golf represents an excellent form of regular exercise. A walk of some seven kilometers (four miles) in fresh air over undulating terrain, punctuated by a few hefty swings at the ball, is good for cardiac rhythm. Even better if one is carrying a bag of clubs. However, the modern commercial trend towards using motorized golf carts is also removing that vital walking element from golf. Purists may object, but golf carts are big business and on many courses, notably in the USA and in tourist resorts, it is obligatory to hire one. So, commercial gain can obviate one of the more obvious benefits of playing golf.

In terms of health concerns, however, most concern has focused in recent decades on the potential risks of turf chemicals applied to golf courses. Public concern is not just for the health of golfers but more particularly the possible effects of pollution of ground water and surface waters, and even contamination of the air through spray drift. This concern is fuelled by the TV image of immaculate golf courses, which intuitively must be heavily treated in order to achieve such "perfection". The sight of golf course superintendents wearing heavy protective clothing, goggles, masks — even moon suits — only adds to the impression that something nasty is being put on the grass.

In 1998, delegates at the annual conference of the Golf Course Superintendents' Association of America were disconcerted by the announcement of research findings they had commissioned, which indicated higher than normal rates of certain cancers in a sample of retired greenkeepers (see box below). Many of these, however, had worked at a time when precautionary measures were less considered and they had handled chemicals long since banned. Nonetheless, even though modern chemicals are more rigorously controlled, the long-term effects of continual exposure and the possible combination effects of different products, can only be termed 'safe' under present knowledge. What is safe for humans may well not be so for wildlife. Environmentalists therefore urge particular caution with regard to the use of pesticides.

Press reports of extreme incidents — someone dying because of a hyper-allergic reaction traced to a chemical recently applied to a golf course — have gained a certain notoriety and have been widely circulated. While it is clearly unwise to engage in that old custom of licking one's golf ball, there is need for some perspective in this debate. In the UK 97% of pesticide use is for agriculture and only 3% for gardening and amenity use (i.e. including golf courses). Overall there are more chemicals used on gardens than on golf courses. A similar situation exists in the US, where the private lawn care industry is a much more significant chemical user than golf courses.

Furthermore, golf courses are more closely regulated in terms of health and safety. Personnel have to be properly trained and licensed to handle pesticides, machines have to be properly calibrated, while the cost of amenity chemicals is such that nobody would choose to overuse them. This contrasts with private gardens, where there is no control on competence, dosage, or protection measures.

However, perception is often more powerful than reality and this has lead some countries and states to impose stringent regulations to limit the number and type of pesticides that can be used on golf courses. Denmark has introduced a total ban on such chemicals for amenity grasslands (i.e. including golf courses) and Germany is in the process of doing so. It is, though, still permitted to use chemicals on agricultural land.

In fact, over-regulation can have some perverse effects. Where the choice of fungicide, say, is limited to just one product, it has been found that pathogens can build up resistance, leading to higher doses being applied, and more frequently, than if a range of products had been available.

substances that accumulate in our tissues. Being higher on the food chain than plants and other animals, humans may be among the last to feel the effects of these chemicals, but we also ingest those which have accumulated in our water, our foodstuffs and "lower" species which are part of our diet.

In *Our Stolen Future* (1996) Theo Colborn and her co-authors carefully describe how a range of synthetic chemicals, alone or in unpredictable combinations, can accumulate in our bodies, leading to problems ranging from cancer to infertility. So-called "gender bending" endocrine disruptors can harm the reproductive abilities of humans and other species.

To list all the studies that chronicle the risks posed to humans by these synthetic chemicals would be fruitless. It is relevant, though, to look at the damage already inflicted upon those species which act as warning signals to our own species: insects, frogs, fish and birds have been disappearing in alarming numbers. Instances of massive die-offs of ducks and geese within hours of feeding on, or in waters adjacent to, farmland, parkland and golf courses that have been recently sprayed are too common to dismiss (Tiner 1991).

Pesticide producers will argue that the safe application of pesticides presents no danger. But what is a "safe" application? That depends on the terrain, the climate, the vegetation, the geology and a number of unknowns. Ignoring the raging technical debate, legions of ordinary citizens are saying, "I don't care what the studies say. I'm scared. I'm concerned for my kids, my pets and myself. I want pesticide use reduced!" In doing so, they are forcing the sporting facilities that they patronize to respond to their concerns.

Recreation officials and groundskeepers are being called on to address public concern over pesticides. The negative effects of pesticides on humans range from allergic reactions and respiratory ailments to nausea, numbness, paralysis, birth defects and even death. The severity of the threat is dependent on such factors as the type of pesticide, the frequency and degree of exposure as well as the person's individual sensitivity. Among those most likely to be affected are those most frequently exposed. This includes park, field and turf maintenance personnel and players of field sports such as soccer, football, cricket, golf and lawn bowling. It also includes children, who spend long hours in neighborhood parks in contact with recently sprayed grass — oblivious to any mandatory warning signs. Several U.S. golf-governing bodies are now funding research on links between long-term pesticide exposure, cancer, and rates of mortality for greenskeepers, players and caddies.

Golf Superintendent — An Occupational Hazard?

A study commissioned by the Golf Course Superintendents' Association of America found that superintendents have a significantly higher risk of dying of cancer and other diseases related to pesticide exposure. The study of 686 deceased members of the Association who died between 1970 and 1992 showed that brain cancer and non-Hodgkin's lymphoma occur at over twice the national average, while prostate cancer occurred at nearly three times the average. The researchers noted that similar patterns of elevated mortalities due to these types of diseases has been noted amongst other occupational groups exposed to pesticides. (Kross, B.C. et al. 1996)

Water Pollution

Local water pollution can present a similar threat to the health and performance of participants in such water sports as outdoor swimming, triathlons, rowing, kayaking, canoeing, sailing and boardsailing. Not only are polluted waters unsightly and the source of noxious odors, they can also harbor infectious diseases and harmful chemical pollutants. Most public swimming beaches are tested regularly for bacteria counts. When those counts exceed acceptable public health standards the beach is usually closed, at least temporarily, and/or notices are posted warning swimmers that they are entering the water at their own risk. Because bacteria such as e. coli are relatively easily identified and are known to be an acute health risk, it is a simple procedure to determine when conditions are safe or not.

In the case of chemical pollutants, testing is much less straightforward and considerably more expensive. There are thousands of chemicals and heavy metals whose effects are frequently unknown or widely debated. Furthermore, symptoms of exposure to many chemicals may take months, years or even decades to appear. Thus water which is laced with low levels of pesticides or industrial effluent may pose no immediate threat to swimmers or sailors and may be declared safe by environmental and health authorities. While regular and prolonged exposure to the waters of the Mediterranean or San Francisco Bay may be harmful to the athlete over the long term, that does not prevent many from training or competing in them.

The dangers of waters polluted with organic materials such as sewage and rotting food and animal waste are well known to water sport participants. Frequent dunkings, accidental swallowing of water or the contamination of open cuts are the most common ways of contracting illness. The vast majority of athletes have the good sense to either avoid such heavily polluted areas entirely, venture into them only during "safe" periods, or take preventive measures such as wearing drysuits, applying waterproof lotions and showering thoroughly. In some cases, exposure to dangerous situations may not be left up to the athlete's better judgment. Just as areas of high air pollution may be selected for land events, polluted bodies of water may be chosen for competitions. With seemingly no regard for the health of the athlete, world championships and Olympic Games have been staged in such cesspools as the harbors of Barcelona, Rio de Janeiro and Buenos Aires.

Carol Anne Alie, a long-time Canadian and world champion boardsailor, can recount an endless list of events held in conditions she describes as "degrading and abusive." The boardsailing course at the 1992 Barcelona Olympics featured rats, condoms and a dead dog. At an earlier event in Buenos Aires, she describes sailing past the opening of pipes that were dispersing raw human sewage into the ocean. Alie has been ill frequently as the result of problems related to water pollution

During the summer of 1998, around 90 athletes who participated in a triathlon in Illinois, USA contracted an acute febrile illness called Leptospirosis, while doing the swim portion of the race in Springfield Lake. This illness is caused by the Leptospira bacteria, which infects animals and then is passed through their urine into local water bodies. The athletes, who represented about 10% of those participating in the triathlon, suffered from fevers, chills, headaches and myalgia. Twenty-three of the athletes were hospitalized with more severe symptom including conjuctivitis, abdominal pain and diarrhea (Center for Disease Control 1998).

The state of the world's oceans and inland waters is such that truly clean water is a scarce commodity, at least anywhere close to a populated area. If the current global practice of treating the oceans as a free dumping ground continues, fish will not be the only endangered species. We might soon have to add to that list sailors, paddlers, rowers, triathletes and even their respective sports, which are running low on decent venues. To quote the technical director for the biathlon in Lillehammer (Haugsjaa and Stromo 1993), whose words are especially applicable to water sports, "If we don't give priority to environmental awareness in the future, our sport will have no future."

An extreme example of pollution affecting sport occurred near Eureka, California, where ocean surfers found their traditionally clean waters getting progressively more and more tainted by the toxic effluents from the plants of Simpson Paper Co. and Louisiana-Pacific. Surfers, who were getting skin rashes and other ailments, sued the companies over their more than 40,000 violations of the Clean Water Act. The surfers won their case, demonstrating how sport enthusiasts can take action to protect their rights to a clean environment (Hawken 1993).

Ultraviolet-B Radiation Exposure

Some of the effects of the depletion of the stratospheric ozone layer are already upon us. Thinning of the ozone layer, a critical constituent of the earth's atmosphere, is expected to have two principal effects. First, it will filter out less and less of the ultraviolet radiation that is responsible for sunburn, snowblindness, eye damage, skin cancer, aging and wrinkling of the skin, weakening of the immune system and altering plant growth. All of these health problems can be expected to increase. Secondly, the ozone layer's traditional role in regulating the Earth's temperature will be affected, likely contributing to climate change and the warming of the atmosphere. The consequences of ozone layer depletion are expected to grow in severity until late in the 21st century.

What this will mean for recreational activity — though it may appear rather frivolous to worry about sport when the biosphere of the entire planet is deteriorating — is a number of profound changes. First and foremost, protection from the sun will become a priority. For the sake of our skin, eyes, and immune systems, it may be essential that we evolve quickly from sun worshippers to sun fearers. Compulsory equipment for those who practice their sport outdoors now includes hats, sunglasses, shoulder-covering clothes and repeated doses of sunblock. As great a nuisance as it may be to have to think constantly of covering up from the sun's dangerous UV-B radiation, the consequences of not doing so may be severe.

Approximately 500,000 cases of skin cancer are diagnosed annually in the United States alone. Of those, 70 per cent are thought to be the result of UV exposure. According to Professor Margaret Kripke of the University of Texas (Scherff 1993), "if ozone decreases by 1 percent, UV-B radiation will increase by 2 percent and the incidences of common skin cancers will increase by around 3 percent in the U.S." Predictions from NASA are that ozone depletion over the northern hemisphere could be as great as 20 to 30 percent.

In addition to skin cancer, the U.S. Environmental Protection Agency (EPA) predicts that as many as 2.5 million Americans born before 2075 will suffer from cataracts who would not have otherwise. Victims will also be struck much earlier in life than is currently common.

The human immune system is also expected to be a victim of increased UV-B exposure. Medical researchers (Shea 1988) fear that UV-B will "lower the body's resistance to attacking micro-organisms, making it less able to fight the development of tumors, and rendering it more prone to infectious diseases," such as herpes, leprosy and tuberculosis.

Particularly susceptible to all of these threats will be those nearest the southern pole, under the reach of the hole in the ozone layer that now appears each spring over the Antarctic. Also especially vulnerable will be those people without the economic means or, perhaps, the education to protect themselves properly. The typical Californian golfer may be able to afford $100 sunglasses and $20 tubes of sun cream, but the Chilean sandlot soccer player, not to mention a field laborer, almost certainly cannot. Similarly, much of the world's population has few options when it comes to recreation. There may be no gymnasium to play in when the sun gets too strong.

The implications of ozone-layer depletion for human health and the practice of outdoor sport are staggering, as are the anticipated costs both of protective equipment and clothing and of healthcare treatment. Next to the costs of treating additional millions of cases of cancer, cataracts and diseases brought on by suppressed immune systems, the estimated economic costs to industry of quick action to prevent further ozone depletion will be a drop in the bucket. For those people or countries with no healthcare coverage or even medical system adequate to deal with UV-B-related conditions, treatment may not even be an option.

Changes in habits so as to reduce the risk of UV-B exposure will in some cases be significant. In addition to whole new ways of dressing and applying protective products, athletes who train and or compete outside will have to rethink nearly everything they do. What time of the day is safest for practicing? What time of day or year should events be scheduled? How long should an athlete stay outside? Can certain training be moved indoors? How can I wear sunglasses/protective cream/protective clothing without interfering with my performance? From the major to the mundane, these are all becoming issues in our increasingly ozone layer-less world. The magnitude of these threats may be enough to put whole sports and ways of life on the cutting block. Sailing, surfing, canoeing, bicycle touring, tennis, even recreational swimming will all have to adapt to the new reality.

Sustainable Sport: For the Health of the Community

Many of the environmental benefits that stem from greening sport are fairly obvious, whereas others are only now beginning to be recognized. Some of the most significant of these benefits follow.

- Less energy consumption means reduced greenhouse gas emissions, air pollution, radioactive contamination from nuclear plants or damming of rivers.

- A reduced demand for water from facilities will lessen the strain on local supplies and perhaps obviate the need to increase infrastructure capacity simply to meet peak-period demand.

♦ Better transportation planning will help reduce the demand for private vehicles, limit traffic congestion and lessen the need for new roads and parking. This translates to less smog, noise, resource consumption and loss of green space.

♦ By reducing or eliminating the use of pesticides at sport facilities, the industry can help protect the quality of surface and ground water, as well as limit harm to flora and fauna.

♦ Green spaces, parks and nature preserves can be protected by placing them off bounds for further development and by limiting both the frequency and the scale of intrusions by sport activities into the most threatened and fragile areas.

While all of these can be described as environmental benefits, every one of them also benefits the community and its inhabitants, beyond the "natural environment". Other "community" or social benefits of pursuing more sustainable sport can be anticipated.

Community Awareness and Local Environmental Improvement

As we have seen, the decision to make a sporting organization, event and/or facility more sustainable can have a profound impact on the community in which the event is held or the facility situated. Any action taken to improve the quality of the sport environment for the sake of participants, will also benefit the health of local residents. Furthermore, the effects of improvements in approach and operating practices are directly felt within the community, through a reduction in the stress being placed not only on natural systems but on public infrastructure such as solid waste and sewage treatment and disposal, energy generation and transportation systems.

But the benefits go beyond these considerations, and into the realm of education, awareness and new habits and attitudes. As we explored above, sport events, organizations and personalities can use their high profile to deliver important messages. When an event is held which has taken genuine steps to "green" its components, organizers and sponsors can benefit from spreading the word that they are running a "green games". Though the media and the public have grown skeptical of hollow claims, any event, which can demonstrate that it has made a substantial effort, should tell its story to the public. The same can be said for a facility, either new or retrofitted, which has incorporated design features and systems, which are more environmentally benign than is common, or than those being replaced.

Once we are past the initial skepticism — which serves the useful task of keeping claimants honest — this is a golden opportunity to demonstrate to the community what has been done and how well it is working. One more sustainable event/facility breeds another. The next event/facility will have a hard time getting away with not attempting to be more sustainable, as the community comes to expect it. Awareness raising of this sort has the potential to extend well beyond the sport industry, into the homes, offices and businesses of the community — wherever the lessons of the sustainable sport approach are applicable. The benefit to the community is that pursuing sustainability can be habit forming.

Applying sustainability to a sporting event or facility is also an opportunity to get the host community directly involved. Since the majority of employees and volunteers come from the host community, they will have the opportunity not just to see how each step is being implemented, but also to be involved in that implementation. Local residents will learn about sustainable purchasing practices, materials and waste management, traffic calming, noise reduction and much more. Appropriate systems will also have to be put in place. When the 1999 Canada Games came to Corner Brook and the 1994 Winter Olympics to Lillehammer, neither had municipal recycling schemes in place. Once they were set up and running for the Games, however, it made no sense to shut them down when the athletes went home. The legacy of a more sustainable event, for the host community, in terms of facilities, systems and education, can be its greatest benefit.

At the simplest level, residents of a community can become personally involved in making sport events and facilities more sustainable. They can also take it upon themselves to use existing sport structures to accomplish environmental goals. A great example of African youths using sport to improve their social and environmental conditions is provided as a case study at the end of this chapter.

Partnerships

In an attempt to find more sustainable solutions to problems related to sport and recreation, individuals and stakeholder groups may be brought together who: (a) might never have had the opportunity to meet and work together and (b) discover in the process that they have common interests and complementary skills which might be applied to other situations. In this way sport can contribute to broader community improvement, as well as sport-specific. Issues such as waste management, transportation and community beautification are among the many to which partnerships and solutions developed for a sport project like hosting a major event or constructing recreational pathways can be applied on a community-wide scale.

Partnerships stimulate the sharing of expertise and experiences between groups. The synergy that can be created may lead to ideas and results that would never have come to light if the two groups worked in isolation on the same problem. By involving Greenpeace and several other environmental groups in the bidding and planning stages of the Sydney 2000 Olympics, organizers benefited from some of the many innovative ideas and the passion brought to the table by these "outsiders" to sport. Perhaps the greatest benefits, however, will be felt by the citizens of Sydney, who have been left with highly sustainable transportation and waste management systems, public sport facilities and a healthy new approach to building and operating major public buildings.

Labor Practices

Recent public protests regarding the conditions under which sport equipment and apparel is being manufactured for the global market have opened up some important public discussions. Manufacturers of leather soccer balls who employ child labor under harsh conditions on the Indian sub-continent came under intense scrutiny in 1996-97. Similarly, the conditions under which sport shoes are being manufactured became the target of several major consumer campaigns and boycotts in 1997-98. While some critics singled out Nike, it is only one of many North

American and European companies sourcing their products (only some sport-related) in countries where health and safety standards and human rights records are far from exemplary.

The symbolism of workers being exploited for the sake of sport (i.e. a "frivolous" item) made for powerful media messages. A positive result may be that many in the sport community have been forced to look carefully at the repercussions of their choices. The response of Nike and the World Federation of Sporting Goods Industries is important. Both have adopted socially progressive codes of conduct and embarked on new courses with sustainability as their guiding principle. It may be that the prominence of sport in this issue has brought it greater attention than had it been the pharmaceutical or computer industry. As a result many average consumers are asking important questions of their favorite brand name suppliers. We can only hope that all industries will learn the lesson and make changes that result in better social conditions for the global community.

This lesson does not only apply to sporting goods companies, equipment manufacturers and other suppliers to your sport organization. Your own organization can benefit from adopting exemplary labor and social practices, including the highest environmental, health and safety standards. The decision to be a leader in this area can have several positive repercussions:

- high employee morale, stemming from the knowledge that they are working for a responsible and caring organization;

- high retention rate of employees, not just because of morale, but also due to reduced rates of injury and disability; and

- a good reputation in the community and among customers/clients/users which may help to attract customers and avoid protests, boycotts, lawsuits, etc.

All of these have financial ramifications, which will be explored in more detail in Chapter 3.

Equitable Access and Opportunity

Applying a sustainable sport approach to facility and program development will grant greater status to the needs of other groups than just professional, elite and mostly adult male athletes. Communities making choices about program funding and groups looking to construct new facilities can use sustainability for guidance in making appropriate choices. By taking a long-term view and considering the needs of all groups who will be funding and must live with the outcome, a sport decision-maker will hopefully give adequate consideration to questions of equal or at least equitable access and opportunity. Should public money and land be used solely to meet the needs of elite athletes, or for a purpose that may be harmful to the environment and the health of neighbors? Or should care be taken to ensure more equitable community benefits?

The design chosen for Victoria's 1994 Commonwealth Games velodrome illustrates this point nicely. The organizing committee had the choice of building a standard elite-level velodrome with steep banks, hardwood floors and a narrow circumference. However, they were aware that public money and public land would be used on a facility that was unlikely to see regular high-level competition. With this in mind, an innovative solution was developed that epitomizes sustainability and community benefit. A cycling track was designed with the following features:

1)   out of doors, to minimize construction and operating costs in Victoria's mild climate;

2)   a concrete surface, to avoid the use of high-maintenance and rainforest-sourced tropical hardwoods; and

3)   a wide-circumference oval shape with the minimum-allowable (for international competition) steepness, resulting in (a) a surface that could be shared by elite and recreational-level cyclists, as well as inline skaters; and (b) an infield large enough to accommodate a standard soccer field.

Case Study

The Mathare Youth Sports Association — Cleaning Up, On the Field and Off

There are several ways to approach a problem. You can sit around hoping that someone else will do something about it. You can lobby and encourage someone else to do something about it. Or you can solve it yourself.

For a group of kids from one of the worst slums of Nairobi, Kenya, the only real choice was the third option. The only people who were ever going to do something about the unsanitary conditions, the crime and drug-ridden streets and the lack of a constructive outlet for their energies were themselves. So a group of Mathare Valley youths set out to pull themselves up by their own bootstraps. Using the popular appeal of sport, they set about tackling the interrelated problems of pollution, disease, crime, addictions and general lethargy from which they suffered.

The Mathare Youth Sports Association (MYSA) is surely one of the most inspiring movements ever to emerge — anywhere! The group has been honoured with the United Nations' highest award for environmental achievement; its teams have won dozens of national and international tournaments; it organises soccer, basketball and netball games for more than 680 teams, 250 of which are female; it holds workshops for coaches and referees, and it coordinates slum clean-up projects with over 2,000 boys and girls taking part every weekend.

When MYSA was formed in 1987, the average lot of Mathare youth was dismal: mothers struggling to feed families of five to seven, fathers working away from home or having abandoned the family entirely, glue-sniffing, prostitution, polluted land, blocked drainage ditches, few job prospects and a high drop-out rate from school. With no facilities for playing sports and no money to build them or get to facilities elsewhere, youth sport activity was limited to kicking a makeshift ball around the narrow streets.

In 1987, some Mathare youth met with Bob Munro, a Canadian sustainable development policy advisor living in Nairobi who had been surprised to learn that no sport opportunities existed for them. Together they discussed how to go about organising a league with almost no financial resources at their disposal. They decided to create a sport association that would be run primarily by the participants. Most importantly, however, the association would be more than just sport-centred; it would also organise slum clean-up activities as a first step in promoting community improvement.

The fundamental tenets of MYSA go along way to explaining its success. There is an emphasis on discipline, respect for others, consensus decision-making and pulling your weight. That message is embedded in one simple overarching rule: "You do something, MYSA does something. You do nothing, MYSA does nothing."

Youths are expected and encouraged to contribute in a number of ways. In addition to showing up for their sport activities, they are obliged to join the team on its clean-up days. Working with limited city staff, they pick up garbage, unblock sewers and drainage ditches and encourage members of their community to observe better hygiene and waste disposal practices. In a shantytown with no electricity, plumbing or running water, good hygiene is often a matter of life and death. Since MYSA kids, like kids everywhere, can't always be counted on to show up for clean-up sessions, the sport leagues award bonus points to teams with good attendance records. Any team that does not have sufficient attendance cannot qualify for the playoffs.

Adult enforcement is conspicuous only by its near-absence. All members are expected to abide by the MYSA Sportsmanship Code (see box). Its ten points are enforced by referees, teammates and, only on the rare occasion, by adult supervisors. The system depends on peer pressure. The same peer pressure that may lure them into stealing and glue sniffing on the streets has been turned to a more positive use, encouraging players to lead a healthier and more responsible lifestyle "for the good of the team." Legend has it that the player who has been smoking or sniffing substances will be threatened with expulsion by his own team-mates if his actions are felt to be affecting the team's play or spirit.

Poor sportsmanship is similarly punished. In the early days, violence against referees was a problem. A simple rule quickly put an end to that. The players decided that anyone touching a referee would be suspended until such time as they had themselves refereed 10-15 games in a younger league. Though the rule still exists, it has not had to be used since 1990.

The discipline which MYSA has helped to engender among the boys and girls who are members has been translated into their lives off the field as well. Dozens of cases can be cited of street kids who have chosen a path far different from what anyone might have predicted. In place of running with the packs of street gangs, they are now running to fit school, community work, MYSA organisational responsibilities and training into their daily lives.

What started out as a sport/environmental clean up program in the late eighties has expanded to include many other initiatives. The MYSA hosts a variety of extra programs that take advantage of the status that the top players have accrued in the slums. These youth leaders have been trained in AIDS prevention to address the serious lack of education on the topic. In a two-year period, they had reached over 30,000 youth with this crucial information. The MYSA encourages youth to stay in school by giving the prize money for leadership awards to the schools that the recipients come from. They also provide part time employment so that the children can pay for their school fees. In addition, the MYSA youth leaders have lobbied for better conditions for children in jail and assist them in contacting their families and help secure their release.

Though social pressures and domestic demands placed on Kenyan girls make playing sports a tougher sell, headway is certainly being made. Through positive role models and opportunities for girl's teams to travel and represent Mathare abroad, the MYSA program has proven that playing soccer is acceptable for women. Some of the older girls are now coaching younger boy's teams and refereeing games.

In a community where survival is of primary importance, there is little money or in-kind resources available for sport. Outside support for the MYSA programme is essential. This consists of a combination of voluntary donations from benefactors — organised by the Friends of MYSA— as well as a range of private and corporate sponsors. Funds, free services and generous discounts on equipment have come from a range of MYSA "friends". Norway, through the embassy in Nairobi has provided large equipment such as trucks and tractors for cleaning and sponsored various teams to represent MYSA at international tournaments.

The MYSA, now over 10 years old, is producing some of the country's best soccer athletes. Recently, Mathare United, a Second Division team made up almost entirely of MYSA graduates, won the National Premier League trophy and the right to represent Kenya at the Africa Cup Winner's Cup. This success provides the younger players with great role models in a society where they are sorely lacking.

It is perhaps a strange irony that the most powerful vision of sport's future should be born not in the wealthy cities of Europe and North America but in the seemingly desperate conditions of an African slum. The sporting vision of MYSA is surely the closest thing yet to a working model of sustainable sport: through shared responsibility and community participation the complementary goals of better human and environmental health, greater recreational opportunity, personal and community growth are all achieved.

MYSA Sportsmanship Code

1. **Be Disciplined:** I will always maintain good conduct and discipline on and off the field. I will always play without endangering my opponents or committing fouls.

2. **Play Fair:** I will never fake an injury or foul, use unfair tactics or indulge in any other unsporting conduct such as using abusive language or gestures.

3. **No Retaliation:** I will never retaliate if fouled, abused or harassed by an opponent.

4. **No Fouls:** I agree to be substituted immediately if given a yellow or red card.

5. **No Appeals:** I agree that only my Captain may speak to the Referee during a game. When a dispute arises I will always remain silent and at least ten steps away.

6. **Respect the Referee:** I will always obey the Referee's decisions. I will stop immediately at the whistle and, without appeals or argument, move quickly into position for restarting play.

7. **Respect the Captain:** I will always obey my Captain during games. In or around the penalty box I will obey my goalkeeper's instructions immediately.

8. **Respect the Coach:** I will always obey my Coach's decisions and instructions. I agree that I should be substituted or suspended for any indiscipline or unsporting conduct.

9. **Respect Team-mates:** I will always support and encourage my team-mates on and off the field. I will never abuse a team-mate who makes a mistake.

10. **Respect Opponents:** I will always treat my opponents with respect. I will always assist fallen opponents and offer to shake their hands before and after every game.

I promise to respect the MYSA Sportsmanship Code at all times. I also promise to share my knowledge and skills by coaching a younger MYSA team, participating in all MYSA training clinics and refereeing at least one MYSA game every week. I will also help organize at least one slum clean-up project every month.

Chapter

Responsible Sport as Good Business

All but the simplest of activities are now somehow influenced by commercial or political pressures. At the same time, the relative importance that sport plays in our lives seems to have dramatically increased during this century, and organized sport has become the predominant form.

Sport is a motivator, a symbol, a diversion, often a passion. If, as Marcotte and Larouche contend, sport is truly one of the great social phenomena of the century, then it is easy to see why there is growing concern over its social impact and economic impacts.

Anyone familiar with athletes and sport organizations will be aware of the gap that exists between the ideals and values we wish were being promoted and those that may actually be — recent Olympics-related scandals, doping incidents and the bad behavior of many professional athletes come quickly to mind. The reality is that the way the sporting community acts, in the boardroom or on the playing field, is entirely consistent with the way society at large acts, which is often counter to many of our ideals.

Lois Bryson argues that since the goal of winning has been placed above such genteel values as fair play, it is entirely consistent that we have allowed a value system to take hold in which all but the most excessive forms of cheating and achieving unfair advantage are tolerated or even encouraged. When you consider the political prestige and the rewards (both symbolic and material) that go to the winner, as well as the profit to be made by other interested parties, is it surprising that "self-regulating gentlemanly codes" have been for the most part abandoned? Bryson goes so far as to suggest that "traditional genteel rules are now antithetical to the commercial and national interests being served by much sport."

While as a society we may wish to preserve and encourage many of the old values, it is important to recognize them for what they are and not to expect too much of them. For while these values may have been relevant to a privileged elite for whom financial gain was of little concern, they can hardly be expected to stand up under the pressures that come with huge financial rewards for individuals and corporations as well as prestige for nations.

Bryson (1990) suggests that we have reached a point where "we need to take a cold hard look at how sustainable are the traditional sporting values," particularly in elite sport. If we are to reduce or eliminate the kinds of pressures that motivate athletes to put their health at risk, inspire communities to spend considerable energy and money on hosting or bidding for major games as well as elaborate recreational programs, and lead to decisions which have a negative impact on environmental health, fundamental changes are necessary. Sport will have to shift its focus away from profit making and competition, away from both monetary and symbolic reward as primary motivations and begin to emphasize participation and cooperation.

The primary goal of this book, however, is to demonstrate to the sporting industry how it can benefit from embracing its environmental responsibilities. So this message of health in no way depends on the downfall of commercialism or competition. However, the sporting industry, society at large and the natural environment can all benefit by establishing a common set of values and a code of ethics/conduct that will promote those values.

Industry has the potential to mature and evolve in such a way that it promotes economic well-being, human and environmental health, and community improvement along with many traditional values. These values will only be promoted, however, if the ethical underpinnings of the sporting community are appropriate to the task, clearly defined and embraced at all levels. What is needed is a common ethic that embodies these shared principles.

This chapter will look at how an ethic that is healthy for athletes, the environment and the community can also be of benefit economically. The industry can be changed for the better with a new approach that, seemingly designed to promote environmental values only, is in fact admirably suited to promoting through sport a broad range of social values such as equality, community, and respect for all living beings. And these changes can be made, for the most part, in economically feasible and even beneficial ways.

Green is the Color of Money

The popular misconception about environmental protection is that it is inevitably expensive. Despite hundreds of examples of companies and organizations whose environmental initiatives have saved them millions of dollars, the myth still prevails in some quarters. Weizsacker, Lovins and Lovins (1997) describe how this perception represents a significant barrier to change, even though it has been demonstrated how organizations can achieve increases in wealth and reduced operating costs, along with reduced pollution levels, by improving efficiency in the way they use resources and through better design and choice of materials.

To be fair, most steps to minimize environmental impact involve an initial expenditure. In some cases that expenditure will be large. In a few cases, the savings may never match the initial expense. In the vast majority of cases, however, money spent to improve environmental performance will bring a significant return on investment. Furthermore, not only will money be directly saved through reduced costs on such items as energy, material inputs and waste disposal, other savings might take the form of lower insurance premiums, fewer accidents and avoided legal costs.

Eco-Efficiency

This win-win phenomenon has come to be known in managers' lexicon as "eco-efficiency." Eco-efficiency means using as few resources as possible as efficiently as possible, thus reducing the waste you must pay to dispose of—either through process changes which produce fewer byproducts or by finding buyers who require those byproducts as their own raw resources. Greater eco-efficiency, though it will often require up-front investments, translates into lower costs, greater savings and greatly reduced waste and pollutant production. Some examples:

◆ Energy demand can be reduced through better building design or renovations, insulation, new lighting technology, and heat and lighting management systems.

◆ A comprehensive materials and waste management scheme can reduce the need for certain materials, guarantee a longer life for or multiple usage of certain materials, and reduce disposal costs through recycling.

◆ Transportation planning can reduce the cost of building new roads and parking spaces, through better siting of facilities and events.

◆ Water conservation measures will reduce the cost of both water purchases and sewage disposal.

◆ Integrated pest management on golf courses and other natural playing surfaces will reduce the need for pesticides and the risk of accidents, lawsuits and fines.

Examples of eco-efficiency abound in sport. It can take various forms and be brought about through a range of practices: facility or process design improvements; input reduction or substitution; output or waste reduction; accident avoidance and appropriate response; operational improvements; better maintenance practices; and avoiding approval delays. Each of these is examined in brief here to illustrate the potential of eco-efficiency. More detailed applications can be found in chapters 6 through 12.

Saving by Design

Probably the most effective way to reduce costs through better "environmental" practice is at the design stage of a project. By designing a facility or a process to require less of certain inputs — for example, less energy as a result of designing for better natural lighting and ventilation features — you can achieve savings at either no additional cost or at a cost premium with a relatively short payback period. Illustrations of saving through design include:

◆ a German sports college which is partially below ground level, reducing the need to heat in the winter and cool in the summer because of the constant ground temperature of eight to ten degrees Celsius;

◆ multi-purpose pavilions at the Sydney Olympic site which incorporate innovative roof designs that draw out hot air, thereby increasing natural air flow to cool occupants at no additional cost; and

- Stadium roofs made of translucent materials that diffuse natural light, creating a more uniform light on sunny days across the playing surface, thereby avoiding the need to turn on the lighting system just to eliminate the stark contrast between sunny and shaded sections of the field.

Cutting Costs by Cutting Inputs

A basic axiom of eco-efficiency is: don't buy things that you don't need or can find some other way of obtaining. This applies particularly to purchasing practices, where there may be ways of either avoiding certain purchases, or of purchasing more durable materials and equipment, or of obtaining products that are less harmful in their use and disposal. Examples include:

- The portable modular trailers which a series of major events, including the Canada Games in Grande Prairie, Alberta (1995) and Corner Brook, Newfoundland (1999) have linked or stacked together to create temporary athletes villages where there was no adequate accommodation and no demand or budget for constructing new, permanent facilities.

- Capturing rainwater from the roofs of the many buildings at an equestrian facility, and storing this water in underground cisterns to be used for irrigation and dust suppression during the dry summer months when facility use is heaviest.

- Renting temporary stands instead of building a permanent stadium to accommodate 36,000 spectators on the campus of the University of Victoria during the Commonwealth Games, when the existing 8,000 seat stands were adequate for the post-Games needs of the university.

Waste Reduction: Don't Pay to Throw Away

Any time materials that have been purchased have to be disposed of at a financial cost to the sport organization, an environmental cost, or both, there may be opportunities to re-use those materials, recycle them or sell them to a broker or a purchaser for whom these same materials constitute a useful resource. Examples include:

- The Rose Garden arena in Portland, Oregon, which was facing a substantial cost for disposing of its construction and demolition materials. Instead of paying to have them carted away, 92% were either re-used on site, recycled through municipal systems or sold to other buyers. Savings in avoided disposal costs came close to $145,000 and revenues generated from resale of materials amounted to $42,000.

- The Atlanta Olympic organizers arranged to have concrete from the demolished Fulton County stadium used for fill under the parking lots of the new Olympic Stadium (now Turner Field). Also, when the Olympic Stadium was realigned for baseball after the Olympics, some temporary seating stands were donated to local high schools to serve as bleachers.

◆ Many golf courses have recognized the savings and nutrients to be captured by composting grass clippings and other organic material from course management and from kitchens. Not only is this a cost avoided, it is a valuable substitute for purchasing commercial fertilizers and soil amendments.

◆ Efforts to re-use and recycle construction waste at Sydney 2000 building sites achieved remarkably high diversion levels. The highest achievers included the Sydney Superdome (98% recycled), Sydney International Shooting Center (87%), Dunc Grey Velodrome (94%), Athletes Village (94%), and the Olympic Stadium (70%).

Saving is No Accident

Taking steps to reduce the likelihood of accidents can be an important step towards avoiding expensive clean-up operations, fines, temporary or permanent loss of staff, and even lawsuits. The most effective way of avoiding accidents is to eliminate the circumstances, materials or processes that are in any way risky. Where these can't be eliminated, stringent operating procedures will reduce risks and clear, frequently updated emergency response plans will help to contain accidents such as chemical spills.

◆ Many U.S. colleges have eliminated hazardous compounds from the cleaning supplies used by custodial staff. This reduces the risk of accidents that might lead to injury of these employees, many of whom have been found to have difficulty reading written instructions for product use. The number of disability claims has also been reduced.

◆ The use of gas chlorinators for pools has been phased out in a number of American states and Canadian provinces, for a number of reasons. Risk, and therefore insurance premiums, can be reduced and equipment corrosion can also be slowed.

◆ Golf courses operating effective Integrated Pest Management programs have found savings. Safe, secure storage for these supplies is costly, as is training and certification for staff that handle them.

Operation Cost Reduction

Probably the most common route to eco-efficient savings lies in renovating or retrofitting facilities in order to reduce operating costs. Bringing down energy demand and water consumption can lead to some significant operational savings in a sport facility, as can reducing the cost of operating heavy equipment and transportation fleets. Since an initial investment may be required if you are renovating/retrofitting, it is important to look at the potential payback and the time it will take to achieve those savings (the "payback period"). Examples of operational cost savings include:

◆ A Massachusetts college that paid $19,871 to install a new lighting and energy management system. Not only did the improvements pay for themselves in energy savings in less than one year, the improved lighting attracted new customers, netting the college more than $40,000 per year.

◆ A Colorado study by the Governor's Office of Energy Conservation found that pool operations account for about one-third of the budgets of the state's recreation centers. The subsequent RSPEC! (Reduce Swimming Pool Energy Costs!) program demonstrated how a series of simple steps could save any public, private or home pool operator upwards of 50 percent of their current bills for energy, chemicals and water.

◆ A typical exit sign in a sport facility (of which there are usually dozens) can cost $25-50 per year to run and an additional $60 per year in labor for replacing bulbs. The cost of replacing incandescent bulbs in all its exit signs with longer-life fluorescent ones, will save a sport facility money in approximately six months, and the bulb may last for up to three years.

Maintaining Your Savings

Although good maintenance of facilities and equipment may not be thought of as having environmental benefits, the decision to keep your facilities in good shape and your equipment running for as long as possible can extend the operating and revenue-generating life of both, and can keep a lot of material out of landfill. Examples include:

◆ Vehicles kept well tuned and maintained will last considerably longer and will save money in fuel and oil consumption and in costly repairs that may result from skimping on smaller regular maintenance tasks.

◆ By keeping on top of maintenance in a sport facility you can reduce the costs of running heating and cooling systems and put off the eventual replacement date. Preventing mold and rot damage and corrosion in swimming pools and locker areas can also delay and reduce the extent of eventual repairs/replacement.

Avoid Delays and You Won't Pay

Sport organizations looking to develop new facilities or expand existing ones are often faced with lengthy approvals and environmental assessment processes. These can be compounded by delays resulting from public opposition, including hearings, court injunctions and even blockades. By following the principles of sustainable design, you can reduce the likelihood that your plans will be rejected or opposed, thus minimizing costly delays. Similarly, by working closely with public authorities to comply with regulations and address their concerns, and through early and frequent consultations with community and environmental groups, you can minimize the likelihood that your plans will be opposed. You may even obtain valuable input.

Some golf course designers have worked in partnership with environmental agencies and community groups to ensure that their proposed development will be acceptable to all and will avoid being slowed by approvals delays or protests. Others have taken a different approach, and paid the price:

◆ A major multi-course golf complex in the French region of Provence has been halted since the early 1990s because the construction went ahead without all the correct authorizations in place. Local environmentalists protested and secured a court order preventing the golf course being used. Much of the original investment was lost. New owners have proposed a scaled-down project but still, over nine years since the first course was completed, it has not been opened for play.

◆ The Domain des Princes near Brussels was a prestigious project that started construction in August 1989. Six weeks later, local activists secured a court order to halt the construction (after all the tree clearance had been done) and to this date the golf project has been locked in the legal and planning systems.

Both these cases show how costly it is to underestimate potential environmental/social opposition to new developments. They are not just isolated incidents. More and more golf courses and other sports development projects are having to take proper account of environmental concerns, and this should be done at the beginning of the project, not as a reactive afterthought when problems arise.

Innovative Financing

The economic benefits of a sustainable approach to sport management are by no means limited to eco-efficiency savings and benefits. A variety of opportunities for generating and preserving business opportunities and new sources of revenue may also be available. One such opportunity is to obtain innovative financing for projects that will achieve environmental, social and community economic development goals that certain funders are trying to promote. Many public utilities will offer grants or subsidies to organizations that take steps to reduce energy demand, water consumption and waste generation.

A host of foundations and grantmaking bodies, both public and private, have chosen environmental projects or initiatives to promote sustainable economic development as priority recipients for their funds. Sport-related projects that meet the criteria of these bodies may be eligible for grants and partial funding. Issues more commonly identified by such groups include reducing greenhouse gas emissions, preserving wetlands and other critical habitat, and protecting or enhancing biodiversity.

Another non-charitable source of financing is the energy service company (ESCo). An ESCo is a company that will help to finance your renovation or energy retrofit in exchange for a percentage of the savings you will accrue. Once the ESCo has been paid back according to the terms of your contract, you will find yourself with a modern, more efficient facility that continues to save you money (see YM-YWCA Case Study at the end of this chapter).

Loyalty: Retaining Customers and Staff

Taking a sustainable approach may also net you a number of less tangible, yet significant economic and social benefits. One of these is the loyalty of staff and customers. Many employees will feel a stronger attachment to an organization which has shown itself to be caring and a responsible corporate citizen — an organization which promotes the health of its employees and clients, their community and the local environment, as well as its own business objectives. These sentiments may result in better morale and worker productivity, and loyalty from existing employees. Considering the cost of hiring and training good personnel, building staff loyalty can represent a significant savings in time and money.

A good corporate image may also help in attracting qualified people to your organization. Several studies have placed environmental responsibility among the elements of "good corporate citizenship" which attract people to certain organizations.

Clients or users may also be attracted to a sport organization (i.e. club, facility, manufacturer) that has earned itself a reputation for environmental stewardship. While this will only be one of many factors in a person's decision some will place it quite highly. Audubon International has reported that a surprising number of golfers have inquired about which golf courses have achieved Audubon certification in an area where they intend to go on a vacation. Clearly the environmental commitment of a golf club is one feature which will attract or sway playing customers.

For some, seeking more sustainable sport facilities may be a matter of life and death, or at least of comfort and discomfort. People with strong concerns about indoor air quality or pesticide use on fields, not to mention health- or life-threatening sensitivities or allergies may only be able to pursue sport in an environment that is safe for them.

New Business Opportunities

Sustainability may also play a role in generating new business opportunities. As described above, this might consist of attracting new customers to an existing facility. On the other hand, there may be entirely new opportunities, such as developing environment-based "eco tourism" or sport and recreation-based programs that highlight nature and yet depend heavily on maintaining the pristine environment that attracts tourists.

Showcasing Innovation

Sport facilities and events that have incorporated more sustainable products, systems and technologies have an opportunity to contribute to local economic growth (if these are locally-sourced) and to the growth of the environmental industry by "showcasing" these features. Any facility or event that adopts such products/technologies can help to draw the attention of the media and the general public to their role in the operation of a more sustainable event/facility. Of course, larger events and facilities with more media appeal are likely to have the greatest opportunity. Hence, the important profile which environmental products have received at recent Olympic Games. Examples include:

- ◆ **Lillehammer 1994 Olympics:** An innovative arena bored out from underneath a mountain, that uses the constant temperature to reduce heating and cooling costs; compostable plates and cutlery made from potato starch; a number of energy-efficient heating technologies; a less-polluting film-processing system; and new "green" purchasing standards which were adopted throughout Norway after the Games.

◆ **Atlanta 1996 Olympics:** A large array of solar panels (the world's largest) on the roof of a pool, used to create electricity and heat water; electric vehicles used as pace cars in the marathon; a huge fleet of cleaner fuel buses.

◆ **Nagano 1998 Olympics:** High energy efficiency in all facilities, including an ammonia-cooled bobsled run that uses one-sixtieth of the ammonia required by Lillehammer's facility; apple pulp-based recycled and recyclable plates; staff and volunteer uniforms made entirely from recyclable materials.

◆ **The Sydney 2000 Olympics:** Building materials, lighting, soil remediation equipment, solar panels, PVC-free plastics, conduit pipes and more. In placing such a great emphasis on more sustainable products and technologies, Sydney did not just give a boost to the producers of these items, but helped to shift the mind-set of many Australian architects, planners and builders, who are now aware of the existence of new ways of building and new materials.

The importance of showcasing is, of course, less for the organization that is doing the showcasing than it may be for the producer or for the local economy. Still, acting as a showcase can help to generate additional interest in your facility or event. The publicity certainly can't hurt.

Your Reputation: Enhance, Maintain or Rebuild It

Another economically important "intangible" is the reputation of your organization. For organizations with a good public reputation, adopting the ethic of sustainable sport can only help to preserve or build that reputation. Those who fail to move in this direction do so at their own peril. It is far easier and less expensive to maintain a reputation than to repair or rebuild a damaged one. The golf and ski resort industries are painfully aware of this business fact.

By allowing, or not recognizing, unsustainable developments and practices in golf course and ski resort construction and operation, both have earned fairly poor reputations. Now almost any building or expansion activity is subjected to extraordinary scrutiny by public officials and local and environmental groups. Not only can this lead to costly delays, some of the better operators have been tarred with the same brush as the "bad apples". A great deal of energy and money is now being spent on improving practices and, industry members hope, their public image.

Partnerships

The social and environmental benefits of developing partnerships, especially multi-stakeholder ones, have already been explored. There are also economic benefits. By bringing diverse, and even divergent, views and experiences around the same table, a sport organization can benefit from the pooling of resources and skills that occur. Ironically perhaps, inviting environmental groups to comment and criticize your operations and plans can often elicit ideas that will result in a better business operation.

Sponsorship Programs

The newest and most promising benefit of adopting and promoting more sustainable practices is that it can appeal to sponsors. While standard business wisdom might argue that sponsors will stay well clear of environmental projects — with many having been stung by the backlash to all of the misleading "greenwash" advertising in the early 1990s — recent experience is showing that certain kinds of sponsors find the combination of sport and the environment a very appealing one.

A sport event with a solid and transparent environmental program (one that does not make outlandish claims that are not supported by fact) will likely find sponsors and donors who wish to support that program and be in some way associated with it. Support may come in the form of environmentally-superior products and services from companies that make and supply these. It may also take the form of cash donations. In 1996, Xerox was a strong supporter of the waste management and recycling initiatives of the Atlanta Olympics. Much of Xerox's support came in the form of staff time and expertise — Xerox is a long-time leader in corporate environmental initiatives.

Sponsors have actively supported some of the environmental initiatives of several Canada Games, the 1997 Ryder Cup, and the 1999 Pan Am Games. SOCOG involved several dozen of its sponsors in supporting the environmental efforts of the 2000 Summer Olympics, and SLOC has developed some innovative sponsorship programs for its Salt Lake City 2002 environmental programs.

Though these are only some examples of the economic benefits that a sustainable sport ethic might bring to the sport industry, they are adequate to dispel the myth that being environmentally responsible is always an added expense. Yes, an initial investment is sometimes required, but it is precisely that: an investment, with an impressive rate of return in many cases. In other cases— good waste management and transportation planning, for example, up-front costs are low and potential savings high.

Case Study

YM-YWCA Energy Savings Initiative

Due to budget restrictions and low risk needs of a non-profit organization, the Ottawa, Ontario YM-YWCA's office, residential and athletic complex had never considered energy management as a high priority. When approached by an energy service company (ESCo) to perform a facility audit without financial obligation, they agreed and when the ESCo offered an energy performance contract that predicted large potential savings, no up-front investment and a short pay-back period, the board decided to go ahead.

The energy performance contract, worth $900,000, was a six-year "first-out—shared savings" contract. Under the first-out part of the agreement, the ESCo agreed to finance the project until all measures were implemented, and would receive 100 per cent of the energy savings to pay back their debt. The shared-savings part of the contract meant that, should the ESCo retire the debt earlier than the contract period stated, the savings would be shared equally between the two parties for one year. This was an incentive for the YM-YWCA to participate in the program.

Once all measures had been implemented, the YM-YWCA took out a bank loan to finance the unretired costs; a loan that the ESCo guaranteed would be paid for with energy savings. The ESCo would pick up any shortfall. With an additional $170,000 from the Ontario Hydro Guaranteed Energy Performance Program, the simple payback period was reduced from 5.8 to 4.7 years. Measures included lighting improvements, low-flow showerheads, an energy management control system, conversion to gas, and hot water system modifications.

The energy performance contract was a successful program at the Ottawa YM-YWCA. Critical to their decision to pursue it was, according to the executive responsible for energy management, the ESCo's flexibility and patience with the organization's uncertainty and their guarantee of energy savings. The YM-YWCA plans to enter into more contracts financed by ESCo loans in the future

Part II
Building the Team

Inspiring and Involving
Staff, Volunteers and Stakeholders

Our sustainability goals — financial, social and environmental — are inextricably bound together, which is why we make such a point of doing well by doing good.

— **Ray C. Anderson**, CEO, Interface, Inc.

It was incredible that people got so involved in this [environmental campaign] that they are willing to make some sacrifices and put some energy and effort to get involved. It brought people together in a way we've never been able to bring our staff together before and haven't since.

— **Ken Hopper**, Scandic hotel general manager
(Nattrass and Altomare, 1999)

Chapter

4 Management Responsibilities: Preparing the Organization for Positive Change

Sustainable sport management—the marriage of good environmental practice with superior economic performance and social responsibility—begins with the establishment of appropriate management structures and processes. An effective environmental management system for any organization can define the organization's environmental and economic goals, policies, and strategies—and then implement them.

Management Responsibility: Top Down and Bottom Up

A good structure for environmental management takes a simultaneous top-down and bottom-up approach. First, support for any major shifts in practices must come from the top. Not only must the most senior people be interested in the cause, they must be seen to be so. They must be champions of the cause, showing vision and leadership. They must demonstrate commitment and a willingness to take risks, if the entire organization is to view this as a serious exercise. "Successful 'greening' of any organization depends on one primary condition—commitment and knowledge at the top of the organization. Modern environmental policy must be anchored at Board level." (Lillehammer Olympic Organizing Committee 1993)

Second, people throughout the organization must be and feel that they are a part of any initiative. They need to believe that they have an equal stake in achieving the goals of management, a better environment for example, and that they will share in its benefits. This requires that all members of the organization be involved in developing, implementing, monitoring, and enforcing the initiative.

Third, stakeholders in the results of any initiative are not limited to the organization itself. A range of outside parties, varying according to organization's size and type, may include investors, sponsors, tax-paying voters, local citizens, environmental groups, educators, and many others. These stakeholders should be partners in both the structure and process.

The most common mistake made by organizations in the early throes of incorporating sustainable thinking into their operations is to assign all environmental responsibilities to a mid- or low-level manager who becomes the one-person "environmental" department. In theory, the manager will receive input from people at all levels and will report to a senior manager, who will then take responsibility for implementing the appropriate action. In reality, lower-ranking employees who are not a part of the process tend to not contribute to it, depriving the organization of their valuable knowledge. And top managers, who may not attach a great deal of importance to the reports of someone with little clout, often put environmental concerns on the back burner.

The ideal structure has two parallel but interlinking tracks, one exclusively within the organization and the other involving outside stakeholders. The diagram below depicts a basic management structure for a medium or large-sized organization, such as a major sport facility or large sport event. A smaller organization, such as a college athletic department, local event or municipal facility would likely not have as many elements (i.e. one committee, including staff and interested citizens, instead of two, and one fewer layer of management).

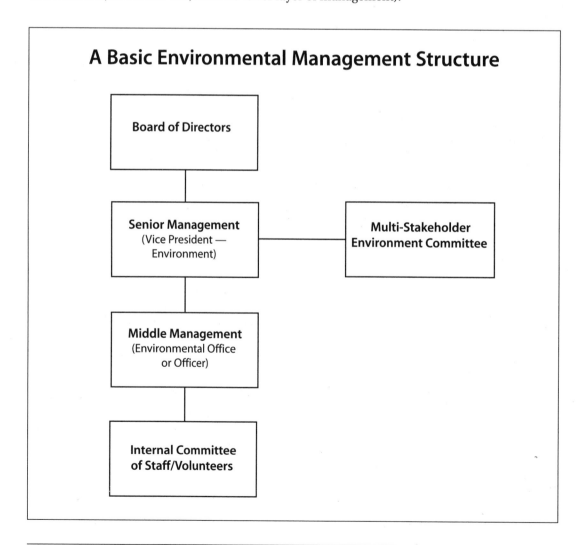

A Basic Environmental Management Structure

Board of Directors

Senior Management
(Vice President —
Environment)

Multi-Stakeholder
Environment Committee

Middle Management
(Environmental Office
or Officer)

Internal Committee
of Staff/Volunteers

Structure Within an Organization

Within the organization, ultimate responsibility should reside with the top person, normally the president or chief executive officer, or volunteer chairperson (in the case of a more informal organization). If a vice president or director for the environment is assigned responsibility for environmental policy implementation, this person must have an effective route for reporting regularly to the top. In addition, where there is a board of directors, environmental management reports should be tabled regularly at meetings of the board.

At the operational level, an environmental division or, in the case of smaller organizations, a single staff person supported by volunteers, may be required to carry out specific tasks related to environmental issues, such as coordinating programs, education and monitoring. A risk that can accompany creating a dedicated group/position of this sort, however, is that the rest of the organization will attempt to pass on to it anything at all related to the environment. It must be made abundantly clear that environmental responsibility resides at all levels and in all functional areas. Essentially, everyone is responsible for incorporating sustainable management into his/her daily tasks. By involving non-environmental operational staff in the creation and execution of their respective action plans, they will acquire both a sense of "ownership" and a better understanding of the rationale behind it. The designated environmental officer or department should be seen as the coordinator and resource person to assist all members of the organization in moving towards sustainability.

"Sustainable development cannot be viewed in isolation or tagged on as a specific issue; all those responsible for every aspect of planning must take it into consideration. Sustainable development is not just ecology: it is the nexus between economics and ecology and therefore needs to be incorporated into all aspects of a business" (National Round Table on the Environment and Economy 1991).

Facilitating Shared Responsibility

For this shared responsibility to occur, all members of an organization must be educated in the relevant environmental issues and goals. Managers must recognize the important role of staff and volunteers (explored in more detail in Chapter 5), both as those who will turn policy into action and as sources of new ideas based on their daily experience. It is crucial, therefore, that management develops a process that encourages participation. For example, in addition to such tools as suggestion boxes and a hotline for information and advice, a large organization should have an Environment Committee, with representation from every department and every workplace function, i.e. cleaners, equipment maintenance staff, groundskeepers, cafeteria staff, secretaries, purchasing managers, accountants, public affairs personnel and volunteers.

External stakeholders can also be a valuable contributor to the process of managing sustainably, if treated as an asset rather than a liability. Most high-level business and governmental managers tend to regard non-governmental organizations (NGOs) such as environmental groups and social activists, with a blend of fear and mistrust. This is unfortunate. More often than not the view stems from a mutual lack of understanding. The more innovative companies and governments have, in recent years, begun to invite these traditional "antagonists" into their meetings and even onto their boards. Those that have done so have often benefited from the knowledge that these NGOs bring with them: a knowledge of public concerns and social trends that may have a profound effect on their future. Sport organizations would do well to invite environmental NGOs to act as their critics and watchdogs.

Community Relations

Under pressure from a coalition of concerned community groups, the city of Toronto initiated a public consultation process and provided intervenor funding to allow citizens to express their concerns for the bid for the 1996 Olympics. The Toronto Organizing Committee (TOOC) showed little interest in this process, however; it failed to incorporate concerned stakeholders — outside of the bid's corporate backers — in the decision-making process. Toronto's bid for the 2008 Olympic Games learned from the mistakes of its predecessor. It included from the outset, a diverse cross-section of community interests on its many committees, including environment and has carried out extensive consultation with a range of interested and affected groups.

Lillehammer's bid resembled Toronto's initially. The LOOC — composed of the typical cast of sport officials, local business leaders, municipal politicians and developers — showed little interest in acknowledging the concerns raised by Games critics. Under pressure from the county government, the Norwegian parliament, the media and eventually the IOC itself, to make the Games "an environmental showcase", LOOC joined a multi-party process to examine how environmental concerns should be addressed. It was recognized that to meet such a goal would require new ways of working, new alliances, and new tools. In 1991, a constructive tri-party relationship was established between LOOC, the Ministry of the Environment and Project Environmentally Friendly Olympics (PEFO). Their unique model of cooperation solved a series of single issues and led to the "green profile" of the 1994 Games.

This so-called second track must be equally inclusive of concerned parties from outside the organization. The importance of involving these stakeholders cannot be over-estimated. This is an opportunity to hear from such diverse interests as local residents, environmental groups, social welfare organizations and others whose voice may be as important to the quality of the event as business groups and elected politicians, but who are rarely granted a forum.

A number of recent bid groups and organizing committees for major games have been including environmental groups as part of the team. Both parties can benefit from such a partnership, as long as it helps them achieve their goals: a winning bid, a better event, cleaner more efficient facilities and a healthier environment.

Such a participatory process should be formalized by creating an environmental/sustainability advisory committee which includes representation from these groups and which gives them genuine input into decision-making. Though public consultation should be a part of such a process, it must go beyond that if it is to be seen as more than window dressing.

With a two-track structure such as this, a process can be created that takes full account of and makes good use of the viewpoints of people within the organization and outside of it.

The Aspen Skiing Company encouraged the creation of a Community Environmental Advisory Committee, made up of local experts, with whom it works closely. "They've become part of our decision-making process," says Pat O'Donnell, president and CEO. (Tomorrow 2001)

Key Steps in Environmental Management Planning
a) Define Your Vision.
b) Determine Your Broad Goals/Objectives.
c) Develop a Detailed Action Plan with Measurable Targets.
d) Identify the Tools You Need.
e) Monitor and Measure the Results You Have Achieved.
f) Reassess your Goals/Objectives.
g) Revise Your Action Plan.

Defining Environmental Goals and Objectives

Any organization committed to better environmental management must first set out a vision. From this vision statement, it can then elaborate a series of fundamental goals or objectives, followed by the policies, strategies and initiatives by which the goals will be achieved. The International Institute for Sustainable Development (IISD), in its Business Strategy for Sustainable Development (Mulligan 1992), states, "management should incorporate stakeholder expectations into a broad policy statement that sets forth the organization's mission with respect to sustainable development." Such a statement should be "both inspirational and capable of influencing behavior." Though this task is likely to be challenging and time consuming, it focuses attention on the commitment.

A policy statement should be supplemented with a series of specific objectives and, where possible, with assignments of responsibility as well as deadlines for completion. They should complement the organization's existing strategies, rather than pulling in an opposite direction.

The RCGA's Statement of Intent

An example of a simple and general policy statement is the RCGA's Statement of Intent (1993).

"The Royal Canadian Golf Association is committed to taking every practical precaution towards ensuring that products and techniques used in the development and maintenance of golf courses present the lowest possible risk to their employees, golfers, the public and the environment."

Here is a sample of environmental objectives set by organizers of the Lillehammer Olympic Games:

- Make people aware of their attitudes in dealing with the environment.

- Be considerate of regional social considerations.

- Encourage sustainable development and growth in industry and business.

- Build facilities friendly to the environment.

- Assure environmental quality in all facets of the Olympic event.

> # OCA Environmental Policy
>
> The Olympic Coordination Authority is committed to the principles of Ecologically Sustainable Development (ESD), in particular the conservation of species and natural resources, and the control of pollution.
>
> In providing, to time and budget, community recreational and associated infrastructure for the Sydney 2000 Olympic and Paralympic Games, and beyond, the OCA's commitment is to:
>
> - protect and enhance remnant natural ecosystems on OCA development sites;
>
> - improve the quality of water entering waterways from OCA sites;
>
> - remediate the legacy of past pollution to ensure land is suitable for its use;
>
> - protect soil and sediments within areas for which the OCA is responsible;
>
> - encourage the use of recycled materials and reduce waste generation;
>
> - minimize the demand for potable water from Sydney mains supply;
>
> - minimize the use of energy from non-renewable sources;
>
> - minimize emissions of greenhouse gases and minimize the use of ozone depleting substances;
>
> - minimize the use of materials which deplete natural resources or create toxic pollution;
>
> - minimize the impacts of noise and night lighting on environmental conservation and neighboring residential areas; and
>
> - minimize impacts on air quality.
>
> The OCA will comply with all relevant environmental regulation including statutory planning instruments and meet the guiding principles of the Environmental Guidelines for the Summer Olympic Games. The OCA will implement development practices for its sites that promote ESD and will involve and communicate with interested parties. Appropriate management systems will be implemented to meet environmental objectives and continually improve environmental performance.
>
> The OCA is committed to sharing its knowledge and experience with others through liaison with key stakeholders to promote and achieve positive environmental values and outcomes.
>
> *Source: Olympic Co-ordination Authority (2000)*

Translating objectives of this breadth and generality into operational terms probably would require numerous changes to an existing organization. In the case of an organization still in the planning stages, changes to the way it is being set up may be required. The IISD describes it as a "rethinking of the corporation." To capture, develop, implement and enforce the types of changes in the above set of objectives requires:

- active involvement of the board of directors and senior executives;

- an effective two-way consultation process to elicit ongoing feedback from stakeholder groups;

- modifying the organization's systems and processes to ensure that the organization's day-to-day activities are consistent with the objectives;

- developing a supportive corporate culture through retraining in new management systems, technical processes and procedures, as well as through reward systems and incentives;

- strategic planning processes modified to reflect the new priorities and the desire to increase stakeholder involvement;

- management information systems to assist managers and employees in planning and controlling their performance against the established objectives;

- marketing that considers the new demands and needs of customers regarding the environment;

- procurement processes that further the organization's objectives by evaluating the environmental profile of products and their suppliers; and

- financial planning that considers the capital requirements for process changes and the ramifications of new processes and procedures.

Precisely how many of these changes might be applied by sport organizations will be dealt with in subsequent chapters. Those that fall primarily within the ambit of management, however, are covered here.

Overcoming Resistance

The challenge for champions of greater sustainability/responsibility — whether they be the lowest on the totem pole or members of the board is to make the case for change and dispel the lingering myths. Scores of organizations are proving that good environmental management is either revenue neutral or ultimately a source of savings or new opportunities. In addition, taking the sustainable path can be shown to have a wide range of benefits:

- reduced risks, leading to lower insurance and clean-up costs;

- improved morale among staff and volunteers, leading to better performance and retention of good people;

- greater appeal to sponsors, donors and partners;

- faster project approvals and fewer expensive delays;

- increased public support; and

- better conditions for sport leading to improved performances and better overall health of athletes.

Where top managers and/or colleagues need to be persuaded of the value of moving to more sustainable practices, arguments should be carefully prepared showing the potential benefits to the organization in the one or several categories that are most likely to prove persuasive. Citing success stories from similar organizations is often a particularly powerful technique. Many such stories can be found in this book.

We now turn to more specific management tools that you can use to address environmental issues more responsibly.

What You Can Do: Large and Medium-Size Organizations

Every organization that is serious about environmental management should conduct an environmental audit, include ongoing assessments, monitor results, and develop solid reporting mechanisms. Medium and larger organizations should step up to the next level and adopt a more formal environmental management system (EMS).

The Environmental Management System (EMS)

Business and government have done a great deal of work recently on developing methods of environmental management that are practical and cost-effective. Different systems have been proposed for various sectors and a range of types and sizes of organizations. In general, an effective environmental management system for any organization is one that is capable of (a) defining the environmental and economic goals, policies and strategies of the organization, and (b) implementing them.

The decision to initiate an EMS must come from the top level of the organization. Either the board of directors or the chief executive officer or the equivalent head of a smaller organization might initiate it. In all cases, for the EMS to be effectively designed and implemented it will require the support of the directors, administrators and, as will be discussed below, all levels of staff and volunteers.

As every sport group is unique, it requires a personalized EMS that is appropriate to the size, organizational structures and issues of particular interest within the community. To construct such an EMS it is not, however, necessary to begin from scratch. There are plenty of models, generic and specific, that might be adopted or adapted. Associations of sport administrators, colleges and universities, national federations, etc. might help to develop an EMS framework that member organizations can easily tailor to their needs.

A good example of this is the Committed to Green program developed by the former European Golf Association Ecology Unit. This has been set up to provide golf clubs with a structured and systematic approach to environmental management without frightening managers with the complexity and bureaucracy of an industrial standard EMS. In fact, Committed to Green was closely modeled on the European Commission's Eco-Management and Audit Scheme but stripped down, branded and presented at a level appropriate for small golf clubs.

Main Elements of the ISO 14001 Environmental Management System

Though many EMS models exist, the increasingly dominant one is that of the International Organization for Standardization (ISO). The ISO 14000 series of environmental standards has an EMS model (14001) that can be applied to any medium-large organization. Smaller organizations can, however, use ISO 14001 for guidance. Whether or not an organization will want to certify as 14001-compliant will depend on its size, objectives and the degree of public scrutiny to which it is subjected.

The ISO 14001 Standard for Environmental Management Systems runs along these lines:

Environmental Policy

Define the organization's environmental policy and ensure that it:

a) is appropriate to its activities and services;

b) supports continual improvement and pollution prevention;

c) contains a commitment to comply with legislation and regulations;

d) has a framework for setting objectives and targets;

e) is documented, implemented, maintained and communicated to all employees; and

f) is publicly available.

Planning

Environmental Aspects

Develop a procedure to identify the environmental aspects of activities, in order to determine those which have significant impact. Consider these when setting objectives.

Legal and Other Requirements

Identify legal and other applicable requirements.

Objectives and Targets

Establish and maintain documented environmental objectives and targets, at each relevant function and level within the organization.

Environmental Management Programs

Establish programs for achieving objectives and targets. Designate responsibilities and determine the methods and schedule by which objectives and targets are to be achieved.

Implementation and Operation

Structure and Responsibilities

Roles, responsibilities and authorities shall be defined, documented and communicated. Management shall provide resources needed to implement the EMS.

Training, Awareness and Competence

Identify training needs for all personnel whose work has a significant impact upon the environment. Make employees or members aware of:

a) the importance of conformance with the requirements of the EMS;

b) the significant environmental impacts of their activities and the environmental benefits of improved personal performance;

c) their roles and responsibilities in achieving conformance; and

d) the potential consequences of departure from procedures.

Communication

Develop procedures for internal communication and handling communication from stakeholders regarding environmental issues and the EMS.

Documentation

Document the core elements of the EMS and direct people to related documentation.

Checking and Corrective Action

Monitoring and Measurement

Develop procedures to monitor the key characteristics of operations and activities that can have a significant impact on the environment. Record information to track performance, relevant operational controls and conformance with objectives and targets.

Corrective and Preventive Action

Develop procedures for defining responsibility and authority for handling and investigating non-conformance, taking action to mitigate any impacts caused and for initiating corrective and preventive action.

EMS Audit

Conduct periodic EMS audits in order to determine how well the EMS is functioning and is being maintained, and provide the results of audits to management.

Management Review

Top management shall regularly review the effectiveness of the EMS, to ensure its continuing suitability, adequacy and effectiveness.

The essential components of Committed to Green are that it is a voluntary participation program, predicated on continual improvement in performance and a commitment to publish results that have been verified by a credible, third party. One important difference from the likes of ISO 14001 is that Committed to Green provides the incentive of its label of recognition on the basis of tangible improvements in performance. In this respect it goes beyond merely being an EMS, to being a mark of accreditation.

Environmental Audits

The environmental audits described here might be performed as part of an EMS (above) or separately, by an organization that has chosen not to develop an EMS.

Environmental audits can take several forms: management audits, compliance audits, performance audits and risk audits. Though compliance and risk audits should be undertaken at some stage to evaluate to what extent an organization's operations and facilities are in compliance with environmental regulations and at what risk their operations and assets might put them, of most relevance to a sport organization would be the management and performance audits. The management audit reviews the philosophy, policies and practices of an organization and, by examining current structures and systems advises on steps that should be taken to improve environmental management. The performance audit, also referred to as a process or operations audit, is the most detailed. It entails a thorough investigation of operations to evaluate environmental efficiency, procurement practices, use of current processes and overall use of resources.

An initial audit should be conducted by an impartial outside specialist versed in leading-edge practices. It is especially important that a risk or compliance audit be performed by experts in this field. Though a management or performance audit can be carried out internally, it is advisable to include at least one outsider in the assessment. The auditing group conducts on-site visits, interviews with management and employees, document reviews, direct measurement, estimation and comparative studies. The auditor's report will then make recommendations for improvements. Depending on the detail of audit requested, an action plan for implementing necessary changes may also be provided. This might include recommendations for improved management structures, consultation processes and financial control systems, as well as strategies for waste management, energy reduction, incentive programs, and purchasing practices.

Ongoing Monitoring and Evaluation

Once an initial audit has been conducted it is essential that follow-up audits be performed, at least annually. Though subsequent audits might be less detailed and performed in-house, the initial audit will be of little value if annual progress is not measured and evaluated. The real value of the audit becomes apparent when performance can be monitored and evaluated from year to year, allowing managers to identify trouble spots and areas of opportunity.

Reporting Procedures

The final step in the environmental management process is to prepare and disseminate reports on the organization's sustainable development objectives and its success in achieving them. Providing relevant, reliable and meaningful information is not only a valuable means of communication with both internal and external stakeholders, it is a further sign of commitment. It can also indicate to the general public, directly and through the media, that organizational effectiveness is about more than sales and profits. Though the typical annual report is limited to hard economic and financial statistics and analysis, Michael Alexander (1973) warns that this is only a part of what stakeholders want, indeed need, to know: "If information is limited to financial and economic matters," he states, the organization "cannot expect to be heard by its employees, its communities and society." These groups are as interested in and concerned by the social and human impact of the organization as they are by the economic.

Every organization should, as a minimum standard, have the following reporting procedures:

◆ Line managers regularly reporting on the extent to which they have met their environmental and sustainable development targets.

◆ Senior management, in turn, providing periodic reports of this nature to the board of directors.

◆ An annual external sustainable development report, included in or to accompanying the corporate annual report.

These management practices can be effectively implemented by virtually all large- or medium-sized sport groups.

A new initiative, Global Responsibility, is developing an environmental reporting method for the sport sector, via the Internet. The platform is based on recognized international standards, notably UNEP's Global Reporting Initiative, which will be adapted to be most relevant to the sport industry. A key concern of Global Responsibility is to enable small companies and organizations to be able to participate and to provide a basis of comparability between different reports. Accountability through transparency will be one of the lead themes for the sport sector, and industry generally, in the coming years.

Small and/or Informal Organizations

Small and/or less formal organizations which have chosen not to adopt a full-fledged, formal environmental management system should nevertheless consider implementing several key elements, such as a simplified environmental audit of compliance, risks and performance; regular monitoring and evaluation of performance, and standardized reporting procedures. This simplified checklist provides a good starting point.

A Simplified Environmental Management Checklist

❑ Create an environmental policy which includes a vision statement that all directors, managers, staff and volunteers will support.

❑ Define specific Objectives in each issue area relevant to your organization (i.e. waste management, energy reduction, purchasing).

❑ Develop a detailed Action Plan, which sets out specific tasks to be performed to achieve the Objectives.

❑ Draw up an Organizational Chart for managing environmental issues, ensuring that there is a clear procedure for reporting.

❑ Carry out an Environmental Audit (i.e. energy and water consumption and waste generation) of facilities, and work with government agencies and local utilities to identify opportunities for energy and water conservation, waste management and reducing the risk of hazardous waste contamination.

❑ Identify key environmental and performance issues to be monitored based on your chosen objectives. On a regular basis (at least annually) monitor performance in each of these areas and report progress.

❑ Refine your Objectives and Action Plan based on performance results.

What You Can Do

Summary of Recommendations for Environmental Management

◆ Develop a structure and a process which gives everybody responsibility for and a stake in good environmental management.

◆ Embrace environmental leadership at the top.

◆ Do not relegate "the environment" to one person or group.

◆ Establish an inclusive process, both internally and externally, that takes account of and learns from the concerns of all stakeholder groups.

◆ Create an internal Environmental Committee.

◆ Create a Citizens' Environmental Advisory Council.

◆ Set up a hotline for those seeking specific information and advice.

◆ Invite an environmental group to act as designated watchdog.

◆ Define an environmental/sustainability policy statement.

◆ Develop a series of specific objectives with assignments of responsibility and deadlines for completion.

◆ Conduct environmental audits.

◆ Perform ongoing monitoring and evaluation.

◆ Create an effective internal environmental reporting mechanism.

◆ Prepare and disseminate an annual sustainable development report.

What to Use

Helpful publications

Crognale, G., P.E. 1999. *Environmental management strategies: The 21st century perspective.*

European Golf Association. 1997. *The committed to green handbook for golf courses.*

Hawken, Lovins and Lovins. 1999. *Natural capitalism.*

Nattrass, B., and Altomare, M. 1999. *The Natural Step for business.*

Noble, Duncan. 2001. *Cool business guide: Lower costs, higher productivity and climate change solutions.*

Romm, Joseph J. 1999. *Cool companies: How the best businesses boost profits and productivity by cutting greenhouse gas emissions.*

Sports Canada. 1998. *Managing and monitoring environmental performance of sports events and facilities.*

Tibor, T and I. Feldman. 1995. *ISO14000: A guide to the new environmental management standards.*

Useful web sites

Business for Social Responsibility: **www.bsr.org**

Coalition for Environmentally Responsible Economies: **www.ceres.org**

Global Responsibility: **www.global-responsibility.com**

Globenet: **www.ISO14000.net**

Integrated Management Systems: **www.solutions.ca/links.htm**

International Institute for Sustainable Development: **www.iisd1.iisd.ca**

Natural Capitalism: **www.naturalcapitalism.org**

Second Nature: **www.secondnature.org**

Whom to Consult

Organizations wanting to develop a formal environmental management system should seek outside assistance from experts in this field. Specialists in EMS as well as Environmental Auditing might be located via your local provincial/state environmental agency as well as professional institutes/associations. Always check references and speak to others who have used the companies' services.

Chapter

5 Inspiring and Preparing Employees and Volunteers: Out of the Blocks Early

The quickest and most visible way to begin moving a sport organization toward sustainability—assuming the appropriate managerial commitment—is among the staff and volunteers and within the offices and the departments that actually run the place, which typically include administration, accounting, purchasing, planning and marketing. It is these offices, through their size, rank and visibility, which will set the trend for the organization.

With the right corporate culture in place, or at least in a healthy formative stage, these offices can use several tools to effect change. The judicious application of several fundamental principles to the way in which all offices are run, the development of responsible attitudes and clear planning, the equipment and materials they use, the way in which purchases are made and the manner in which resources are ultimately disposed of, can have a far-reaching effect within the entire organization. The decisions you make in how you run an organization and its offices can profoundly affect almost every other organization that these offices deal with, since these decisions are most visible to people inside and out.

Though a commitment to sustainable management should come first, it is fruitless to wait for all managers and employees to be "onside" before you take the first practical steps. In fact, the more dubious members of an organization can be brought into the believers' camp when they see how well initial changes are working.

Developing a Supportive Corporate Culture

Attempts to implement sustainable policies and procedures will not get far in an organization whose corporate culture is not open to such changes. Both managers and staff can balk at change. Most will need to be persuaded of its benefits and equipped to make changes as effortless as possible.

Managers can take several steps to help develop an organizational culture (involving all employees and volunteers) that is flexible and open to changes in procedures and practices; steps that, as an added bonus, have the fortunate effect of improving the working atmosphere for all. Many organizations that have introduced advanced environmental management practices have in the process experienced a new type of organizational renewal.

Those at the top can best demonstrate the organization's commitment by becoming personally involved. This point cannot be overstated: "The active and visible involvement of senior executives and the board of directors can be a powerful force in forming attitudes and creating a supportive culture for sustainable development" (International Institute for Sustainable Development 1992).

As part of the prerequisite step of ensuring that environmental responsibility is introduced at all levels, employees are made to feel a part of these positive changes. The International Institute for Sustainable Development (1993) observes that "the increased involvement and participation of employees in these programs not only generates positive practical ideas, but also increases energy and enthusiasm for the programs. Most customers and employees want to be part of organizations that are committed to operating in a socially responsible manner." Numerous human resources studies have shown how job satisfaction and employee pride can be significantly higher in organizations that are socially and ethically progressive.

There are four additional ways in which to spread the appropriate corporate culture:

1. Establish effective means of communication.

2. Train and educate staff and volunteers to rethink their behavior.

3. Create reinforcing incentives.

4. Designate adequate resources.

Communication

Employees and managers must be given full and advance warning of what they can expect from any shift to new practices. People must understand the policies and objectives that are being established. They must also have a means of expressing their concerns. Any major shifts in policy or practices should be preceded by thorough consultation. Once a decision has been taken regarding the precise stages and timing of change, employees should be given advance warning. Finally, assistance should be provided to allow employees to embrace the new program with confidence: training, education and any new "tools" that may be required.

Training and Education

Appropriate training and education programs must accompany any sustainable development initiative. While these should certainly be tailor-made to cover the specific tasks and responsibilities of the target audience, it is equally important that all members of an organization be informed of the broader rationale for changes. This should include an explanation of the general environmental and economic context in which the initiative has been launched, for example, the issues of climate change, ozone depletion, waste disposal and pesticides—their global and local impact as well their relevance to the operations of the organization.

All members of the organization should receive adequate information and training. Most often neglected by educational programs are senior managers and volunteers. The former may feel they are already adequately informed and far too busy to set aside a day for training whose immediate application is not obvious to them. The latter tend to be wrongly dismissed as marginal members of the organization who do not merit the expense of such instruction. This is unfortunate, not only because volunteers can outnumber paid staff, but also because they are often the public face of the organization at a major event.

Training can be provided by outside consultants or qualified staff. Larger organizations with ongoing training programs should consider offering environment/sustainable management-related training and materials on a regular basis. New staff/volunteers should receive a basic introduction to corporate environmental practices as part of their initial orientation program. Smaller organizations may need to rely on less formal training and education. Useful tools include a basic tour of facilities and demonstration of equipment by a qualified staff member as well as a standard "manual" covering practices, procedures, resources to consult and answers to frequently asked questions.

Incentives

Incentives can go a long way towards building an appropriate corporate culture. Existing disincentives can be equally destructive of such a culture.

Training for Sydney Organizers, Staff and Volunteers

Both of the principal groups preparing for Sydney 2000 instituted formal training programs. The OCA developed a curriculum for all staff, which combined general environmental management education with specific Games-related material. Construction-related tradespeople were provided training regarding on-site health, safety and materials management issues, including materials storage for reuse and waste separation for recycling. Those who completed the course received a "Working Greener" sticker for their construction hardhats. SOCOG developed an environmental training session, which was a mandatory part of initial orientation for all staff and volunteers. Updates and explanatory material were also regularly displayed or circulated at SOCOG headquarters.

The simplest example of a practical incentive comes from Bell Canada's Zero Waste initiative. Having been informed in advance, employees arrived at work one Monday morning to find a blue recycling bin and a small plastic bag for disposal of non-recyclables, where their garbage cans had been. From that date onward the blue box would be emptied nightly while the plastic bag would be replaced each week only. It would be up to them to take their non-recyclables to the one large bin allocated for each floor. By reversing the services to which people were accustomed, a powerful incentive to recycle was created.

One form of disincentive to reduce waste is common in many large organizations: at fiscal year-end, financial managers rush to spend any remaining funds so as to justify receiving a similar amount in the next year's budget. Money that has not been spent is viewed as a sign of bad forecasting, as opposed to one of fiscal responsibility. This can lead to a situation like that of one government office which had ten laser printers in an office of nine people, two of whom could not type. Organizations must ensure that established disincentives are not canceling out any new incentives.

Designating Adequate Resources

Sufficient resources must be allocated up front to properly implement an environmental management initiative. An initial investment is required to make system and process changes, to introduce effective communications and to train and educate people. Failing to provide sufficient funding for people to carry out their assigned tasks is certain to sabotage the initiative and dampen enthusiasm.

The most important point for managers is that front-of-the-pipe spending (e.g., on waste reduction and pollution prevention) is far more effective and less costly in the long run than end-of-the-pipe measures such as waste disposal and clean-up, or paying fines. Managers should consider: (a) how urgently must changes be made? (b) how much money can be saved by making necessary changes? and (c) what is the bare minimum cost of training courses, educational material, consulting fees, etc. required to get the job done?

Creating an Action Plan

Two key building blocks for any organization — creating an appropriate management structure and an environmental management system (EMS) — were explored in the previous chapter. Your organization will have chosen to take a formal or less formal approach, as appropriate to its needs. Whatever route you opt for, the key stage for translating policy into action is the environmental "Action Plan" or program.

Once you have established which issues need to be addressed by your organization, based upon the results of any environmental audits, impact assessments, internal or community consultations, you will be ready to move forward to preparing an Action Plan. The Action Plan should follow a logical progression, starting with your environmental policy, followed by the definition of goals, more detailed objectives and, finally, specific targets.

Not all organizations will require a comprehensive Action Plan, nor will they necessarily have the knowledge or resources to implement one. For smaller organizations, and those new to environmental management, a basic Action Plan may be sufficient. It is often better to tackle a smaller number of top priority issues, and to do a good job, than to achieve mixed results on an overly ambitious list of issues. In Chapter 12, you can find examples of both a basic Action Plan and a more comprehensive plan for event organizers.

The elements to be addressed by an organization vary enormously, depending on size, geography, funding, local challenges, sport involved and the environmental literacy of staff, volunteers and participants. An overview of the issues to be addressed by several types of sport organizations is provided below.

Governing Bodies

Bodies responsible for setting and enforcing the rules and technical requirements which govern sport and selecting the hosts of key events have an enormous influence over the way facilities are designed and operated and events are staged. These organizations, particularly those at the top of the pinnacle like the IOC, International Ski Federation, United States Golf Association and National Collegiate Athletic Association, can use that influence for the better by ensuring that their rules and decisions work to further sustainable sport rather than to hinder it.

Major sport bodies should reexamine their current technical requirements, rules of play, codes of conduct, criteria for selecting event hosts, and their own corporate practices, for opportunities to promote sustainable sport and to remove any unnecessary impediments.

This process of adopting the concept of "sustainable sport" under various names (green games, environmentally-friendly) by governing bodies is underway. Various national and international sport federations and associations are committing themselves to principles and policies, codes of conduct and host selection criteria that educate and help to further the concept. For example, environmental criteria are now used as part of the host city selection process by the IOC, the Canada Games Council (below) and the International Cycling Union.

Canada Games Council Environmental Criteria for Bids

A. Environmental Policies, Plans and Structures

1. Has an Environmental Policy been adopted by the organization?

2. Has an Environmental Plan been developed with specific targets and objectives?

3. How will the Host Society be structured to encourage environmental responsibility at all levels?

4. Have all stakeholders likely to be affected by the event been consulted during the bid preparation process?

5. What partnerships have been formed with external stakeholders?

6. Have Environmental Impact Assessments been done for new or renovated facilities?

B. Human Health

1. What steps will be taken to protect the health of the competitors and all other participants?

2. What will be done to reduce or eliminate threats to participants from environmental factors such as:

   ◆ air pollution and smog?

   ◆ exposure to dangerous ultraviolet rays?

   ◆ impure drinking water?

   ◆ polluted water at venues?

   ◆ poor indoor air quality?

   ◆ hazardous chemicals, building materials, etc.?

3. What standards have been adopted in the above potential risk areas?

C. Resource Conservation and Pollution Prevention Measures

1. What steps will be taken to conserve energy?

2. Will the use of renewable energy sources be encouraged?

3. What waste management targets have been set and what strategies are planned to meet them?

4. What steps will be taken to reduce the impact of the Canada Games on:
   - air quality?
   - water quality?
   - soil quality?

D. Environmental Protection

1. Will any existing natural spaces or wilderness be developed?

2. Will any events be held or facilities built or expanded in protected natural areas?

3. Has an environmental impact assessment been completed for any such events/facilities?

4. What steps are being taken to protect natural spaces, habitat or species?

5. What restorative or rehabilitative measures will be taken?

E. Facilities construction and management

1. What new facilities will be built?

2. What purpose will they serve following the event?

3. Are they designed to meet the needs of both the event and post-event use:
   - in size?
   - in technological features?
   - in location?

4. Can temporary facilities serve the needs of the event equally well?

F. Transportation

1. What will the impact of the event be on transportation levels and infrastructure?

2. How will any anticipated demand increases be addressed?

3. What steps will be taken to encourage use of public transportation and active transportation by competitors, participants and spectators?

G. Legacy

1. What steps have been taken to ensure a positive legacy from the event:
   - economically?
   - socially?
   - environmentally?

Reprinted courtesy of the Canada Games Council

Environmental codes of practice have been adopted by the North American Mountain Biking Association, the International Equestrian Federation and many others. Specific environmental programs and projects have been launched by the International Rowing Federation (FISA) and the European Golf Association (EGA).

Major Games

While every "major games" will differ, they share such common elements as: multiple sports; multiple facilities; large numbers of participants; accommodations in an "athletes' village" of some description; transportation requirements; media interest; and a duration of several days or weeks. Planning for a major event must begin at least several years in advance. For major games to achieve greater sustainability, it is critical that any sustainable event initiative be adopted at the earliest possible stage.

Though Lillehammer will go down in history as the first attempt to green a major games, it must be remembered that the LOOC only embraced the idea of a "green profile" at a relatively late stage in the preparatory process and only after heavy prompting from other stakeholders. The first Olympic Games to have incorporated the goal of a sustainable event from the outset was Sydney 2000. As a result, Sydney 2000 was the first major games with the opportunity to embed the goals and objectives of a "green games" into all areas of the organization and all aspects of the event itself. Taking this early and comprehensive approach meant Sydney was able to realize benefits well beyond those achieved at Lillehammer.

The Salt Lake Organizing Committee has also created an environmental program for the 2002 Winter Olympics. An outline of the SLOC 2002 environmental platform can be found at the end of this chapter.

The sustainable major games will incorporate sustainable sport thinking and translate it into action. It will also use its positive profile to advantage both for publicity and as a means of leverage for getting stakeholders involved in a positive way. Once the objective of sustainable sport has been adopted by all governing bodies and federations and built into the host selection process, all major games will be required to take steps to improve sustainability.

Issues to be addressed at a Major Games or Event:

- Environmental management
- "Sustainable Office" practices
- Purchasing
- Partnerships with stakeholders
- Working with the media
- Sponsorship and donations
- Materials and waste management
- Transportation

- Facilities construction / operation

- Accommodation

- Food services

- Event legacy

- Sustainable travel/tourism opportunities

Minor Games and Championships

From the point of view of improving sustainability, the differences between what we consider major games and minor games and between them and single-sport championships are remarkably few. Running a minor multi-sport event can be as complex as organizing a major event.

Where there are differences, they tend to fall into two areas: budgets are smaller and/or a narrower range of facilities is required. Both of these serve to restrict the amount of building that is done specifically for the event and the size of projects that can be undertaken by event organizers and local communities. Smaller sport events rarely have new facilities built or roads expanded for them. They also tend to house athletes in existing accommodations rather than in dedicated athlete villages.

Despite these differences, smaller events have many of the same operational needs as major games and face similar challenges. As a result, the list of areas where these minor events can improve their sustainability is almost as long as that for major games found above. Though minor events should follow a similar process and tackle all applicable issues, they will likely have fewer resources with which to do so. They may therefore want to stress solutions that come with a lower up-front price tag or none at all. The cheapest way for a sport organization to benefit from sustainability is to emphasize good environmental management and eco-efficiency.

Issues to be addressed at a Minor Games or Championship:

- Good environmental management

- "Sustainable Office" practices

- Eco-efficient systems, processes and practices

- Renovating and retrofitting facilities with an eye to pay-back on investments

- Developing partnerships with stakeholders

- Working closely with sponsors, donors and suppliers

- Materials and waste management

- Transportation

- Promoting a positive legacy

Professional Sport

Professional sport tends to be characterized by a series of short events confined to one sport. Given its duration, it is remarkable how much of an impact one such event can have on the environment, let alone a series or entire season of such events. The impact of a professional sport event tends to be confined mostly to the facility in which it is held or it's near vicinity. It is therefore at this facility and on its grounds and neighboring streets that the professional sport organization, its governing body and the facilities operator should be looking to implement solutions.

The 1997 Ryder Cup at Valderamma — "Committed to Green"

Measures to "green" the event formed an important part of the 1997 Ryder Cup, and ran in tandem with the environmental initiatives at the Valderrama Golf Course in Spain. The following are several environmental initiatives taken as part of the Ryder Cup's "Committed to Green" campaign:

Transportation

The use of shuttle buses to transport 8,000 visitors to and from their hotels, plus a park and ride scheme considerably reduced congestion, noise and air pollution.

Waste Management

A recycling operation was sponsored by Eastman Chemical Company through their Good Sports Always Recycle campaign. PET recyclable plastic materials used for Cups and bottles for the event were made from Eastpak Polymer, so that they could be recycled and used for new applications such as clothing and packaging.

Materials Management

The event installed purchasing policies for environmentally preferred materials, with the emphasis on reducing where possible and then seeking materials that can either be reused or recycled.

Infrastructure and construction

As an existing facility, relatively little new construction was required at Valderrama. New car parking facilities were built on sites already designated for future development. Catering and hospitality centers were all temporary structures sited to avoid removing mature trees.

Energy Efficiency

Additional energy was brought to Valderrama from the new clean-burn natural gas power plant in Tarifa. On the golf course many quieter, less polluting vehicles were used for official use.

Communications and Public Awareness

Feature articles on "Committed to Green" were published in the official Ryder Cup Program and the Daily Magazine. Six interpretative panels on Valderrama's wildlife and local ecology were on display around the course and additional display panels at key entrance points announced the initiative. A special Valderrama Environmental Statement was also published. Environmental briefing notes were distributed to TV and radio commentators and "Committed to Green" was formally launched at a press conference by European Community President Jacques Santer.

Both the professional sport organization or franchise and its governing body must first recognize their connection to the community that supports them. A team that relies almost entirely on community support must nurture that relationship and acknowledge its responsibilities to its supporters. Those supporters include both the active fan and the taxpayer who allows municipal facilities and even funds to be used by the team. Where the professional organization contributes to smog, traffic congestion, solid waste, noise, energy demands, sewage volume, etc., it has a responsibility to contribute to solving these same problems.

By building sustainable thinking into its operations, the professional sport organization can take advantage of both the short- and long-term savings available. Unlike one-time events, most sport teams and facilities will be around long enough to benefit directly from the savings that eventually accrue from their investments in greener systems and technologies.

Given the high profile enjoyed and encouraged by professional sport over a prolonged period, an opportunistic organization committed to sustainability can legitimately develop a positive image for itself. Companies that are seen as caring and committed to their community, not to mention the planet, will enjoy a big leg up in the sport marketing game. That reputation can be enhanced even further by work with the community on joint initiatives and education campaigns and by supporting local groups in their environmental work.

Issues to be addressed by professional sport organizations

- Environmental management
- "Sustainable Office" practices
- Purchasing: establishing criteria and partnerships with suppliers
- Partnerships with stakeholders, especially concerned community groups
- Partnerships with sponsors
- Materials and waste management
  - Reducing the vast quantities of waste generated by spectators
- Food services
- Ceremonies and entertainment
- Transportation
  - Improving accessibility by public transportation
  - Reducing traffic congestion, pollution and noise
  - Discouraging private vehicle dependence
- Facilities construction and operation
  - Building design, equipment and materials
  - Tendering for supplies and services
  - Energy and water conservation
  - Indoor air quality

The Individual Athlete: Roles, Rights and Responsibilities

Often forgotten at the big-business levels of sport is the athlete or participant. It is the athlete who suffers most from a degraded recreational environment, and yet the athlete has not traditionally had much input into changing the situation. If this is to be corrected it will be up to the athlete to recognize the role that he/she can play, one which revolves around certain rights and responsibilities. Athletes, like everyone else, should have the right to live, train and perform in an environment that does not put their health at risk. By the same token, the athlete has the responsibility not to contribute to environmental degradation, either through sport or daily activity. The athlete should assume the role of advocate for his/her individual rights and those of all athletes, and assume responsibility as an environmental steward, both on the field and off.

Issues to be addressed by athletes

- Organize with other athletes to create an effective lobby that defends your right to a healthy environment in which to train and compete.

- Call for strict guidelines governing how facilities should be built, events run and sites and venues selected.

- Adopt a sustainable sport ethic and promote more sustainable sport in all your activities.

Spectators

The spectator is accustomed to being passive. Here is a chance to make a difference and to promote the sustainability of your favorite sports.

Issues to be addressed by spectators:

- Push for more sustainable events and facilities in your community.

- Volunteer for clean-up activities and promote the sustainable sport ethic.

- Take the least resource-intensive means of transport to an event.

- Reduce the amount of resources you consume as a spectator.

- Reuse or recycle consumer products and put trash in its place.

Energizing Through Education: The Rethinking Process

The most effective anchor for creating a more sustainable organization is the responsible office. More than just a nice place to work, this responsible, environmentally healthy office is a concept. It is a rethinking and it involves fresh planning. A program of stewardship is one that promotes use of the most appropriate materials, equipment, and routines in every conceivable situation. It includes everything from choice of paper and office equipment, to cafeterias, washrooms and responsible waste management. It extends into every task performed by the office workers, staff, and indeed the team. Though many of these same issues and practices arise in other situations (and will be discussed in that context in subsequent chapters), the idea of a responsible, a green, office as a place where so many environmental issues converge and are positively addressed, is a particularly useful starting point.

In managing offices the goal is to make the most efficient use of resources and to reduce waste so as to limit environmental impact. Both measures generally translate into long-term savings, even if some initial investment is required.

The challenge in creating a responsible use of materials is generally one of changing behavior patterns. Getting people to recycle can be achieved relatively easily by making it convenient for them. Encouraging reduction, however, requires a shift in thinking: do I need a copy of this? Do we need new binders for this report, or can we collect last year's and reuse? Better yet, can we issue the report without binders? Here communication, education and incentives can play a critical role in an organization: communicate the purpose and the benefits of reducing and reusing; explain clearly how to go about doing it; and design the system so that it rewards responsible thinking and action—as opposed to penalizing it.

Reducing, reusing and recycling apply to many of a sport organization's functions and operations, well beyond the office. These are examined in more detail in subsequent chapters on materials, operations, and waste management.

Rethinking Purchases

The responsible office can have a huge impact by establishing criteria for buying products and services; it will then have power not only to screen what it is paying for, but also to exert some influence over its suppliers. The objective is to purchase, wherever possible and feasible, the most environmentally responsible products on the market. In order to do so, it is first necessary to establish criteria and guidelines for determining which products and services are responsible and sustainable (for a guide to environmental criteria for purchasing see Chapter 6). It is also essential to establish just how far, in terms of cost and time spent, the organization is willing to go to implement its responsible procurement policy. Environmental considerations must, after all, be integrated as far as possible with other criteria, such as performance, life expectancy, quality and value for money (cost).

This approach to purchasing can be a positive and potentially groundbreaking one. As we will explore in the next chapter, an organization can set new trends in the types of products and services on the market by demanding that certain criteria be met and, if they do not yet exist, by working with suppliers to develop them. If a client is big enough and important enough, a supplier can go to great lengths to meet its demands. Once a supplier has gone to the trouble and expense of developing a new product or service, they are likely to seek additional buyers for it. A number of suppliers to Sydney 2000 made available new, more sustainable products and materials to organizers (e.g. non-PVC cables). Not only did most use this opportunity to launch these products to the wider Australian market, several actually set up new distribution networks (electric vehicles) and even manufacturing facilities (solar panels) in Australia, creating new jobs!

Rethinking Energy

Saving energy is a matter of technology and behavior. By getting people thinking and acting in an energy-conscious manner, electrical and heating bills can be cut with little if any expense. Solutions can be as simple as turning off lights and computers and making fewer photocopies and laser prints. This is often best accomplished by reviewing existing routines and habits, identifying wasteful ones, and establishing new routines.

For example, a specific routine for shutting down computers and printers and turning off lights should be established for the last person out of the office. Sometimes, however, the principal culprit is the technology itself. No matter how conscientious the office staff is, it may be the heating and lighting systems or other office machinery that are simply inefficient technologies. It is therefore essential to assess the efficiency of existing machinery and evaluate the economic payback of retrofitting or upgrading systems and equipment.

Rethinking Transportation

Employees and managers can reduce the impact of their transportation choices, both when they travel on office business and when they commute to and from the office or recreational center. As a manager, you can help them think through travel issues, hold discussions, get feedback and suggestions, and implement changes that will benefit the entire organization. The type of transport used (public vs. private), the choice of vehicle (truck, van, car, bicycle), its fuel type (gas, propane, electric) and efficiency, as well as various maintenance and operating practices should all be considered.

Organization policies should also be reviewed: are official vehicles evaluated for their environmental impact? Are drivers instructed in fuel-saving practices? Does the office encourage or assist car-pooling, the use of public transport or bicycling? Can you subsidize bus passes? Is there protected bicycle parking? Do you provide cyclists with change rooms with showers?

All of these are part of responsible thinking. While some steps will save the organization money, others will contribute to human and environmental health.

Rethinking Print Materials and Publications

Though the sport industry, outside of equipment and apparel manufacturers is not generally considered a producer or manufacturer of materials, many events and professional franchises pump out an incredible volume of material. Almost all of it is paper: advance information for participants, spectators, sponsors and the media; registration packages for participants; promotional material to attract spectators and sponsors and to bring recognition to those sponsors; programs, statistics and tourism information. Inevitable? Perhaps. But there is often a right way and a less right way of doing things.

Most who produce such materials would argue that it is a key part of the sport business. They are half right: most of the information they are disseminating is considered essential by most of the recipients. But they are also half-wrong: not all of this material needs to be produced, and that which does can be printed and distributed in a less harmful and far more cost-effective manner. There are three related issues: (1) how much printed material is produced; (2) the way it is produced; and (3) how it is distributed.

Communications

Energizing people must occur through communication. But how an organization communicates involves various expenditures of time, effort, energy, and resources. As a manager, it's useful to examine your communications practices from time to time, both for the tools that are used and the effectiveness with which messages are delivered. This is a thinking and planning process that benefits you as a manager, but training athletes and staff to do likewise also can benefit them and the entire organization. You work as a team, getting off the blocks all the quicker for it.

The effectiveness with which environmental objectives and practices are encouraged within the organization should be considered. Is there a good system for delivering information and providing assistance to people? Do people know what they are supposed to be doing and why? Are they given regular progress reports? Do they have a simple means by which to express concerns and offer suggestions? An effective management uses various communications tools to make this possible: suggestion boxes; a hotline; bulletin boards, either physical or electronic; environmental coordinators; and committees.

You can view the workplace in a holistic fashion. It is not something separate from our home lives and community. The office, like the entire organization, is a part of the community and of the larger environment. Being consistent in our concern for the planet may have a positive influence in two directions: People who have already adopted less wasteful practices in their home lives can influence colleagues and the organization for which they work, saving them both money; and a vibrant, responsible office style (described in greater detail in Chapter 8) can influence the thinking of those who have not yet adopted many conservation practices at home. The leader, whether it is the organization or its membership, influences the follower.

Engaging Volunteers

A critical link in many sport organizations (particularly smaller ones and those hosting events) is the corps of volunteers. The extent to which volunteers are trained and motivated will generally dictate how well they perform and how smoothly they can provide services to participants and spectators. Volunteer training should include a clear explanation of the environmental goals and objectives of the organization, the steps that will be taken to meet those goals and the ways in which volunteers can contribute, and should be as thorough as possible. As important as training, however, is seeking the input of volunteers on ways in which an event or organization can be made more sustainable. Volunteers frequently have considerable experience in dealing with the issues that arise at an event and a strong knowledge of what works and what doesn't.

Hints for Training, Motivating and Engaging Volunteers

An attempt should be made to green all aspects of the volunteer corps:

◆ Training manuals should be limited to only the material that they are likely to need and read. Rather than provide all volunteers with a huge binder on all aspects of the event/organization, several copies should be made available for consultation at a central location and posted on a web site.

◆ Mailouts of training and background information can be consolidated where several people from a family are volunteering.

◆ Uniforms should be made from appropriate materials and issued to those who need them for ease of identification. Uniforms should not be excessive, nor should other "freebies", a typical way of rewarding volunteers, be too numerous.

◆ The real reward for volunteers lies in good treatment, not in the number of free hats, t-shirts and key chains they get. Issuing a standard uniform to all workers (paid staff and volunteers) helps avoid resentment, in addition to saving money. Identification tags can be used to distinguish between people for reasons of access and security.

◆ Volunteers should be able to ride public transportation and/or shuttle vehicles during an event, with their identification tags serving as passes.

Planning

Advance planning is an important principle of good management. It happens also to be one of the keys to more sustainable decision-making by managers, staff and volunteers. For it is in the early stages of a project (such as building or renovating a facility, organizing an event or preparing to launch a new program) that the most significant decisions are taken regarding land use, resource consumption, purchasing, etc. By asking the question, "what is the most sustainable course of action", in the planning stage, greater efficiency is likely to be achieved, waste reduced and unnecessary costs avoided.

Forecasting

Determining "need" is one of the great challenges for any manager, sport being no exception. What sort of a facility does the community need, can it afford, and will it use on a long-term sustainable basis? What level of activity can a piece of land or body of water tolerate before it begins to deteriorate? These are all questions that rely to a considerable degree on good forecasting. Good forecasting itself relies on a combination of experience, careful research, attention to trends and, last but not least, even a dose of intuition.

For example, the most crucial decision related to document production is whether the item is needed at all. Far too many publications are created with neither a reason for being nor an audience. At the closing ceremonies of the 1993 Canada Games, a $3 souvenir program was on sale at the gate. Almost none were sold. People had already received a sufficient, simpler program along with their admission tickets. With better planning and coordination, the document might not have been produced at all.

What You Can Do

Summary of Recommendations for Preparing Employees and Volunteers

- ◆ Encourage a supportive corporate culture.

- ◆ Establish effective means of communication.

- ◆ Provide training and education for staff and volunteers.

- ◆ Create reinforcing incentives.

- ◆ Designate adequate resources.

- ◆ Adopt responsible office practices in all parts of the organization.

- ◆ Encourage frequent rethinking of practices.

- ◆ Review policies on a regular basis.

What to Use

Helpful publications

Elkington, J. 1998. *Cannibals with forks: The triple bottom line of 21st century business.*

Frankel, C. 1998. *In earth's company: Business, environment and the challenge of sustainability.*

Moxen, John; Strachan, Peter A. (eds.) 1998. *Managing green teams: Environmental change in organizations and networks.*

Sport Canada. 1999. *Environmental management and monitoring for sports events and facilities — A practical toolkit for managers.*

Case Study

Salt Lake City Organizing Committee Environmental Platform

Salt Lake City's bid for the 2002 Olympic Winter Games included a commitment to the following environmental platform:

Management

To integrate environmental sensitivity into every aspect of the Games in its administration through budgetary, organizational and procedural means.

Environmental Design and Construction

To ensure that design and use of Olympic facilities adequately assess and minimize environmental impacts and complement natural surroundings.

Temporary Facilities

To ensure that temporary facilities can be reused in a manner that benefits the entire community. Also, to restore any natural areas that are impacted by the installation and removal of such facilities.

Energy and Water Conservation

To build facilities and adopt practices that conserve our valuable natural resources.

Materials Management

To responsibly manage material selection, use, consumption and disposition to minimize environmental impact.

Office Suppliers, Contractors and Sponsors

To work with suppliers, contractors and sponsors to ensure that products and the methods in which they are delivered are environmentally responsible.

Cultural Events and Ceremonies

To use high profile events to further environmental education and to serve as a model for environmentally responsible events management.

Sport and Sport Organizations

To encourage Olympic teams and sport organizations to develop environmental messages and profiles that are suited to the sport itself and to the Olympic spirit.

Environmental Education

To realize the Games as a unique vehicle to educate both children and adults regarding environmental issues.

Transportation

To minimize transportation impacts and their related environmental problems, encourage mass transit and other environmentally responsible modes of transportation.

Lodging and Food Services

To provide environmentally sensitive lodging and food services for our visitors.

Environmental Monitoring

To monitor the progress of Salt Lake City Organizing Committee in meeting its environmental goals.

Chapter

6

Connecting with Stakeholders: Involving Your Community in the Challenge

Sports administrators, event organizers, facilities managers, parks and recreation directors and workers interact with their stakeholders in many ways and at many different levels. Stakeholders might include athletes, facility users, spectators, the media, sponsors, donors and suppliers.

In all of these interactions there is an opportunity to promote sustainability through education, partnership and joint projects. This chapter explores some of the various groups you might work with and the different types of initiatives you and they should consider to promote a sustainable approach to sport activity.

Educating the Public for New Practices

A high-profile organization, facility or event offers the publicity and often the resources to initiate programs that can help to instill more sustainable practices and ways of thinking. Sport organizations that have embraced environmental change are in a unique position to share their concern and knowledge through a variety of educational programs and community ventures including:

- ◆ informing industry of ways they can cut pollution while saving money;

- ◆ encouraging more efficient and cleaner use of transportation;

- ◆ educating shippers and boaters on ways to reduce water pollution;

- ◆ advising individual sport enthusiasts of ways they can protect themselves and do less environmental harm;

- ◆ developing educational programs for schools; and

- ◆ creating community initiatives.

By getting the community closely involved in environmental projects and showing people how they have a stake in this process, the effects of an organization or an event can reach further and last longer than one might ever expect. The local community should be invited to participate in the

Salt Lake Organizing Committee's Environmental Education Summit

An Environmental Education Steering Committee was formed in Salt Lake City as a result of a successful environmental education summit organized by the Salt Lake Organizing Committee for the Winter Olympics of 2002 (SLOC). The committee makes recommendations on environmental curricula and demonstration projects to SLOC.

The one-day summit, organized by SLOC and attended by over 100 participants, focussed on developing a sport and environment curriculum and education program that would take place before, during and after the Games.

Participants identified a number of specific projects and explored curriculum ideas both for schools and for all ages. Recommendations included partnerships among a variety of groups, Internet and media delivery and hands on activities related to real-life issues. Environmental messages that could be included in various projects were discussed. The formation of the steering committee was seen as critical to the success of the environmental education program that would continue independently after the games.

planning and running of sport initiatives. Furthermore, all steps initiated as part of an event should include plans for the development of infrastructure and the continuation of program long after the event is over. By training and educating employees and volunteers from the community and from various walks of life, including private industry, a sporting event can leave a profound legacy for the community.

When Lillehammer hosted the Winter Olympics, for example, its organizers encouraged schools to learn from its experiences through a series of projects, special seminars and activities. They encouraged the study of how environmental issues relate to sport, play, outdoor life and natural resource management. The general public was informed of the committee's environmental initiatives and involved through the training of advisers in the municipalities, volunteers, and army personnel. The public even participated in a major "Olympic Forests" tree-planting program.

Instilling New Habits

The least tangible but perhaps most pervasive legacy that a responsibly managed sporting facility or event can leave is a heightened awareness in the community of the value of a more sustainable approach to sport. This awareness will manifest itself in the new management approaches instilled in sport organizations and in the staff and volunteers who will disseminate what they have learned into other sectors and activities throughout the community. The high expectations raised during the games will remain in the public consciousness for a long time. The end of the event need not signal an end to the pursuit of sustainable communities. Quite the opposite: people may expect all

organizations, events and facilities to mirror and even build on the successes of the games. A critical mass of people will have acquired the necessary skills and habits, learned to question conventional thinking and come to believe sustainability to be a goal worth pursuing.

Corner Brook Games Carry Over

As a direct result of environmental initiatives that were carried out during the 1999 Canada Winter Games in Corner Brook, Newfoundland, several other community and sport organizers have asked for help in developing an environmental program at their events. This list most notably includes the 1999 ITU World Cup Triathlon race and Newfoundland and Labrador Federation of Municipalities conference.

Working with Schools

Environmental awareness should be introduced into school studies in the form of an overriding ethic and as a component of study in physical and outdoor education. By learning to better appreciate their place within the natural environment and the role that it plays in their survival and good health, students will be more likely to act responsibly on its behalf. Once children understand that playing sports in a polluted environment can counterbalance the positive effects of that exercise they will begin to see the importance of protecting the environment.

Furthermore, learning which involves physical activity has always proven to be more effective than sedentary learning. Therefore, developing curriculum that teaches environmental concepts through playing physical games and activities is worthwhile. These techniques are often used successfully in outdoor education programs and can easily be transferred to a school setting (Henley 1989). In addition, taking children out into nature on field trips, such as hiking or canoeing, brings them directly in contact with nature.

The concept of sustainability and its relevance to sport and recreation is appropriate for students at all ages. It is a natural accompaniment to sportsmanship and developing a positive ethic. A myriad of school activities and events can bring the concepts alive to younger students. Students should learn to identify sustainable behavior and to promote it in their own lives through classes, special events and excursions, and at home. School-sanctioned activities and excursions themselves can be models of an organization according to principles of sustainability. At the elementary and high school level, physical education and health curricula should include an environmental component.

Students at the college and university level in physical and health education, recreation studies and sport administration courses all would be well-served by an environmental component in their curriculum. More detailed academic studies of the principles and technology of sustainable sport, and discussion of responsibility and a sustainable sport ethic are needed.

Sport event organizers should look for ways to collaborate with schools and universities on environmental education projects. Developing materials for schools on the environmental initiatives in the sport arena will be well received by educators and often incite a willingness to participate in these projects, whether it be a tree planting campaign or recycling at the local recreation center. In addition, many post secondary instructors and students are interested in applying their expertise to innovative new projects and can be a useful community resource.

Recommendations for schoolteachers and administrators

1. Design curricula, which study the relationship between sport/recreation and the natural environment in which it takes place.

2. Define a school environmental goal and code of practice which promote environmental stewardship and sustainability in all activities, including a commitment to sustainable sport and greener games.

3. Ensure that all school sports and recreation activities are guided by a "green games" approach and work to promote the goal of sustainability.

4. Include in the curriculum:

    ◆ "minimum-impact" outdoor living and travelling skills;

    ◆ understanding of basic ecological processes;

    ◆ awareness of local and global environments;

    ◆ understanding of human dependence on environmental resources;

    ◆ awareness of human influence on natural environments;

    ◆ study of the impact of growing quantities of human-generated waste; and

    ◆ study of the ability and limitations of natural systems to recycle waste.

5. Teach principles of conservation: sustained yield, maintenance of life-supporting environments, maintenance of species diversity.

6. Develop curriculum that harnesses children's natural affinity to physical activity for the teaching of environmental concepts.

Public Relations

With the commitment to sustainable sport comes an opportunity, perhaps even a duty, to show that you are doing things in a new way. The opportunity is not just for the organization, which stands to receive positive publicity for its efforts, but for the promotion of the broader goals of sustainable sport, and environmental and community health.

Of course your initiatives will be closely scrutinized by the media, the public and environmental groups. This is only natural. In the early days of popular environmentalism everyone was trying to pass themselves off as "green." Similar superficial attempts by companies to paint themselves or their products green without any genuine commitment have put the public on guard against "greenwashing." If you want to get good publicity these days, you had better be open, honest and demonstrably committed.

Fear of criticism leads some organizations to shy away from drawing attention to their community and environmental initiatives. This is both good and bad. It's good that those whose efforts may be little more than a marketing ploy are less and less able to get away with it. It's bad if fear of criticism is preventing some groups from even trying. You only have something to fear if you have something to hide. A genuine commitment speaks for itself through action. The organization dedicated to improving its environmental performance will ultimately be recognized as such, even if its current practices have some way to go.

Regrettably, the media tends to focus excessively on the negative. People who are working hard to make their practices more sustainable may receive unduly harsh criticism for things they have not yet been able to address or for which a workable solution has not yet been found. This should not discourage anyone from trying, however.

There are two overriding principles to follow when publicizing your organization's efforts: (1) make your actions consistent with the message you deliver; and (2) be open and honest about your level of commitment, your successes, and your failures.

The Body Shop, a worldwide retailer of body care products, and its founder Anita Roddick have received an enormous amount of international publicity for their commitment to promoting social and environmental change. From the beginning they have been forthright about their goals and open to public scrutiny. Any mistakes they have made seem to have been ignored or forgiven, when weighed against their accomplishments and unwavering commitment.

When you have nothing to hide, it is relatively easy to promote and publicize your commitment and your objectives. Any publicity, as has been noted, will ultimately benefit both your organization and the broader goals of sustainable sport. Any media or publicity strategy should therefore be designed to emphasize: (1) your commitment to reducing the environmental impact of your event/facility/organization, (2) your commitment to the community; and (3) your dedication to sustainable sport and its attendant environmental and social benefits.

Setting an Example for the Community

By publicizing your sustainable sport initiatives, you are making an important statement: that the community's health and well-being matters. You are going on record with your belief that your sport organization can and must become more sustainable. When such a strong statement comes from sport, it has the potential to reach a very wide audience. It can also reach people who may not be getting or absorbing messages about the importance of environmental stewardship from traditional sources of information and education. During the opening ceremonies at Lillehammer, the importance of the environment was mentioned no less than six times. Television viewers learned of its importance to Lillehammer, to Norway, to the International Olympic Committee and to sport. This may have been the first time that many viewers were ever confronted with the thought that there is a connection between sport and the environment. This high-profile occasion was used successfully to spread the message of sustainable sport to millions.

Not many organizations will ever reach a billion television viewers. What they will have that may put them ahead even of the Olympics, however, is personal contact. The vast majority of sport organizations are small, community-oriented groups which deal face to face with the people whose lives are directly affected by their choices. This means that messages can be delivered far more directly and more effectively when face-to-face.

A young soccer player may not read in the local paper that community fields will no longer be sprayed with certain chemicals. She will notice, however, the sign on the field announcing that this step has been taken and explaining why the turf has changed slightly. This may lead her to learn more about the effects of spraying and, with her new awareness, to question why her parents and neighbors are spraying their lawn. Sport is the catalyst.

Promotion strategies have as much to do with the medium as with the message. Novel ways of delivering a message can be as valuable in making a point as the message itself. For example, instead of a soft-drink sponsor announcing that it encourages the recycling of its disposable cups, that same company might work with organizers to reduce or eliminate the need for disposables by supplying and promoting the use of a reusable mug.

Marketing

The principles of the sustainably managed sport organization extend fully to marketing efforts as an important facet of public relations. Attempts to attract sponsors, sell tickets to an event, attract members to a club or users to a facility are important functions of the administration. They are also highly visible. Whatever form these marketing efforts take, they must be consistent with the organization's environmental commitment. This can pose a challenge to the marketing mindset, which tends to eschew restrictions. Marketing people must recognize that not all means of selling a message are equally appropriate. Lavish and wasteful techniques should make way for ones that, though less glossy, are perhaps even more effective. This approach need in no way impinge on creativity. In fact, with a general public that has grown tired of, and unresponsive to, the loud and brash approach, there is a golden opportunity for innovative marketing. Marketing can be made more sustainable in various ways: these will be explored in later chapters.

Merchandise

The phenomenon of sport merchandising—selling peripheral products adorned with team logos, event names or the marks of corporate sponsors—became a major part of the sport scene in the eighties and nineties. Merchandising is now a large source of income for everyone from universities and professional franchises to the Olympic Games. With the highs there have also been lows. When people's names began to appear on material of poor quality and dubious taste, organizations were forced to crack down. The IOC, realizing that its name and symbols would in fact lose their value if they were not better controlled, has become very careful about their use.

Many sport organizations have now developed criteria for deciding where and on what their trademarks should appear. The primary criteria tend to be the quality and appropriateness of the product. Added to this list should be environmental and social impact. Only those products that are manufactured by companies with a good environmental and social record should be considered. Those that are manufactured by companies and factories with poor environmental and labor practices should be avoided. As the buying public becomes more vigilant about the source of merchandise (e.g., avoiding "sweatshop" goods), it will pay to take the high road in sourcing of merchandise.

Mizuno's Recycled Olympic Uniforms

Mizuno, an ISO 14000 certified sporting goods company, has stated in its code of ethics: "It is our duty to consider the global environmental consequences of our actions". Many Mizuno products contain recycled materials. For the 1998 Winter Olympic Games in Nagano Japan, Mizuno supplied staff and volunteer uniforms made entirely from recycled nylon. Mizuno has also led the way in the World Federation of the Sporting Goods Industry initiating the development of an environmental committee and promoting environmental conservation activities within the sporting goods industry.

Recommendations for Good Public Relations

1. Develop a strategy for promoting your environmental commitment and initiatives

2. Ensure that your actions are consistent with your message

3. Be open and honest about your level of commitment

4. Set an example for the local community and other stakeholders

5. Involve as many stakeholders as possible in planning and implementation

6. Plan your initiative with the long-term legacy in mind

7. Involve the private sector in partnerships of benefit to all

8. Promote and publicize all the great things you are doing

9. Be ready to defend what you're not doing as well as what you are doing

Working with People in the Media

One of the underlying ideals of journalism is a commitment to objectivity and balance. Objectivity in the media, like amateurism in athletics, is more myth than reality, however. Michael Keating (1993) in his book for the media Covering the Environment states: "In theory, the media mirror the world. But, by what the media choose to write about most, and comment on, the media also influence the public agenda." The truth is that the majority of reporters, editors, publishers and producers bring several biases to their roles. They may bring their personal assumptions and preconceptions, or they may be influenced by what they believe their editors, readers and the organization's owners will want to read, hear or see. Though many in the industry do their utmost to approach each story with an open mind, this is difficult to achieve. Others, whether intentionally or subconsciously, use the influence of the media to pursue a personal agenda, typically to promote their own vision of how the world ought to be. To paraphrase Noam Chomsky, the media is often a "manufacturer of consent" promoting what is thought to be the dominant world view of that particular time and society.

Modern sport has always been profoundly influenced by the media. Indeed, sport, like other forms of entertainment, is in many ways dependent on the media for the attention and coverage that helps to generate public interest. This dependence can evolve into a relationship that is anything but objective. The most common critique of sport journalism, however, is that it can be dangerously close to boosterism. Knowing the passions of the fans, who are after all the same audience for both the media outlet and the sport organization, the journalist must be careful in his/her coverage. Criticism of an athlete, a team or an event can be viewed by some as one step short of treason. Journalists who oppose bids for the Olympics, who criticize public bailouts for foundering franchises or who question the need for a new stadium frequently feel the heat of blistering attacks. The fan, after all, is biased by definition. It is not surprising, therefore, that sport journalism in many cultures is known for its soft coverage and uncritical approach to the status quo of sport.

At the same time, because sport is dependent on the media, it is ready to hand over an extraordinary amount of control to the media industry. This is especially true for professional and elite events, which have come to rely heavily on coverage, primarily television, to generate interest and revenues. Often events are scheduled, facilities built or renovated, venues selected or changed and even the rules of a sport modified to meet the demands of the media.

The influence of the media is especially visible in its ability to fashion what is seen, read or heard. Acting as the "gatekeeper" who decides how much coverage, if any, is given to a sport, an event or a particular team, the editor can exercise a profound influence over what we expect from sport. By emphasizing elite, male sport, most journalists and broadcasters are actually defining sport as something relatively narrow and exclusive. By implication, what is not covered—women's sport, youth events, disabled games and "minor" sport—is not really to be considered important sport. Issues like gender equity, equal access, participatory recreation and the environment, by virtue of their not being explored, do not appear to matter to sport.

To propose that the media should accept and even embrace environmental stewardship and take its responsibility for promoting sustainable sport is therefore running head-on against both the myths and the hard reality of sport journalism. If the media is to elevate social responsibility to the point of actually promoting sustainable sport, is this not abandoning its sacred trust of objectivity and non-intervention? If the media is to approach its task with a more critical eye, might this not jeopardize the sports institutions that its readers covet most? The answer to both questions is simple: like any institution with power, journalistic organizations and practitioners have an overarching ethical responsibility to the constituents that give them power — all of the constituents, not just the sport industry. Ironically, by playing the role of environmental steward, the media will ultimately help rather than hinder the sport community as a whole.

There are a number of ways the media can promote sustainable sport: by making its own activities responsible and reducing its own impact; by providing better coverage of the environmental issues relevant to sport; and by promoting the idea of sustainable sport as an apolitical social objective.

Limiting the Negative Impact of the Media

Media organizations and individuals must, like those in any other industry, commit themselves to sustainable practices. These include management practices, environmental principles, and other initiatives particular to their tasks. Though such a genuine commitment can only be made voluntarily, sport organizations which are themselves committed can take several steps to help the process along by ensuring that the media is not exempt from the rules and guidelines which govern an event or a facility.

All environmentally-responsible management practices must apply equally to the media:

- Media kits should be kept to a minimum in frequency, quantity and size, and should follow sustainable publishing guidelines.

- Electronic means of communication should be used wherever possible.

- Ways to reduce, reuse and recycle should be explored and implemented.

- Equipment provided should follow guidelines for energy-efficiency, etc.

- No-smoking policies should apply equally to media centers and press boxes.

- Media transportation planning should attempt to limit the number of vehicles required and the emissions of those vehicles.

- Private media vehicles should conform to the same standards and rules as others.

Journalists or organizations interested in sustainable sport should consider themselves partners of the organizers/managers and work with them to explore ways to fashion a new approach to sport journalism and a code of practice that is consistent. What this may require from the media is a conscious attempt to reduce its demands for certain services, resources and special infrastructure, for example:

- fewer vehicles;

- a willingness to share transportation;

- background information to be provided on demand rather than automatically;

- a willingness to work with existing facilities rather than demand new construction or renovations;

- fewer demands for special treatment of the press, who are often accorded better facilities than athletes; and

- an acknowledgement of the environmental and cost pressures of media demands and a commitment to keeping these in check.

The media can equally demand many of these things when they find themselves more environmentally conscious than the event organizers/facility managers. Opportunities for playing a positive and constructive role are many: e.g., demanding recycling facilities, asking that smoking be forbidden or requesting state-of-the-art photo chemical recovery equipment. There is nothing to say that the media cannot be the agitator rather than the dinosaur. The media has been known to agitate for plenty of other changes, why not environmental ones?

At the Sydney 2000 Olympics, the media played an important role in telling the public about what had been accomplished through Sydney 2000's environmental commitments and initiatives. While this positive message was being delivered by many media outlets, however, some of the worst waste management practices were observed in the media center and, more notably, in the compound of the host broadcaster, where large quantities of non-recyclable materials were thrown out, in flagrant disregard for SOCOG's waste management system.

Improved Coverage of the Environmental Issues Relevant to Sport

One of the most effective roles for the media is in committing itself to pursue stories that explore the issues relevant to sustainable sport. Can the media rise to the task of pursuing related stories in its own region? Will other sport organizations be pressured to become more sustainable, and will unsustainable practices get the investigative coverage they deserve? The media has begun to play a critical role in shaping public opinion about the state of the planet's health. In so doing, according to Keating (1993), "it has influenced millions of citizens to be more concerned about the environment, plus to demand more action to restore and sustain it." This power to influence the masses confers a special responsibility on the media. Will sport journalists, or the media in general, rise to meet this responsibility?

To do so will require either greater environmental literacy on the part of the sport media, or greater interest in the sport industry on the part of journalists who cover economic, political and social issues. Keating calls on journalists to try to understand the issues, seeking a balance between underplaying and overplaying risks. He argues, "The media have a heavy responsibility, because they are the primary source of environmental information for most people. Environment stories influence government policies, corporate investments, educational programs and the shopping choices of millions of individuals."

Promoting the Idea of Sustainable Sport as an Apolitical Social Objective

To argue that the media has no place as an advocate for safeguarding the planet is akin to saying the media has no responsibility for helping to maintain law and order. Media institutions evolve along with the demands of society, and society as a whole is crying out for steps to be taken to save the natural environment. There should be no fear of appearing to side with one political view or another; sustainability is an apolitical objective. When the issue gets political is when the media begins advocating means of achieving sustainability that favor vested interests. That is where the media should exercise its much vaunted balance and objectivity. Whether to save the planet is not a choice, it is an imperative. How to do it involves weighing options and exploring strategies.

Media organizations should themselves become active as partners with industry, government and community and environmental groups in developing means to make sustainable sport possible: sponsoring workshops, publishing books, contributing research, funding community activities, etc. If a newspaper can bill itself as the 'official' paper of a professional sport team, surely it can be the official supporter of sustainable sport!

Recommendations for Working with the Media

In working with media representatives, advocate their involvement in responsible management and partnership with your organization by requesting that:

1. media organizations become environmental stewards;

2. media organizations develop their own sustainable sport Code of Conduct;

3. alone or in partnership with sport organizations, the media develop and implement alternative practices with less environmental impact;

4. media eliminate unsustainable demands on events and facilities;

5. there be improved coverage of the environmental issues relevant to sport;

6. the idea of sustainable sport as an apolitical social objective be promoted; and

7. debate on the best means of achieving sustainable sport be fostered.

Working with the Active Public

When working with the public to instill new habits and sensibilities regarding the environment there is probably no more a receptive group than the active recreational public. The following outlines some of the specific ways that sport administrators, organizers and interested individuals can make a difference by tapping into the interests of public.

Recreational Programs

The greatest number of practitioners of active sport are found not at the elite level, but at the recreational level, whether in organized recreational programs or simply as users of recreational facilities. It is therefore incumbent that any sustainable sport campaigns target these people, the sporting majority.

In some areas recreational programs and facilities have been hard hit by cutbacks in funding by local governments. After several decades of strong development of both programs and facilities, the public has come to expect high standards and availability of both. The challenge faced by parks and recreation officials is how to continue to provide the same caliber of service but at a lower cost. Sustainable sport comes to the rescue. Many steps can be implemented to allow program organizers and facilities managers to provide the same or even better quality of service and reduce their costs in the process.

In certain cases, these changes will be to systems, practices and technologies, subtle changes that the majority of users may not even notice. Changes in parks and turf management, better waste management strategies, and personnel looking to replace hazardous materials with more benign ones are all steps that can save money while improving the quality and safety of the recreational experience for users as well as staff.

In other cases, changes will be noticeable and will depend on the cooperation of users, and on their willingness to embrace more sustainable sport practices. These might include discouraging private vehicle use by limiting parking and banning idling; encouraging the use of public and active means of transport; naturalizing playing fields and parklands; and conserving water.

Though recreation takes diverse forms, some common routes to greater sustainability do exist:

1. Assess your needs carefully. If 20 softball diamonds are needed for one summer holiday weekend but only ten are used the rest of the year, insist on building ten and locating temporary substitutes in neighboring communities or on other fields. Most people will have just as much fun at a basic facility as they will at one with all the latest frills.

2. Investigate how to make facilities as flexible, durable and energy-efficient as possible. Work with participants to figure out how facilities can be shared and can serve more than one type of user. Hold discussions to help think through how facilities can be easily adapted to meet changing needs and fashions over the years. Team up groups of recreation enthusiasts that together can hire expert consultants for technological advice. Often by designing facilities to delay major renovations, they will be far more economically viable. Maintenance and operating costs can be kept to a minimum.

3. Design programs to minimize the need for expensive or harmful facilities or services. Efficient thinking should be incorporated into all activities so as to reduce their impact and in order to inform and educate participants about the importance of sustainable sport.

4. Encourage users to get actively involved in treating the environment responsibly and caringly as they participate in games. Promote, the concepts of Active Living and Healthy Communities, emphasizing the ideas that by living actively you can reduce your impact on the environment and improve your own health and that of your community at the same time.

Key Issues for Parks and Recreation Administrators.

- Facilities construction and operation
- Environmental management systems
- Materials and waste management
- Transportation
- "Sustainable Office" practices
- Purchasing
- Printing
- Promotion and public relations
- Partnership with stakeholders
- Food services

Community and Local Events

Events organized by or for smaller communities and local residents range from the very small and low-budget to the large and well-funded. What these events tend to have in common with one another is a relatively low-frills approach: facilities and services tend to be modest; out-of-town athletes and other participants are either billeted or expected to pay for their own accommodation; and volunteers do most, if not all, of the work.

Considering these constraints, two things are surprising: the amount of waste and inefficiency — and hence the potential opportunities — that can exist; and the wide range of issues that the environmentally minded organizer must somehow tackle. The local event must focus its efforts on reducing, limiting costs to the bare essentials. Waste generally denotes inefficiency that can be ill afforded, especially in these times of scarce sponsors and donors. This does not mean a dull event. The focus should be on helping participants and spectators to make the most of their experience, without expecting unnecessary services, handouts and entertainment that detract from enjoyment of the main event.

Key Issues for Local/Community Event Organizers:

- "Sustainable Office" practices
- Purchasing
- Printing
- Promotion and public relations
- Partnership with stakeholders

- Materials and waste management
- Transportation
- Food services
- Signs and banners

Surfrider Foundation Catches the Wave of Environmental Concern

The Surfrider Foundation is an excellent example of an organization that has tapped into the ecological concern of folks who love waves, beaches and coastline and want to protect them. They represent more than 25,000 surfers, swimmers, divers, bodyboarders, kayakers and beach enthusiasts around the world who have a vested interest in preserving the ocean environment. Their mission statement defines the foundation as "an international environmental organization dedicated to the rehabilitation, restoration and protection of the world's waves and beaches through conservation, activism, education and research." The foundation's guiding principles reflect their desire to protect the environment for its own sake as well as for the benefit of practicing water sports. Surfrider has captured the imagination of a large portion of the public that is beginning to understand the relationship between sports and the environment. See **www.surfrider.org**

Outdoor and Wilderness Activities

That unspoiled nature has both an intrinsic value and a right to exist seems to have been accepted by a surprisingly small percentage of the general population. Even some regular parks and wilderness users seem to have trouble with the idea that these are not solely commodities for their enjoyment. Fortunately a growing number of those who rely on wilderness for there pleasure or their livelihood—guides, outfitters, operators of resorts—recognize that without wilderness, there is no wilderness adventure.

This growing awareness has generated a grassroots movement to ensure that all who use wilderness adopt a voluntary ethic that grants priority to the integrity of natural spaces and that demands a sense of environmental stewardship from everyone. Around the world, park wardens, scout troops, school groups, adventure holiday guides and legions of campers and hikers are among those who have begun and must continue with renewed vigor to promote such an ethic.

Wilderness users will have to take responsibility for attempting to restore certain places to their original condition. That may mean climbers carrying a garbage bag to bring down the litter from previous expeditions, canoeists rebuilding eroding riverbanks or mountain bikers adopting a trail to be restored and then maintained. Nowhere is the vested interest of the sport/recreation community more apparent than in the area of outdoor and wilderness activity.

Leave No Trace

Leave No Trace is a national non-profit public education organization with a mission to promote and inspire responsible outdoor recreation through education research and partnership. As increasing numbers of people seek the beauty and exhilaration of outdoor recreation, our collective mark on the environment and natural processes increases. Leave No Trace champions techniques that are designed to minimize social and environmental impacts.

Their outdoor ethic contains six basic principles which are:

- ◆ Plan Ahead and Prepare.
- ◆ Camp and Travel on Durable Surfaces.
- ◆ Pack It In, Pack it Out.
- ◆ Properly Dispose of What You Can't Pack Out.
- ◆ Leave What You Find.
- ◆ Minimize Use and Impact from Fires.

Showing the Sustainable Side of an Event or Ceremony

For many people sport is considered simply a form of entertainment. Spectators at sport events expect to be amused by a bombardment of expensive and often unsustainable shows, gimmicks and prizes. This section discusses how organizers can cut down on resource consumption and waste production when it comes to putting on a show for the fans. Chapter 12 covers event management in greater detail but here are some highly visible issues that affect the public directly.

Accompanying Entertainment

Though peripheral performances and various forms of side entertainment are nothing new to sport, they have been elevated to a new level in the made-for-television manner in which so many sport events are now staged. This trend becomes an environmental issue when one considers the energy consumption necessary to put on these extravaganzas. With each new way to incorporate sound, light and other resource-consuming activities, is the event getting more sustainable or less so? Event organizers should be looking for energy-saving means of putting on their event or toning it down and finding creative ways to put on a simpler show that is just as entertaining.

The extravagance of the opening ceremony at the Olympics has often been taken as a given. However, several recent Olympic organizing committees, such as in Lillehammer and Nagano, have opted for simpler but no less effective ceremonies.

Taking this one step further, organizers could creatively weave in an environmental message into their halftime shows or contests without compromising the entertainment value of the event. In Lillehammer and Nagano the opening ceremonies were about the celebration of culture and nature thereby sending a message about the significance of the environment for these host cities.

Finally, there is a growing public concerned about the noise pollution and negative health effects resulting from the extremely high volume at music events. Sport event organizers should also take heed of these concerns when planning their music entertainment.

Awards, Ceremonies and Prizes

The awards ceremony tends to be a relatively simple affair. Where questions of sustainability and environment enter is in the award itself. The refusal of Canadian skiers to accept a trophy from a tobacco company raised the issue of appropriate sponsorship for sport. But while more and more people are questioning who is giving the money and prizes, not many have taken a good look at the prize itself.

There is little to be concerned about in the standard trophy, medal or cash prize. Where a product or usable item is given, however, the challenge is to ensure that these are appropriate to the recipient, the event and the commitment to sustainable sport. Larger prizes tend to come from, and are therefore determined by, the event sponsor or a donor. A common prize is a car. Though this can be expected where an automobile company is the donor, the fact is this is a resource-consuming and pollution-creating prize, which is not entirely consistent with the sustainability message. Further, the vast majority of recipients at the level of event where cars are given as prizes will already have a car, or several. Donors, and event organizers, should consider alternative prizes that do not encourage excess consumption of this sort: perhaps a gift certificate on the purchase of their next vehicle.

Even awards and door prizes that consist of appropriate sport equipment can encourage waste. Recipients will often already have the same equipment/clothing or better, or quite simply not want or need it. Again, offering gift certificates or the option of making a donation in the recipient's name to a charity of his/her choice would be less wasteful and more educative. Though it is difficult to say no to donated prizes, it is important for event organizers to emphasize to donors that they are seeking appropriate awards. A good way to do this would be to develop a list of criteria that all awards and prizes should meet. Awards ceremonies can thus be effective in raising awareness of sustainability through sport.

Non-material prizes can serve an educative purpose. Donating money to charity is one example, as is making a donation to a scholarship fund or bursary. Funds for young, low-income athletes or for athletes wishing to pursue further education are particularly appropriate. A category which has yet to be fully developed involves donating money to environmental projects of the recipient's choice, planting trees in the recipient's name, or offering scholarships to athletes who wish to pursue studies in a subject related to sustainable sport. In each community and at every level, there are dozens of potentially appropriate 'alternative' awards such as these waiting to be created. While helping to reduce unnecessary material consumption, this type of award can also be a powerful educator. The spectator who learns that money has been donated to an environmental organization or a sport-related charity in the name of their idol also learns that something deeper than material reward really does matter to the sport community.

Recommendations for Events or Ceremonies

◆ Creatively reduce the consumption of energy and resources needed to put on the ceremonies.

◆ Limit noise, pollution and waste produced by ceremonies.

◆ Work with sponsors to avoid inappropriate awards and prizes.

◆ Seek alternative, non-material awards and prizes that inform and educate.

Partnerships with the Private Sector

One particularly effective way to spread the sustainable sport message is to involve the private sector in different types of partnerships. Contractors, sponsors and suppliers can be brought on board through various means of improving the services and materials that they supply, making them healthier for the community. It is a win-win situation: the event/facility benefits from increased sustainability, while the private sector partner benefits from the publicity and the knowledge it gains in the process. This knowledge and experience might give the company an edge over its competitors in other markets or at similar sport events/facilities.

Working with Sponsors

Even at the best of times, finding corporate sponsors can be a challenge. When someone comes along who wants to give you money or in-kind products and services, it is hard to say 'no'. But there are plenty of reasons for not being too hasty to accept sponsorship, or at least not without asking some fundamental questions. For an organization that has worked hard to demonstrate its commitment to environmental stewardship, accepting a renowned corporate polluter as your major sponsor could spell the death of that image in the eyes of the public.

Fortunately, there is a more positive side to this issue. Sport organizations can actually work with potential sponsors, encouraging them to embrace environmental stewardship, assisting them in adopting more sustainable practices, and helping them to develop a legitimate green profile. As we will see below, "legitimate" is the operative word.

Choosing Appropriate Sponsors

As difficult as it may be to turn down an offer of sponsorship, there are times when a sport organization must do so. Sponsorship is intended to be a mutually beneficial relationship: the sponsor makes a financial or in-kind contribution that benefits the recipient (be it an event, team, facility or athlete); in return, the sponsor benefits by having its name attached to that of the recipient. What is being "bought" is the reputation of, let's say, a particular event. The sponsor is counting on improving its profile and sales as a result of this name association. The event hopes to benefit materially from the deal as opposed to from the reputation of the sponsor. While a sponsor will therefore go to great lengths to choose the right event, that event rarely has any comparable screening process for selecting sponsors.

The danger here is that the recipient, if it fails to properly consider the implications of having a particular sponsor attached to its own name, may in some cases actually have its reputation tarnished well beyond the value of the sponsorship. Dr. Andrew Pipe contends that "many people in sport are oblivious to the damage an inappropriate sponsorship does to the image of sport in general and an event in particular." Should a sport event be sponsored by a tobacco company? Should an organization committed to sustainability accept money from a Union Carbide or an Exxon? While some might argue that polluting industries like petrochemicals, mining and auto manufacturers should be excluded outright, the matter is not so black and white. In fact sponsorship, like most environmental issues, should be seen in shades of gray. What shade of gray, then, is acceptable?

Each organization may have to develop its own criteria for judging who is acceptable and who is not. Those criteria are likely to reflect the values and commitment of the organization itself. As a starting point, you may want to ask potential sponsors some of the following questions:

- What environmental policies have you adopted?

- How are you going about implementing these policies?

- Have you conducted an environmental audit?

- If not, why not? If so, what did the audit conclude?

- Have you acted on the recommendations of the audit?

- Have you ever been found guilty of breaking environmental laws?

- If so, what measures have you taken to prevent a similar recurrence?

Companies that refuse to provide a satisfactory answer to these or similar questions and that are unable or unwilling to verify their responses should be ruled out. Even if satisfactory answers are provided, some independent verification should be sought. Fortunately, since few sport organizations have the financial or human resources or expertise, there are two relatively easy ways of doing this. The first is to ask environmental and community groups in the region of the company's head office or national office for their views on the firm in question. If the company has earned itself a bad reputation, these groups would be aware of it. Secondly, in many countries organizations exist which monitor the ethical performance of most major firms. These include groups like Co-op America and EthicScan Canada or non-profit consumer, labor and church groups. Ask not only for their assessment of the company in question, but also for the criteria by which the firm was judged.

Companies can be evaluated on more than their environmental records. Some groups screen for such factors as labor relations, gender and racial equality, community involvement and ties to weapons manufacturers or repressive regimes. What is useful about getting such a full evaluation is that you can decide which criteria are most important to you. It is up to the sponsor-seeker to decide on what grounds a prospective sponsor should be ruled out.

As a minimum standard, the sponsor should be: (1) publicly committed to improving its environmental management and performance; (2) willing to work with the sport organization to limit the environmental impact of its products and services; (3) willing to meet all of the environmental standards established by the particular sport event, facility or organization; and (4) able to demonstrate that it is working to improve its environmental performance. In addition, the sponsor must demonstrate openness and candor on environmental issues. If a company is unable to meet this minimum standard but is still accepted as a sponsor, the recipient sport organization had better be prepared to defend its decision.

Will adhering to standards such as these rule out some traditional supporters of sport? Likely yes. Organizers who have gone to great lengths to run as green an event as possible would jeopardize their profile by accepting sponsorship from a chemical company which is polluting the local river. But this gets right to the heart of the matter: some of the planet's major polluters go to great lengths to legitimize themselves by building a good corporate image. Oddly enough, the biggest polluters seem to have ample treasure chests when it comes to public relations. Is it not time to reveal some of the skeletons in the closet, or at least to get these firms to put their closets in order?

Should the sport community be afraid to take on such a role for fear of losing supporters, they would do well to remember that many of the traditional corporate powerhouse industries which were key supporters in the past will not be the supporters of the future. Structural changes around the globe are taking money out of the hands of resource extraction companies, heavy industry and manufacturers. The baton is being passed to high technology firms, information and service vendors and even environmental industries. This is where the sport community should be looking for its sponsors.

There is also an opportunity for sport groups to lead companies to better practices which could, conveniently, save them big money.

Developing Innovative and Alternative Methods of Sponsorship

Sport should look to an ever-widening field of new and greener potential sponsors: software developers, renewable energy equipment makers, pollution and waste treatment firms and electric vehicle makers. In some cases this is starting to happen already; the telecommunications, office equipment and financial service sectors now provide a significant portion of sponsorship money for major events. Where the real opportunity lies, though, is in attracting those new and growing sectors which not only need the exposure but also have something to offer.

Many major events, such as the Sydney Olympics, Salt Lake City Olympics, Pan Am Games, Ryder Cup, and even smaller events such as the Canada Games are all raising sponsorship with an effective environmental program. Companies are attracted to the positive image that comes with being associated with sustainable initiatives and many are more than willing to demonstrate their environmental policies at a high profile sport event. During the 1996 Atlanta Olympics one

ACOG official estimated that $10-40 million in additional revenue was lost by not having a stronger environmental program.

Never has there been a better time for innovative and alternative forms of sponsorship. In-kind sponsorship and donations programs have the potential to raise the profile of the sponsor while actually reinforcing the environmental objectives of the event or facility. The more obvious examples include: vehicles which use cleaner, alternative fuels; passive solar design features for new buildings and retrofitted buildings; water conservation fixtures, energy-efficient office and maintenance equipment; photovoltaic systems and wind generators for powering remote sites; non-chlorine pool treatment processes; graywater recycling systems and water purification technology. These are but a few of the types of mutually-beneficial partnerships that should be explored. The sport event or facility is precisely the type of high-profile demonstration site that a company with a new product or process needs to gain exposure.

Innovative Sponsorship at the 1999 Canada Winter Games

The environmental committee at the 1999 Canada Winter Games in Corner Brook Newfoundland was given no funds for its operating budget. Nevertheless, several environmental initiatives were carried out during the Games due to a successful appeal to various provincial and community businesses and corporations with innovative sponsorship opportunities. Newfoundland Power supplied transportation vehicles for the collection of materials for recycling, as well as providing 1000 low flow showerheads and 1,400 stickers to remind athletes and coaches to turn off lights. Genesis Organics offered to process all the compost wastes for free and the Municipality of Corner Brook offered to transport food waste to composting sites. The Municipality also gave a discount on public transportation fares for athletes, volunteers and spectators. The Multi-Material Stewardship Board donated 250 recycling bins to the Games, which remained at the various facilities so the recycling program could continue after the Games. Pepsi, one of the Games major sponsors agreed to supply reusable water bottles and water towers instead of thousands of plastic throwaway containers. Finally, a local mental health patient organization, West Lane, offered to collect and process the recyclable materials in return for the three-cent deposit on the aluminum cans.

Pan Am Games Cashes in on the Environment

The environment committee of the 1999 Pan Am Games in Winnipeg, Manitoba acquired a substantial amount of sponsorship for their environmental program. In many cases it was the sponsor or partner that initiated these programs, coming to the organizing committee with proposals. For example, the Manitoba Products Stewardship Corporation donated approximately $300,000 in services and in-kind time to organize the waste management and recycling at the Games. Manitoba Hydro, a major sponsor donated over $75,000, retrofitting with energy -efficient lighting accounted for $37,000 of that amount. Manitoba Environment, paid for an environment administrator to complement the organizing committee. Manitoba Education and Training subsidized the hiring of several environment interns to assist the venue management teams. A conservative monetary estimate of all the donations to the environment program is approximately $500,000, proving that there is a big financial incentive to fostering environment sponsorship at a sport event.

Helping Sponsors Develop an Appropriate Profile

Once the sponsor has demonstrated a legitimate environmental commitment, the sport organization can begin working with that sponsor to help it develop its green profile. Many sponsors are accustomed to thinking that a statement of good intentions is sufficient to make them "environmentally friendly" in the eyes of the public. These firms will need to be led through the process of evaluating all of their activities and/or products and developing alternative products and processes which meet the standards set by the sport organization.

Checklist for sponsors, donors and suppliers

- ◆ Respect all local and national environmental legislation.

- ◆ Meet or exceed best current practices.

- ◆ Seek innovative means of supporting sustainable sport.

- ◆ Take responsibility for retrieving and safely disposing of non-recyclables.

- ◆ Leave behind a positive legacy for the community.

As soon as a sponsor has taken credible steps to promote more sustainable practices, it deserves to be recognized. The sport organization should develop as part of its publicity and public relations strategy, a system for giving recognition to those firms or groups which have been supportive of its environmental programs. This could take the form of press releases that elaborate on the type of contribution made, an environmental honor roll to congratulate those who have played a significant part, and a press conference or reception in honor of sponsors.

Though it may seem a bit excessive to be heaping praise on companies, especially when some of them will likely have been coerced into going green, it is important to do so for two reasons. First, a pat on the back and a bit of good press will go a long way to encouraging these companies to carry on with what they have learned in all aspects of their work, as well as inspiring others to take a similar approach. Second, a green profile for sponsors goes hand in hand with promoting the green profile of the event/facility/organization itself. In this way the message of sustainable sport will be effectively disseminated to the public.

Working with Suppliers and Donors

As with sponsors, it is important to work closely with donors and suppliers to ensure that their products and services are supportive of the green cause, by establishing a standard contracting process. Though the process will differ slightly for donors, who do not typically go through the sort of tendering and bidding process that a supplier will, both should be encouraged, or even forced, to follow a hierarchy of preferences. Such a hierarchy can be spelled out through the criteria that the sport organization uses to select a supplier or product. The buyer/recipient can use criteria such as reduced packaging, reusability, non-toxicity or a high recycled-material content, to pursue its goal of sustainability.

Organizations that have green purchasing policies have discovered that a learning period is generally required by both their purchasing managers and their suppliers. Purchasers need time to

Coca-Cola Responds to Heat from Greenpeace

Greenpeace's aggressive Olympic campaigns demonstrated how quickly corporate action on environmental issues can be achieved with effective pressure. Nothing focuses the media spotlight better than an Olympic Games, and Greenpeace leveraged this publicity to elicit a positive response from Coca-Cola on the issue of global warming.

Greenpeace and Greenfreeze

One of Greenpeace Australia's central campaigns during Sydney 2000 preparations focussed on the phasing out of hydro fluorocarbons or HFCs in refrigeration systems. They specifically targeted recalcitrant companies in their pre-Games report called "Green Olympics, Dirty Sponsors". The report outlined how several of the Olympic sponsors, Coca-Cola, McDonalds and Unilever in particular, were using HFCs in their refrigeration systems at the Olympics in Sydney even though the environmental guidelines explicitly state that "Sydney is committed to use of CFC-, HFC- and HCFC-free refrigerant and processes".

Greenpeace demanded that Olympic sponsors:

- commit to a 100% Greenfreeze technology (non ozone-depleting and greenhouse gas producing equipment) at the Sydney Olympic Games and all future Games;

- abandon their corporate refrigeration policy of HFC use;

- specify all new equipment to be Greenfreeze; and

- abandon all CFC/HCFC/HFC use by the 2004 Athens Summer Olympics

HFCs are considered to be among the worst greenhouse gases in existence, however they are used pervasively in the refrigerant business since CFCs have been banned in most countries. The most frequently used HFCs have a global warming potential of over 3,000 times that of carbon dioxide, the most common greenhouse gas.

Coca-Cola Responds to the HFC Challenge

In response to Greenpeace's climate change campaign Coca-Cola announced a new environmental policy for cold drink equipment in Sydney Australia, on June 28, 2000.

Coca-Cola pledged to:

- no longer purchase new cold drink equipment using HFC where cost efficient alternatives are commercially available;

- expand its research and development program of alternative refrigeration technologies between now and 2004;

- require suppliers to use only HFC-free foam insulation and refrigeration in all new cold- drink equipment by 2004; and

- require suppliers to develop equipment that is 40-50% more efficient by the end of the decade.

Coca-Cola also announced that it had made an agreement with one of the largest commercial refrigeration companies in the southern hemisphere, Skope, to develop large, single-door coolers using hydrocarbon (HC) gases, which they claim have negligible impact on global warming. In 1999/2000 Coca-Cola worked with several partners in Denmark to develop small single-door coolers that reduce energy consumption. One hundred of these small drink coolers using the HC refrigerant were installed at Sydney Olympic Park for the 2000 Olympics. Unfortunately this only accounted for 5% of Coca-Cola's refrigerators on site.

settle on an initial list of criteria, to determine which products they might easily phase out entirely and to judge the quality and performance of some of the greener alternatives. Suppliers will need advance notice to locate and develop greener alternatives as well as modify existing products, processes and packaging.

The first step should be to establish and communicate a philosophy or statement of principle in order that your staff, suppliers and donors have a full understanding of what you are trying to achieve. A typical statement might read:

Statement of Environmental Preference

To reduce waste and to promote environmentally preferred purchasing, our organization will amend specifications for the acquisition of goods and services to encourage: the elimination of packaging, the use of durable and reusable products, and products which contain the maximum level of recycled and recyclable content, without significantly affecting safety, performance or price.

A product might be considered "environmentally preferred" (EP) if it is demonstrably less harmful to the environment than other products with the same end use, when its life cycle (e.g., storage, use and disposal) is taken into account.

By communicating your intentions as clearly as possible to suppliers and donors and by seeking their input on the criteria by which you will evaluate bids and select products, you will help to develop a constructive partnership and thereby increase the likelihood of getting the products and services you want at the price you want. A good supplier who fully understands what the buyer needs will go out of its way to provide it. This gives the sport organization, particularly a large one, extraordinary leverage: once a supplier has gone to the trouble and expense of developing a "greener" product or process, that supplier will go out of its way to sell it to other markets. Sport can thus play a role in speeding up the availability of environmentally preferred alternatives.

Criteria for Donors, Suppliers and Service Vendors

Clear and concise criteria by which EP quality will be judged are essential. These will need to cover a number of functions (e.g., packaging and cleaning) as well as several different environmental issues (e.g., waste reduction and energy efficiency). This means that in some cases EP qualities could come into conflict. Where this occurs, the following hierarchy, taken from Transport Canada's "Choose Green Procurement Guide" (1993) should be followed:

Hierarchy of Environmental Preference

High priority: High recycled content, low toxicity, high biodegradability

Medium priority: Durability, reusability, upgradability, conservation of fuel, energy or other resources

Lower priority: Recyclability, packaging qualities.

Another helpful checklist, published by the National Round Table on the Environment and the Economy (1996) for environmental purchasing is as follows:

Pre-purchase considerations

❑ Is the product necessary?

❑ Are all the features/elements necessary?

❑ Can the product be shared, borrowed or rented rather than purchased?

❑ Can a used or re-manufactured product be substituted for the new product requested?

General Questions

❑ Is the product certified "green"(e.g., EcoLogo [Canada]/Green Seal [U.S.]/ Blue Angel [Germany] or another recognized independent program)?

❑ Is the product durable/long lasting?

❑ Is the product easily repaired?

❑ Is it easily updated or upgraded by replacing or adding a part?

❑ Has a full life cycle environmental evaluation been carried out on the product?

Manufacturing /Use/Disposal

❑ Does the product contain recycled material?

❑ Does the product contain toxins banned or restricted substances (e.g., CFCs) or ozone-depleting substances?

❑ Does the product design minimize use of resources (i.e. energy, water)?

❑ Is it easily maintained and repaired?

❑ Is it reconditionable or recyclable after use?

❑ Does the product require special disposal considerations (e.g., hazardous materials)?

Environmental Profile of Manufacturer, Supplier, or Service Provider

❑ Does the company have a written, formal, environmental policy?

❑ Does the company have an Environmental Management System (EMS)?

❑ Does the manufacturer comply with any environment performance standards (e.g., ISO 14000)?

❑ Does the company apply stricter environmental standards than required by law?

❑ Has the company made a commitment to cradle-to-grave product stewardship?

A sport organization should use these and any relevant additional criteria to develop its own purchasing specifications. These specifications must then be clearly communicated to donors and suppliers, at the earliest stage possible. Appropriate weight should be given to EP considerations, in addition to factors such as cost and performance. Suppliers who are selected should be held contractually to the agreed specifications. Bidders who are not selected should be informed if environmental factors played a part in the decision, so as to encourage them to raise their standards.

Companies and groups that sponsor, supply or donate to a sport event, facility or program must assume their own role in the quest for sustainability and greener games. Any organization has the responsibility to promote environmental stewardship within its society, through its own operations and through its interaction with others. A wide range of literature exists to guide you through the process of moving toward sustainability, at whatever level you require (see What to Use section at the end of this chapter).

What You Can Do

Recommendations for Working with Sponsors, Donors and Suppliers

- Encourage potential sponsors to embrace environmental stewardship.

- Decline offers from organizations which could tarnish your image.

- Seek innovative and alternative forms of sponsorship.

- Work with supporters and suppliers to develop a legitimate profile for sustainability.

- Encourage and assist suppliers to provide more sustainable products and services.

- Adopt and enforce environmentally-preferred purchasing practices.

- Recognize publicly those sponsors/suppliers who are committed to environmental stewardship.

What to Use

Helpful publications

Lyons, Kevin. 1999. *Buying for the future: Contract management and the environmental challenge.*

National Round Table on the Environment and the Economy. 1996. Development of criteria for green procurement. **www.nrtee-trnee.ca**

Russel, Trevor. 1998. *Greener Purchasing: Opportunities and Innovations.*

Useful web sites

Certification Bodies

Canadian Environmental Choice: **www.terrachoice.ca**

Committed to Green: **www.committedtogreen.org**

Nordic Swan: **www.ecolabel.no**

US Green Seal: **www.greenseal.org**

German Blue Angel: **www.blauer-engel.de**

European Union Eco-label: **www.europa.eu.int/ecolabel**

Sport Industry

Nike Inc.: **www.nikebiz.com**

Patagonia: **www.patagonia.com**

Mizuno: **www.mizuno.com**

Purchasing

Buy Green: **www.buygreen.com** (not updated recently but provides many useful links)

U.S. Environmental Protection Agency (EPA): **www.epa.gov**

Integrated Management Solutions: **www.solutions.ca/docs/pwgsc_links.htm**

King County, WA: **www.metrokc.gov/procure/green/**

Case Study

Partnering with Sponsors for Sydney 2000

Sponsors helped Sydney 2000 meet its environmental commitments in many ways. They provided environmentally-friendly goods, sponsored environmental projects or used the Games as an opportunity to change corporate culture.

It is now clear that major companies are taking heed of the need to be more accountable and transparent in environmental and social issues. This will impact more and more on sport, as sponsors want to be sure their exposure is not jeopardized by poor management and communications. In turn, more sustainable sport will be more attractive to sponsors seeking better risks.

Examples of corporate support for the Green Games included:

- Energy Australia supplied PureEnergy electricity generated using solar, wind, hydro and landfill gas power.

- Holden showcased an experimental Ecommodore vehicle during the Torch Relay. This vehicle halves the fuel consumption of a full-sized family car. The lead car in the Marathon races was a zero-emission HydroGen 1 fuel cell car.

- Ramler Furniture provided biodegradable cardboard tables and bookshelves for a number of venues.

- Nike's Stand-Off Distance Singlet made of 75% recycled soft drink bottles was available to runners in the Olympic marathon. This consumes 43% less energy in production, uses no dyes for colouring and all printing is done through a water-based screen printing process.

- Carlton and United Breweries provided recyclable PET beer bottles and PET beer cups; Lindemans Wines provided recyclable plastic wine glasses.

- Olex Cables developed a PVC-free electrical cable, which was used in most venues, and was also responsible for managing the project to bury overhead transmission lines that formerly crossed Homebush Bay.

- Fuji Xerox supplied 'Green Wrap', a high-performance recycled paper, and was also a sponsor of the Olympic Landcare community tree-planting program.

This is not an exhaustive list. Throughout the Games, sponsors and suppliers worked closely with the Environment Program to seek practical solutions to procurement issues. Above all, Sydney 2000 clearly demonstrated that sport sponsors are willing to engage in environmental issues and many of them saw this as a value-added component. Indeed, some sponsors only came on board because of the environmental commitments.

A sponsor's view

"Coca-Cola developed a very ambitious new policy on refrigerants on the occasion of the Sydney Olympics. It was also the starting point for a whole re-thinking of our approach to environmental stewardship.

We started learning the hard way: we were initially the target of a Greenpeace campaign. The Greenpeace campaign was based on specific requirements set by the Organizing Committee, which had been elaborated — several years before the games actually took place — together with Greenpeace and had been part of the "green" Olympic bid by Sydney. We were not at all involved at that time and understood what the situation was only very late. Our first instinct was simply to erect defensive walls and to prepare to defend ourselves. Then, we understood that the way out from our perceived siege was a rather different one: we established a dialogue, built engagement and, through better mutual understanding, agreed on how to move forward.

Sydney was for us an eye-opener and a good lesson on the force of green procurement standards. More importantly, we understood how a global brand can raise to the challenge posed by such standards, contribute in minimizing environmental impact and actually benefit from the process."

Salvatore Gabola, Director Public Affairs, Coca Cola West Europe Group
(From Stubbs, 2001)

Part III

Facilities for Sport and Recreation

Designing, Building and Operating More Sustainably

By skimping on design, the owner gets costlier equipment, higher energy costs, and a less competitive and comfortable building; the tenants get lower productivity and higher rent and operating costs.

— **Hawken, Lovins and Lovins** in *Natural Capitalism*

Chapter

Facilities Design and Construction

The most visible and substantial environmental impact of any sport event or organization is determined by its facilities — what facilities are used, where they are located, and how they are run. No event or activity can take place without a venue. That venue may be anything from an untouched mountainside to a state-of-the-art dome stadium, or from the genuine natural environment to the developed natural environment and the built environment. This chapter will focus on developed and constructed environments for sport — those we term "facilities" — in an attempt to identify opportunities to reduce both the environmental and economic costs of building and running a sport facility.

Facilities Construction: When to Build and How

Before even beginning to contemplate the actual shape or location of a sport facility, it is critical that to ask some fundamental questions. Is a facility needed? What kind will best serve all potential users? What will the long-term costs be (financial, social and environmental) and who will pay them? This is a critical juncture, for it is here that the savings can be most easily found, needs met, clashes averted and financial and ecological disasters avoided.

Planning, Consultation, and Awareness-Raising

As important as asking the right question is asking the right people. The planning process must do more than ask easy questions of supportive experts. A meaningful planning process — one which is most likely to yield the most helpful information — is open and inclusive. That means posing questions whose answers are not predictable, to stakeholders whose interests do not necessarily coincide with those of the project initiator. It also means disclosing as much information as possible to the people who will be affected. Such an open process, perhaps surprisingly, tends to elicit the most useful results. Though far more difficult to achieve, the truly inclusive process gets people working together to seek common ground and, ultimately, an end result which they all can live with. The additional up-front effort put into good planning and consultation will pay off, metaphorically and tangibly, many times over down the road.

Pre-Design Questions

In the early stages it is essential to ask fundamental questions. A manager can set the agenda, requesting input from others whom you involve in this planning process.

1. **Is this facility needed?** Consider the existing alternatives, the purpose to which it will be put both immediately and in the future, and other types of facilities that might be more appropriate.

2. **What will be the true financial costs of the facility and who will pay them?** This requires an honest attempt to estimate not only likely cost overruns, but also maintenance and operational costs over the life of the building.

3. **What might be the environmental and social costs?** You should study what the potential impact of the facility — both its construction and operation — will be on the local community, the local ecosystem and the regional and global environment.

Principles of Sustainable Facility Design

- Enhance ecosystems during development and protect them during ongoing use of the site.
- Offer a safe and high quality environment for people who work at or use the site, and a highly desirable recreation destination.
- Reduce demand for water from potable drinking supplies.
- Achieve high levels of energy efficiency, and purchase energy requirements from sources that are renewable and/or which emit low levels of greenhouse gases and other pollutants.
- Minimize the use of materials which deplete natural resources or create toxic pollution in their manufacture, use or disposal.
- Preserve or recreate significant areas of open and natural spaces for current and future enjoyment.
- Avoid ozone-depleting substances.
- Minimize impact of noise on local community and other resident species.
- Minimize impact of lighting on local community and other resident species.
- Protect the quality of water leaving the site via run-off or infiltration.
- Improve the quality of soils wherever possible, and protect soil and sediments within the developed area.
- Maximize the appropriate use of recycled materials and minimize the generation of waste in all development and ongoing operational activities.

Assuming that a relatively unbiased summary of these and other questions and concerns has been prepared and made public — one which does more than dismiss the arguments of "non-boosters" — the planning process should culminate with a decision: to build or not to build?

The Building Decision: Renovate or Build? Temporary or Permanent?

When you and your cohorts think a new facility is required, the question to ask before proceeding is: "Can an existing facility be suitably renovated at a comparable cost?" Though it often appears cheaper to build from scratch than to renovate, there are hidden costs which may not have been calculated. These may be tangible (land purchases, demolition expenses, dumping costs for demolition waste) or intangible (dumping of non-renewable resources in the case of a demolition, appropriation of green space where a new site is selected, energy and water consumed in the building process and pollution generated by building and transportation). The typical renovation consumes far fewer resources — and therefore creates less waste — than building a new facility.

The decision to renovate or build should take full account of life cycle costing and payback periods. Will the building last as long as forecast? How long will it be before significant new capital costs are incurred for repairs or upgrading? Can the building be easily adapted to changing fashions and demographic trends? These are all questions that should be answered by your design and engineering professionals. If you want to be certain, ask for second opinions from other reputable experts in your region.

Where renovation is the option of choice, the environmental impact of the renovation process can be minimized. Workers should be fully protected from dust, asbestos, lead paints and other hazardous materials; nearby communities should be protected against unnecessary dust, noise and fumes; dangerous materials should be sent to appropriate disposal sites, not ordinary landfills; and any recyclable or reusable materials should be diverted from the waste stream.

> ## Greener Financing for Technologies and Retrofits
>
> Subsidies from utilities and government grants are often available to assist facility operators with installing or converting to energy-efficient equipment and systems and innovative technologies, especially if they are locally or domestically produced. All such grant and subsidy programs should be explored. In addition, preferential rates can be negotiated on loans and mortgages with some financial institutions who recognize the long-term savings that will be achieved by a facility and therefore perceive their loan/mortgage as a lower risk. The most promising current trend is toward projects financed by an ESCo (energy service company) which typically provide the client with turnkey services including: performing an initial energy audit; designing and specifying energy-saving measures; managing the tendering process; commissioning new equipment; training staff; and monitoring/verifying post-retrofit energy use.

Check with government environmental protection and enforcement bodies if there are new regulations/bylaws related to construction, renovation and demolition. These bodies typically

The Trend Toward Multiple-Use Facilities

The ideal facility is one that is designed to be adaptable to shifting demands. The most economically sensible direction for planners and architects to take is to design facilities that are appropriate for multiple uses and able to weather the heavy demand. Coincidentally, a single, well-built, multi-use facility is far greener than several initially inexpensive, single-use ones.

Examples include:

- indoor stadiums with multi-configurable seating, running tracks and climbing walls;

- covered speed skating halls with hockey/figure skating surfaces on the interior and running tracks around the outside;

- outdoor velodromes usable for inline skating as well as cycling, and with multi-use turf pitches on the infield.

A number of designers have developed multi-configurational stadiums that provide sport/entertainment facilities with multiple event modes that can be rapidly switched over. These permit a single facility to host many different types of events thus providing the revenue necessary to make the facility financially self-supporting.

One such concept involves a grass playing surface located on a "barge" which floats in and out of the stadium. Thus, there are three surfaces available for use inside and outside the stadium, concrete, grass and water. Multi-configurational means increased use of facilities and revenue and a decrease in land requirements. The environmental benefits include the maximum use of materials and energies, less waste of land space, and less energy and materials spent resodding an indoor field.

provide guidance on minimum requirements and suggested approaches. Also, spell out as much as possible in clear terms in contracts with your contractors and builders. They may be aware and helpful. On the other hand, they may be unaware and/or uncooperative. Either way, it is their job to know and follow national, state and local regulations. Let them know how important it is to you that they take the environmentally responsible path. It could save you money and headaches.

Where the decision is to build on the old site, similar steps should be taken: notably, a careful demolition should be requested, whereby contractors divert all reusable and recyclable materials. Again, you will need to work with contractors. Emphasize your concerns, listen to theirs and write appropriate language into your contracts. Copper, brass and other valuable metals and non-metals can often be sold to brokers. Part of the cost of demolition can be covered in this way. Reducing the amount sent to landfill will also save thousands of dollars in trucking and dumping fees. Decide who should keep the money received for re-sold materials. You may want it to defray your costs. On the other hand, allowing your demolition contractor to keep the money may bring in lower quotes, thus lowering your costs.

If a new building is required, one option might be to use a temporary structure. Smaller events have almost always been forced by low budgets to use rented, temporary structures. Many major events are rediscovering this option. This is a common choice faced by event organizers.

A temporary structure might suffice for registration areas, change rooms, toilets, media centers, broadcast booths, spectator seating, ticket and refreshment kiosks. By leasing tents, awnings or pre-fabricated huts wherever use and climate permit, building costs can be slashed. With foresight, even purchased temporary structures can be sold or donated, intact or in part following an event. Furthermore, impact on the site can be minimized if a non-permanent building is used. The temporary media village for the Lillehammer Winter Games, for example, was erected on posts over agricultural land following the autumn harvest. By spring, those same fields were again being cultivated!

The decision to build a permanent site should never be taken lightly. Too many sport mega-projects go ahead based on overly optimistic scenarios prepared by consultants who know what favorable recommendation is expected from them. All too frequently politics plays a deciding role. The belief that a shiny new facility will provide employment, economic development, boost tourism and "put the city-region-country on the map" tends to hamper rational decision-making. Hence the frequent need for taxpayer's money to be used to prop up white-elephant facilities, or to subsidize new arenas to house professional franchises that may or may not be committed to staying in the community.

Three Cases of Facilities Choices

Victoria Commonwealth Games

For Victoria organizers, a tight budget meant making the best use of construction money. Most events were held in existing facilities, renovated where necessary. The use of tents for a variety of functions was aided by Victoria's moderate climate. Those new facilities that were built were designed with accessibility and multiple use in mind. The Juan de Fuca cycling track is designed to accommodate, not only competitive and recreational cycling, but roller-blading, skate-boarding and, in the infield circumscribed by the track, various field sports.

Lillehammer Winter Olympic Games

Although Lillehammer constructed several permanent facilities that had been listed as temporary in their original bid, and several more which they had not planned to build at all, extensive use was made of temporary buildings for everything from athletes and media accommodation to broadcast booths and ticket kiosks. The majority of these had already been assigned post-Games destinations prior to the event. Pre-fabricated modular units were assembled to create larger structures at many sites. It was thus relatively easy to disassemble the modules and send them to other towns to be used as school classrooms and community centers. Collapsible A-frame kiosks were donated to the Red Cross as emergency shelters. In this way, Lillehammer was left with very little construction material to dispose of.

Albertville Winter Olympic Games

In contrast to Lillehammer, many of Albertville's temporary structures and permanent facilities were victims of a lack of foresight. Just two years after the Games, several temporary structures, though disassembled, lay in pieces on the ground. The press center at La Lechere is one of several permanent structures not being used as planned. A number of offices and hotels, constructed in the flurry of pre-Games building activity, lie empty. Some hotels have gone bankrupt.

Location is Everything

As any real estate agent knows, location is a critical determinant of business success. It is also an example of where economic and environmental sustainability coincide. The right location for a successful sport facility is often the better environmental choice as well. The best site for a stadium tends to be as close as possible to where potential users live.

But as important as proximity is accessibility. Some of the most central locations are poorly served by roads and public transportation, a recipe for traffic congestion. From the perspective of access, as we explore in the transportation chapter, the optimal site is one which is centrally placed within its community of users but is well served by a network of public and private transportation routes. At the same time, however, it should not disrupt regular traffic flow or disturb neighboring communities; this is often as much a question of scheduling as it is location.

Hockey Before Agriculture

The Ontario Municipal Board allowed the owners of the Ottawa Senators National Hockey League team to build the Corel Center on protected agricultural land, despite the objections of a small agricultural protest group. Dwindling farmland was lost when the sport facility was built on a remote suburban/rural site, to which users get primarily by car. It is not in walking or even cycling distance of the majority of the market.

Thinking for Long-term Health

The tendency in North America throughout the 1960s, '70s and '80s was to abandon downtown locations in favor of suburban or even rural ones, taking advantage of lower land prices and plenty of parking space. Because car access was so easy and so many people own cars, access by public transportation was rarely considered. This is a prime example of how full environmental costs are not factored into our economic system. Although there is an enormous long-term cost to turning farmland into a sport stadium and parking lot, that cost is not reflected in the price of a ticket for the spectator because it is often borne by the taxpayer at large, immediately or well into the future, rather than by the arena or franchise owner. In the case of ecological damage, the only measurable harm is done to the voteless flora and fauna. Harm to humans is so hard to quantify that it is generally dismissed.

Protecting Precious Land

Parklands and wilderness areas are endangered spaces and must be protected from further sport facilities development. Though a case can be made for allowing careful use of protected wilderness parkland for sport purposes, further construction of facilities will only hasten the demise of these remaining global heritage sites. Existing facilities within park lands, such as Canada's Banff and Jasper National Parks or the U.S. Yosemite and Grand Tetons, should be allowed to remain, but under one strict proviso: that no expansion or upgrading which increases the degree of impact

---

Keeping Games out of Protected Spaces

The question of using parks for sport facility development has been an issue for a number of major games, such as Olympic proposals for Denver, Calgary, Nagano and Atlanta. In each case local opposition groups have succeeded in halting or limiting the use of protected wilderness. The fact that these battles have had to be fought, however, demonstrates just how fragile the concept of "protected" is in most parts of the world. Is something protected only until a "better" use is proposed for it? To reinforce the protected status of parkland, the IOC and other governing bodies must refuse to consider bids that include building facilities in parkland. Sydney has worked to ensure that none of its facilities will encroach on significant natural or cultural environments.

---

be allowed; and that every attempt be made to reduce the environmental impact of existing facilities and services. So little wilderness has been preserved worldwide — especially in the relatively populated regions under greatest pressure — that any land designated as protected must be strictly off bounds for all recreational use save perhaps non-mechanized, temporary visits.

Environmental Impact Assessments and Audits

An effective tool for keeping facilities out of sites where they might cause significant harm, as well as ensuring that their design and operations have a minimal environmental impact, is the Environmental Impact Assessment. The EIA is a process whereby all aspects of a plan to build, renovate or upgrade facilities, or run an activity, are assessed by a neutral body of experts. A resulting EIA report should attempt to determine the best- and worst-case scenarios for all aspects of a proposed project and for the project as a whole. The environmental costs and benefits of the project should be listed both in quantifiable and non-quantifiable terms.

Almost all countries, states and/or municipalities have legislation requiring that EIAs be performed on projects of a certain size or dollar value or for proposed activity in sensitive areas. Your environmental authorities can tell you if an EIA is required for your project. They can also provide guidance on what is required, including potential costs and time frames.

EIA requirements can vary enormously from one jurisdiction to the next. A qualified environmental consultant that specializes in performing EIAs should be engaged. Your yellow pages are the best starting point. Be sure to check the references of any consultant. A good one will save you time, money and hassles by avoiding delays.

The EIA is a potentially valuable technique, which is unfortunately susceptible to misuse for political ends. While it can be very useful in underlining the likely impact of a project on the local and global environment, the weakness of the EIA is that its results are frequently a mix of tangible and intangible costs and benefits. Unlike its purely economic cousin, the cost/benefit analysis, the EIA must be couched in softer language, often without any dollar figures attached. This makes it easy

The Argument for a Balanced Approach to Wilderness Development

Some skiing industry developers believe it is possible to build, even within protected wilderness preserves, given adequate guidelines and a clear and respected Environmental Impact Assessment (EIA) process. They argue that there will continue to be pressures on parks from potential users and that rather than implement an outright ban or moratorium, governing bodies, concerned citizens and the ski industry can work together to ensure a "balanced approach". Such an approach would include careful adherence to any national or state/ provincial parks legislation as well as the mandated successful completion of an EIA by any proposed new project. The ski industry, for its part, could set an example of sustainable tourism, and operators within protected areas use there privileged position to educate users about environmental issues.

for anyone with a vested interest in seeing the project proceed to argue that the economic benefits (jobs, tourism, etc.) will outweigh the environmental harm.

This is changing, however. With more and more people recognizing that sustainability requires both a strong economy and a healthy environment, the EIA is taking on a growing importance in its own right. What the sport industry, like any other, must realize is that a negative environmental impact is still a loss to society, no matter how great the potential economic benefit. For an EIA that warns of severe consequences to be overridden by economic arguments is not sustainable thinking.

Any project of consequence should be subject to an EIA. The size and nature of the project will determine the extent of the EIA. If it is to be more than a public relations exercise, the government or sport organization must decide beforehand that its recommendations will be respected. If the EIA warns of severe environmental harm, the project should be scrapped or a better alternative found. If potential consequences are identified but steps can be taken to prevent or alleviate them, a full commitment must be made to taking those steps.

It is rare for any major project to be launched these days without an EIA. To do so is to invite economic, ecological and public relations trouble. To do an EIA but ignore the results is equally risky. A number of infrastructure and sport facility projects for the Albertville Games either ignored the warnings of geologists or did too little to address the risks. The resulting landslides proved very expensive and embarrassing.

The environmental audit is another useful tool. An audit identifies areas for improvement and proposes steps to increase sustainability. A specific audit of the potential environmental consequences from the construction process and the eventual functioning facility should be done before work starts. In fact, three or more audits of this sort would be wise: a pre-construction audit, a mid-point audit to detect where changes might be made while it is still feasible and relatively cheap to do so, and a post-construction audit to determine how well goals have been met and if any further action is required. Auditors might keep a close watch on such construction concerns as energy consumption, cleaning and maintenance routines, indoor air quality, systems for handling or eliminating harmful compounds, waste disposal plans and treatment of soil and vegetation. For the small-scale facilities manager who may wish to attempt certain audits in-house (i.e. energy efficiency, waste management) useful guides are available and may be adequate. Otherwise, professional help is available from consultants, often the same as those who performs EIAs.

Design, Equipment and Material Selection

In the design of any facility, there are many opportunities to pursue greater sustainability. A building can be designed to take advantage of sunlight, for natural lighting and passive solar heating (see chapter 8 also for more information on good, natural energy systems). It can be partially buried or sheltered by a hill or trees to reduce heat loss or, in hot climates, to remain as cool as possible. Similarly, a facility's systems, machinery and construction materials are important economic and environmental considerations. In many cases, the choice of the better environmental option will actually lower operating costs, even if initial capital construction costs are higher. Certain energy- or water-conservation devices or better insulation may begin to save money less than two years after construction. In other cases, the greener choice may never be as inexpensive as a traditional item or material. The benefit may lie in cleaner and healthier air or a reduced contribution to local environmental problems.

The types of equipment, fixtures and materials selected by any sport facility will be a key determinant of its environmental impact and its eventual operating costs. Categories to consider include energy-conserving systems and devices, water conserving systems and fixtures, the composition, flexibility and durability of building materials, the ease of assembly and disassembly of components and the presence of harmful compounds in any of these materials (see chapter 8).

Building materials have come a long way. Shortages of certain resources and rising prices have acted as a powerful incentive to innovation in the industry. Traditional wood framing products have been supplemented by ones using a fraction of the amount of wood and by completely different materials, such as recycled steel studs. Some of these cost less, are more durable or offer specific advantages. Others simply perform the same task using fewer materials and creating less waste.

Oberhaching College Halves Energy Demand

Germany's new College of Physical Education, in Oberhaching, is a remarkable achievement in ecologically responsible design and construction. In a comparative study done with a similar physical education college in the same region, the Oberhaching College shows a 50% reduction in energy requirements.

The impressive array of energy saving technologies includes:

◆ an integrated energy system that uses natural gas as its main supply

◆ heat recovery systems and low-temperature surface heating and ventilation systems:

  ◗ two condensing boilers equipped with gas heat-recovery systems;

  ◗ 75% of the heated rooms equipped with low-temperature underfloor heating; and

  ◗ filter back-flushing water and waste water from the pool showers fed to a collection vessel for heat recovery.

◆ pool water treated by ozonation, flocculation , combination filtration and chlorination

◆ ozone added to pool filter systems downstream from the circulation pumps

The significance of these energy conservation systems is measured by:

◆ heat exchange rates of 90% and an all-year rate of 80%.

◆ the high investment cost of the heat-recovery systems offset by lower costs for installation of heat and cold generation and the lower consumption of gas and electricity. (For the recovery of 1kW of heat energy, only 0.03-0.05kW of electrical energy is required).

◆ reduction in the amount of heat discharged into the atmosphere by approx. 2,500,000kWh.

Preferable construction materials include those that use byproducts that would previously have been wasted, such as laminated woods and particleboards. Others have a high recycled content.

Steps for selecting building materials

◆ Seek maximum recycled content.

◆ Choose durable, easily reparable or interchangeable items.

◆ Select materials which do not require hazardous or toxic products to apply or remove.

◆ Choose products which will not need to be disposed of as hazardous waste.

Look for building materials that do not off-gas potentially noxious fumes, particularly composite woods, carpets, paints and other finishing products. More healthful indoor conditions begin with better air. Healthier products of this type are reaching the market as the risk of indoor chemical and biological pollutants becomes increasingly recognized and better understood. Ask your suppliers to provide materials that will not harm indoor air quality. Ask them for third-party certification or evaluation of their products. Above all, ask questions and emphasize your concerns. A growing number of resources (books, trade journals, web sites) provide guidance in this area.

Tendering Criteria for Purchasing and Contractors

The most effective means to promote more sustainable building practices and the use of greener equipment and materials is to build appropriate criteria into tendering documents for contractors and suppliers. Bidders should be required to answer questions concerning the environmental profile of the materials and processes they will use, their cleaning and maintenance routines, their use and treatment of hazardous chemicals or compounds, and any plans they might have to reduce waste, noise, pollution or habitat damage. Their responses should be carefully considered as part of the bid evaluation process. The firms awarded contracts must then be reminded of their environmental commitments and held responsible for any failures. If necessary, fines should be imposed on contractors who fail to follow environmental guidelines. (A fine of $10,000 was threatened for every tree disturbed at the Lillehammer bobsled and luge site — sufficiently daunting that no trees were damaged.)

Sydney OCA Tendering Process

The Olympic Co-ordination Authority for Sydney 2000 committed to designing facilities, selecting building materials and choosing products and services with a strong emphasis on their environmental attributes. In putting this commitment into practice, the OCA used a tendering process that put the onus on bidders. The OCA provided general environmental guidance and descriptions of important issues that it wanted to see addressed, instead of precise criteria and quantifiable targets. By emphasizing how the environmental attributes of each proposal would strongly influence its overall score, the OCA effectively challenged bidders to "out-green" each other, without telling them exactly what product, material or design to provide. The benefits of this approach are multiple: education of designers, architects, planners and builders; stimulation of innovation; less workload for purchasing officers and specification writers; competitive pricing for environmentally-superior results; and greater legal defensibility.

Aesthetic Concerns

Amidst all the worry about cost, technical performance and deadlines, the aesthetic side of facilities construction is often forgotten. Function tends to take precedence over form. Yet there are some aspects of modern society which few can find attractive: highways, neon signs, telephone poles and transformer stations. Most societies have grown to accept these as part of modern civilization. The same can be said for many of the standard accoutrements of sport: signs, advertising billboards, parking lots and disposable containers. It is interesting to note that Baron Pierre de Coubertin actually called for aesthetically appropriate Olympic facilities almost a century ago.

> ## Keeping Lillehammer Beautiful
>
> Clearly Norway is one country where appearance has a strong pride of place and the people are not so quick to accept all of sport's trappings. The determination of Lillehammer residents not to allow the Olympics to change the fundamentally modest and historic look of the town began with an attempt to spell out the aesthetic values they did not want altered. From this novel starting point the LOOC developed four main principles for facilities construction: Norwegian character; environmentally friendly design and construction; unity and coherence; and work by leading Norwegian designers. From these, a number of more specific Guidelines were also spelled out.

Clean-up, Landscaping, Rehabilitation

Going beyond the purely aesthetic, a number of measures can be taken during and following construction to improve the cleanliness and ecological health of a site.

Steps to preserve the cleanliness of the site

- Take all possible steps to avoid pollution and contamination.

- Carefully remove and dispose of construction materials and equipment.

- Clean up immediately any spills of compounds that are not benign and readily biodegradable.

- In the case of more severe spills where seepage may have contaminated soil, surface water or ground water, complete remediation is essential. Authorities must be immediately notified and no expense spared to limit the damage.

The final step is to return the appearance and composition of the grounds to as natural a state as possible. Any trees that were transplanted during construction should be replaced. Where trees and other flora may not have existed, consider a naturalization program to recreate a healthier and more vibrant ecosystem. Only native species should be considered; others run the risk of creating unexpected problems.

Diverting construction waste and materials, thus, becomes a final part of the construction process. Construction waste, unused materials and those from dismantled buildings — as mentioned early in this chapter — can often be diverted from landfill. Doing so saves money and extends the life of local landfills, to the benefit of local taxpayers and those areas that might have become new landfills.

Contractors should be encouraged to reduce waste in the building process. This can be achieved by making them contractually and financially responsible for separating reusable and recyclable materials and for finding markets or brokers. Many contractors are already working to limit waste in construction as part of good business management. Materials wasted are materials that were unnecessarily purchased and which cost money to dispose of. The brokering of reusable building materials is an up-and-coming industry in most countries.

A New Use for Polluted Land

The Old Works public golf course in Anaconda, Montana, is a model for putting polluted land back into safe, productive use. Energy giant ARCO, which was responsible for cleaning up the former site of its copper smelter, struck a deal with local government officials and the U.S. Environmental Protection Agency to spend roughly $40 million cleaning up and capping the contaminated area and building the golf course, then handing it over to the city. Lime was applied over the toxic soil, which was then capped with plastic liner, clay and then clean soil, before being seeded. Water bodies are closely monitored to detect any possible leakage of pollutants. Designed by Jack Nicklaus and opened in May 1997, the Old Works course is the first built on an EPA Superfund site, and one which the EPA would like to see replicated elsewhere.

Rose Garden Shows the Way for Recycling and Reusing Construction Waste

The contractors for the Rose Garden arena in Portland, Oregon showed how to save money and to create less waste through construction and demolition (C&D) debris management. The construction of the arena produced nearly 50,000 tonnes of C&D waste. At the rate of $75 a tonne to dump this waste at the nearest landfill, over 150 miles away, this would have cost $158,000 in disposal and transportation costs. However, with initiative and teamwork, 92% of the waste was recycled or reused. Furthermore, they generated $42,000 from sales of the materials.

What You Can Do

Summary of Recommendations for Facilities Construction

- Consider all possible alternatives before building a new facility, including renovation, retrofitting and temporary facilities.

- Use an integrative design process: involve all stakeholders in planning and consultations.

- Conduct an Environmental Impact Assessment and respect its findings.

- Conduct pre-, mid-, and post-construction environmental audits.

- Locate the facility to maximize economic and environmental advantages.

- Never build new facilities in protected parkland; operate existing parkland facilities with utmost caution.

- Develop environmental criteria for building-material selection.

- Use environmental criteria when tendering for materials and services.

- Use payback studies to determine which energy-saving and water conservation features to install.

- Take steps to ensure good indoor air quality.

- Consider renewable energy systems for facilities and equipment.

- Consider aesthetic, noise and light pollution when building and operating a facility.

What to Use

Environmental Impact Assessments and Audits

For consultants specializing in this work, contact industry associations or professional institutes, as well as the yellow pages for your area. Always ask for references.

Green design, construction and purchasing

Helpful publications

Lawson, B. 1996. *Building materials, energy and the environment: Towards ecologically sustainable development.*

Lopez Barnett, D., and W. Browning. 1995. *A primer on sustainable building.*

Mumma, T. 1997. *Guide to resource efficient building elements, 6th ed.*

Strain, L. *Resourceful specifications: Guideline specifications for environmentally considered building materials and construction methods.*

Sustainable Systems. 1997. *Greening federal facilities: An energy, environmental and economic resource guide for federal facility managers.*

Thompson, G., and F. Steiner, eds. 1997. *Ecological design and planning.*

Useful web sites

E Design Online: **www.edesign.state.fl.us**

Environmental Building News: A monthly newsletter on environmentally responsible design and construction. **www.ebuild.com**

Green Building Information Council: **www.greenbuilding.ca**

GEO Green Building Resource Center: **www.geonetwork.org/gbrc**

Oikos: A searchable database on green building products/materials. **www.oikos.com**

Energy Efficient Building Design/Operation

Useful web sites

US Department of Energy: **www.eren.doe.gov/buildings**

Helpful publications

Pennsylvania Dept. of Environmental Protection. 1999. *Guidelines for creating high-performance green buildings.*

Steven Winter Associates. 1998. *The passive solar design and construction handbook.*

Suozzo, M., et al. 1997. *Guide to energy-efficient commercial equipment.*

Tuluca, A. *Energy-efficient design and construction for commercial buildings.*

Watson, Donald, FAIA, Kenneth Labs, *Climatic Building Design: Energy-efficient building principles and practices.*

Indoor Air Quality

Useful web sites

US EPA web site (**www.epa.gov/iaq/iaqinfo.html**)

Helpful publications

Bearg, D. 1993. *Indoor air quality and HVAC systems.*

Canada Mortgage and Housing Corporation, *Building Materials for the Environmentally Hypersensitive.*

Immig, J., S. Rish, and S.K. Brown. 1997. *Indoor air quality guidelines for Sydney Olympic facilities.*

Levin, H., ed. *Indoor air bulletin: Technology, research and news for indoor environmental quality.*

Miller, N., ed. 1995. *The healthy school handbook: Conquering the sick building syndrome and other environmental hazards in and around your school.*

Whom to Consult

Certification bodies for various products and services

Useful web sites

U.S. Green Seal: **www.greenseal.org**

Canadian Environmental Choice: **www.terrachoice.ca**

Committed to Green Foundation: **www.committedtogreen.org**

European Union Eco-label: **http://europa.eu.int/ecolabel**

Nordic Swan: **www.ecolabel.no**

German Blue Angel: **www.blauer-engel.de**

Forest Stewardship Council: **www.fscoax.org/**

Governments

Contact federal and state/provincial environmental authorities for your region/country.

Chapter

8 Facilities Operation: Going Further with Less

Any sport facility, new or old, big or small, can operate more sustainably. Sustainable facilities operation may be the result of better technologies, better practices, better purchasing, or some combination of all of these. In most cases economic benefits can be realized, in the form of cost savings or increased revenue. Challenging the myth that environmental protection is inevitably more expensive, sustainable facilities operation often showcases ways to provide superior opportunities for sport and recreation at an equal or reduced cost. Improvements and innovation can be achieved through more efficient natural resource management (energy, water), pollution prevention (air, water, noise, light) reduced demand for materials and supplies, and elimination of and appropriate handling of hazardous materials.

Saving Money by Saving Energy

The cost of energy is rising everywhere and will only continue to do so. This, combined with the fact that many of our principal environmental problems are energy-related is a powerful motivation for conservation. Many cost-effective steps can be taken to reduce the energy consumption of any facility. In fact, a study by the Rocky Mountain Institute concluded that if the best electricity-saving innovations already on the market were installed in all U.S. buildings and equipment, three-fourths of the electricity now used would be saved, with an average payback period of slightly more than one year, and with equal or better services (International Institute for Sustainable Development 1992).

Most utility companies have initiated comprehensive energy conservation programs. These are typically designed to encourage and assist customers by offering consulting services and incentives, such as rebates on the installation of more efficient technology. Sport organizations should take full advantage of this type of assistance.

For example, one YM-YWCA received a subsidy of $170,000 from the local utility towards its projected $900,000 energy retrofit project. This helped to reduce the payback period from 5.8 to 4.7 years. Many community and school ice rinks, pools and indoor sport halls have received similar assistance from their local utilities, who have a vested interest in keeping a lid on electricity demand, in order to avoid expensive construction of new power plants. Games organizers can work with city recreation officials to improve the energy performance of either new facilities or older ones undergoing retrofits in order to host an event. Both the Victoria Commonwealth Games and the Kamloops Canada Games worked with their provincial utility, BC Hydro, to implement the "Power Smart" energy conservation program in many of their facilities. This step saved them money on the purchase and installation of equipment and insulation and will save the facility operators hundreds of thousands of dollars over the lifetime of the buildings. Georgia Tech worked closely with the U.S. Department of Energy to install solar panels and improve the energy performance of the pool used for the 1996 Atlanta Olympics.

Bundles of Savings in Etobicoke

Since 1983, the City of Etobicoke, Ontario has been designing, implementing and updating comprehensive conservation programs, resulting in reduced energy consumption and costs. Steps taken at its pools, arenas and other recreational and non-recreational facilities cost over $2.5 million (with $500,000 covered by grants). The result has been a cost saving of over $7 million: a 35% reduction in energy consumption. The table below breaks down the various components of the energy conservation project.

Energy Conservation Program/Project Highlights

Project/Program	Cost ($CDN)	Anticipated Savings/Year
Gihon Springs Outdoor Pool / Solar system	9,443.00	2,625.00
Central Arena / Brine pump controller	14,000.00	3,039.85
Centennial Arena / Water recirculation system	12,050.00	5,000.00
Pine Point Arena / Heat reclaim system	11,080.00	3,200.00
Etobicoke Olympium / High efficiency boilers	44,743.00	8,000.00
Etobicoke Olympium / Computerized control system	53,720.00	25,000.00
Pine Point Arena / Low Emissivity Ceiling	25,400.00	5,207.00
Pine Point Arena / Ice pad lighting redesign	4,197.00	1,579.00
Etobicoke Olympium / Heat recovery systems	137,758.00	23,626.00
Alderwood Pool / Thermal pool blanket	8,877.85	9,184.20

Heating, Ventilating and Cooling

To improve the efficiency of the heating, ventilation and air conditioning (HVAC) systems — which account for 60 percent of energy consumed in the average building — the main step is to reduce air leakage. By tightening the "envelope" of the building, less heated or cooled air will escape, and occupants will be more comfortable. In an extremely well sealed building, however, maintaining the quality of indoor air is especially important. This will be dealt with in more detail later.

The envelope of a building is tightened by stopping air leakage and reducing conduction. To plug air loss, all joints between one surface or material and another should be examined for gaps and cracks. These include windows, doors, ventilation systems, foundations, joints between walls and openings for air conditioners, lights and electrical conduits. Gaps and cracks can be sealed with caulking, weather-stripping and other forms of insulation. Dilapidated doors and windows can be replaced with newer, airtight models; although these are initially more expensive, they will pay for themselves many times over. New construction should make full use of recent advances in airtight building methods and materials.

Conduction is the transfer of heat from one area to another through a separating material.

Steps to reduce conduction

♦ Use better insulated doors and advanced windows.

♦ Install high levels of insulation or upgrade existing levels in areas such as walls, ceilings and roofs, and foundations.

♦ Block off unused/unnecessary doors, windows and other openings.

Chicago Facility A Model of Energy-Efficiency

Seven Bridges Ice Arena in Chicago Ill. is one of the largest ice skating facilities in the U.S. holding three rinks, a fitness center, with a weight room and various studios, a restaurant and pro shop. There the planners designed a heating, ventilation, air-conditioning (HVAC) system with various innovative measures to conserve energy, protect the environment, and save money (Louria 1996).

Refrigeration of the ice surfaces provides the means by which most of the other systems run. The refrigeration plant is equipped with compressors that use ammonia and therefore have zero ozone depletion potential. The refrigeration process produces an enormous amount of energy that the arena could not afford to loose. Instead the waste heat is recovered to provide the facilities heating and domestic hot water. However, not only does the refrigeration process provide heat, it also provides the energy for the space cooling and dehumidification, the snow-melt pit and the evaporation condensing systems.

For space heating a water and glycol mixture is circulated in piping which was heated by the refrigerant's hot gas loop. The mixture is also used for the necessary sub floor heating of the ice rink in order to stop frost build up and heaving of the rink floor. A recovery waste heat exchanger was installed in the refrigerant hot gas loop to heat the domestic water. Furthermore, the heat from the lighting systems is recovered and spot heating is used for spectators in the rinks themselves for more efficient heat energy use.

The energy-conservation features have a payback period of less than three years.

◆ Shade south-facing windows with awnings or shutters to reduce solar gain in summer.

◆ Plant trees or install other windbreaks against prevailing winter winds.

◆ Design buildings to maximize solar gain or protect against it, depending on the climate.

The HVAC system transfers heat or cold throughout a building by using air or water. Heat can be generated from almost any type of fuel, whereas cooling is typically achieved through the use of CFC, HCFC and HFC coolants. HVAC systems can use less energy by reducing demand, improving efficiency or upgrading to alternative technologies.

Steps to reduce energy consumption

◆ Switch from electricity or oil to natural gas, a cleaner-burning, more efficient alternative.

◆ Install automatic set-back thermostats and set them at optimum levels.

◆ Encourage seasonal attire — most buildings are over-heated in winter and over-cooled in summer.

◆ Shut down HVAC as fully as possible at night and over weekends and holidays.

◆ Eliminate heating and cooling from unoccupied areas such as storage, where contents are not temperature sensitive.

◆ Ensure that hot/cool air is properly circulated and eliminate cold/hot spots.

◆ Install ceiling fans and consider portable fans as an alternative to air conditioning.

◆ Discourage the use of electric space heaters.

◆ Keep unnecessary lights and equipment shut down in summer to reduce heat.

Steps to improve the efficiency of the HVAC system

◆ Replace older systems (50 to 60 percent efficient) with a new (up to 90 percent) one — the pay-back period may be as little as three years.

◆ Have the system inspected, cleaned and tuned up annually.

New technologies such as heat pumps and heat recovery systems provide good ventilation while minimizing the loss of energy to the outside. For new buildings or during renovations or HVAC upgrading, consider the installation of a heat pump, which uses outside air to heat or cool depending on the season. During extreme cold or heat, the heat pump will supplement the existing primary system. Heat exchangers can capture hot air (from boilers or other heat-generating machinery), which would normally be directly vented to the outside, and use it to pre-heat incoming air or the water supply.

Geothermal pumps offer an increasingly popular and cost-effective method of heating and cooling. Similar in effect to heat pumps using outside air, geothermal pumps circulate a solution such as water and methanol antifreeze through a system of pipes buried at least two meters (six feet) under ground where a constant temperature of 10-12° Celcius (50-55°F) naturally exists. The solution returns to the facility, where it can pre-heat/cool everything from air, to pool or shower water.

> ## Selkirk Arena Pumps Savings from the Underground
>
> Selkirk Arena in Selkirk, Manitoba uses geothermal technology to heat/cool a professional-size ice surface, change rooms, a banquet hall and offices. The arena, which has no conventional heating system, uses one-third of the energy of a conventional recreational facility of this type.

Lighting

More efficient lighting practices include a reduction in the use of lights, upgrading to energy-efficient alternatives and making better use of daylight. The keys to reducing the amount of lighting are to provide only as much light as necessary for the task and shut off lights entirely whenever and wherever practical.

Steps to improve lighting practices

- Reduce over-lighting by lowering brightness to a level appropriate to the task.

- Provide as little light as is practical and safe in storage and transit areas.

- Install "intelligent" timers and sensors, such as motion detectors and daylight sensors that turn lights off, on, or up as needed.

- Locate switches where employees/users can turn lights on and off on demand.

- Install additional switches so that lights can be turned on only where required.

- Remove all excessive bulbs, fixtures and ballasts.

Advances in energy-efficient lighting alternatives give the sport facility a wide range of choices. Fluorescent and compact-fluorescent bulbs are becoming common in office settings. They and other technologies such as metal halide and high-pressure sodium are considerably more energy-efficient than the mercury vapor systems common in most older facilities. As important as energy efficiency, however, is the effectiveness and quality of light. Fortunately, most newer technologies provide better as well as cheaper light. Look for full-spectrum or broad-spectrum lighting systems, which provide more balanced, natural lighting that is easier on the eyes of facilities users.

Steps to improve lighting systems

- Carefully consider all lighting needs prior to specifying products for construction or upgrading.

- Choose energy-efficient fluorescent tubes with advanced ballast where possible, and compact fluorescents if appropriate.

- Consider hiring a specialized lighting engineer for major systems such as arena, gymnasium and field floodlighting — you will make back any money spent.

Some of the simplest steps to save lighting costs involve maximizing natural light:

◆ Design facilities to make the maximum use of daylight and consider increasing south-facing windows when renovating.

◆ Arrange workspaces to take advantage of daylight.

◆ Use light-colored paints and fabrics when decorating or renovating to enhance and reflect natural light.

◆ Install curtains or blinds that can be easily opened/closed to reduce harsh glare or excessive heat from strong sunlight.

Better Lighting = More Business

Merrimack College in Massachusetts installed a metal halide lighting energy management system in its ice arena and gymnasium at a cost of $19,871. The system saves $21,874 annually in reduced energy costs. The improved atmosphere led to increased bookings of the facilities from outside users, giving a total annual monetary benefit of over $41,000.

Hot Water Systems

The energy consumed to heat water can be reduced by using less hot water, turning down the temperature, shutting down the system during periods of non-use, improving the efficiency of the system, and insulating pipes and tanks. See the next section on water conservation as well for additional ideas on savings.

Steps to cut hot water use

◆ Install low-flow showerheads and faucet aerators.

◆ Promptly repair any leaks in the system.

◆ Install automatic shut-off faucets in sinks and showers.

◆ Use timers to shut off water heaters and circulation pumps over weekends and holidays.

◆ Turn down water temperatures to recommended settings for the specific purpose 41°C for showers and sinks, 71°C for laundry and 82°C for dishwashing.

◆ If your water is electrically heated, try to perform tasks during off-peak hours.

◆ Insulate all pipes and hot water tanks.

◆ When installing new heaters, place them near the main area of use.

◆ Where feasible (i.e. during renovations) consider replacing electrical heaters with more efficient gas-fired ones.

◆ Consider installing heat pumps or recovery systems which pre-heat water.

◆ Consider using passive solar systems to heat water.

Motors and Equipment

Sport facilities, especially larger ones and those connected with cafeterias or hotels, often use motors and machines for everything from cooking, laundry, elevators/escalators and pool filtration to rink cooling systems. For many of these functions, newer equipment has become available that is cleaner, quieter, and far more energy-efficient. Consider updating equipment when you renovate or have funding to work with older buildings. When building or renovating, consider spending a little more money on more efficient equipment. The payback period is usually short and a more efficient system generates less heat and pollutes less, in addition to saving energy. Here are steps to reduce energy consumption with older and newer motorized and electronic equipment.

Steps to reduce energy consumption by equipment

- Install timers to stop or slow down motors when not in use.

- Keep all equipment well-maintained and clean.

- Replace inefficient and trouble-prone equipment with energy-efficient models.

- Install the right equipment for the job; over- or undersized motors are not efficient.

Water Conservation and Treatment

Water, like energy, is an increasingly scarce and expensive commodity whose use has enormous environmental repercussions. Unfortunately the prices most users pay for clean water do not come close to covering its real cost. Moves are afoot in a number of countries, however, to develop pricing mechanisms which transfer the real cost of water to the consumer. Since the price can only go up, the sport facility that has taken steps to reduce its water consumption may be only marginally affected.

Sustainable water use involves more than lower consumption, however. The way we handle the water that we do use, and the substances that we do or don't dump into it have a profound effect on not only the downstream quality of water, but also the price that we will someday be paying for it. By reducing water consumption, you reduce your bills and the need for expanded treatment plants. By reducing the hazardous materials that go down the drain, you help reduce the cost of making it drinkable again — and our waterways livable for every creature that relies on them.

Large volumes of water are typically consumed by sport facilities for indoor pools, landscaping and turf maintenance. Artificial snowmaking is another major water consumer. Action that specific facilities such as these can take to save water will be suggested in chapter 9. Meanwhile, here are some effective general steps.

A Site-Wide Water Solution for Sydney Olympic Park

The Olympic Park at Homebush Bay is serviced by an ambitious site-wide water recycling plant called the Water Reclamation and Management Scheme or WRAMS. WRAMS sources sewage and storm water from within Homebush Bay and treats it for non-potable reuse at Homebush Bay venues. The $1.3 million system produces an estimated 800 million litres of treated water each year (the equivalent of 258 Olympic pools). This water is used for toilet flushing and irrigation and can provide 50% of the water needs for Homebush Bay and save $640,000 of potable mains water per year. It also reduces the amount of sewage being discharged into local sewage systems and water bodies.

Recycled water cannot contaminate the mains supply of potable water, as it is piped to end users through a separate, dedicated supply system. Signage clearly identifies it as recycled, non-potable water. Although it is clear and odourless, it is not intended for drinking, washing, swimming or washing clothes or pets. It costs 15 cents per kilolitre less than drinking water.

WRAMS is complemented by a wide array or water-saving initiatives across the Olympic Park site, including the capture and re-use of rainwater, landscaping with native drought-tolerant plants and grasses and the installation of water-saving devices in all facilities.

Indoor Water Use

The principal areas of indoor water consumption are washrooms, showers, and the kitchen/cafeteria and laundry rooms.

Steps to improve water conservation

- Instruct and remind washroom and shower users to shut off taps fully.

- Repair drips and leaks promptly.

- Instruct cleaning staff to check for and report leaking faucets and toilets.

- For automatic flushing systems, check that timing cycles are appropriate for the frequency of urinal use. Shut them down entirely after hours. Manual flushing is far less wasteful than automatic systems. Consider switching during renovations.

- Install low-flow aerators and automatic shut-off valves on taps.

- Install low-flow showerheads and pressure-activated taps — tests show that people not only take shorter showers but stop to soap before re-starting the shower.

Killington Ski Resorts Go Green with Blue Water

A wastewater recycling system at Killington, Vermont, installed in 1987 saves the ski resort up to 30,000 gallons (90,000 liters) of water per day and nearly 3 million gallons per year. The innovative system reclaims water from various non-sewage uses, treats it and reuses is for flushing toilets and urinals. It is completely separate from the water used for drinking and in kitchens and washbasins, so there is no danger of contamination. As an added precaution, a harmless blue dye is added after treatment so that the water can never be confused with fresh supplies. Signs in each toilet stall ask "Why is this water blue?" and go on to explain to users how the novel system works. In this way public education is combined with an environmentally sustainable and economical practice.

◆ Retrofit toilets to reduce water consumption or install modern ultra-low-flow models. (Be sure to research models and makes that work effectively — there is no point in having a low-flow toilet if you have to flush twice! In some countries "dual flush" low-flow toilets allow the user to decide whether to use a half- or full-tank flush)

Steps to take in the kitchen and laundry room

◆ Check and maintain all plumbing systems and attachments.

◆ Adjust water usage to the size of dish or laundry load, if possible, or run machines only with a full load.

◆ Purchase dishwashers and washing machines that use less water and that allow you to select load sizes. Many newer machines are also quieter and more energy efficient.

Outdoor Water Use

Facilities such as golf courses and playing fields spend heavily on keeping their turf healthy and green. In fact, we have come to equate turf health with greenness, but the truth is often just the opposite. Watering during dry spells actually works against the health of the ecosystem as a whole by depleting water reserves elsewhere. Sport facilities can reduce demand for irrigation by helping encourage an evolution in the attitudes of users to the point where turf that is less than forest green is acceptable.

This is especially a problem in drier climates, such as the western United States, where exorbitant water usage and waste have already drastically depleted water tables. Are you recreating an artificial environment that is unsustainable without continual and expensive input of resources (water and fertilizers)?

An enormous contrast is evident between traditional "links" golf courses (natural, un-irrigated turf which goes dormant and brown in summer and dry spells, but recovers with the first rains) and modern highly-irrigated "pudding greens" which have changed the character of the game. This color-driven problem is exacerbated by the broadcast media who do not appreciate the environmental consequences of the pursuit of perfection, as defined by lush green grass at all times (Royal and Ancient, 1997).

Steps to reduce outdoor water consumption

◆ Plant only native vegetation or species suited to the climate.

◆ Limit watering of turf and vegetation to newly planted sod or seeded areas and to playing surfaces that receive heavy use.

◆ Reduce demand for water through sound turf maintenance: mowing higher and less often during dry spells, aeration, top dressing and fertilizing with organic matter.

◆ Water only during the evening and overnight to reduce evaporation.

◆ Use trickle or soaker hoses rather than aerial sprinklers.

◆ Use brooms rather than water to sweep walkways and driveways.

◆ Collect and store rainwater for irrigation.

◆ Use mulch wherever possible to protect trees and shrubs, retain moisture and reduce soil temperature.

◆ For parking lots and roadways, use permeable asphalt or bricks to allow rainwater to return to the soil, streams and ground water.

◆ When designing buildings or renovations, consider ways to capture gray water (used water from sinks and showers) for re-use in irrigation.

Many newer sport facilities are designed to capture rainwater for re-use. The Manchester United soccer team collects rainwater from the roof of its stadium and stores it in an on-site cistern. Enough water is captured to meet all of the facilities' turf irrigation needs. Many of the facilities built to host Sydney 2000 Olympic events both collect rainwater and re-use gray water (from showers, kitchens, etc.).

Treatment of Discharged Water

Any water that has to be discharged must either be free of hazardous materials or treated to remove them. The former is by far the more sustainable option. Discharging polluted water is not only fouling the very water your community relies on, it may also lead to heavy fines or even criminal charges, depending on the seriousness of the offence.

◆ All employees should be trained not to use sinks, toilets or sewers for disposing of substances labeled as corrosive or poisonous or banned from drain disposal such as solvents, paints, toxic cleaners and automotive maintenance fluids. Reminder signs should be placed above sinks in all areas where people work with such materials.

Mount Washington Ski Resort Produces Wastewater Safe for Discharging into Local Stream

Mt Washington Ski Resort on Vancouver Island was planning a major expansion in the summer of 1996 but had to take into account that their effluent discharge is directed into a nearby creek. The provincial Ministry of the Environment requires very low nutrients levels in the effluent from the sewage treatment plant and the existing plant was already operating at capacity.

The resort hired a wastewater engineering company to design a new wastewater treatment facility that allowed the resort to expand while protecting sensitive aquatic environments. The process incorporates biological treatment and membrane filtration in order to produce effluent of near drinking water quality. Sensors monitor water flow and quality in the creek and the information is relayed to the control station.

Mount Washington's wastewater treatment facility sets a high standard for ski resorts in reducing negative impacts on sensitive alpine aquatic environments.

♦ Hazardous materials should be safely stored and a standard procedure implemented for collection and removal to treatment facilities.

♦ All hazardous products used in a facility should be examined with a view to finding less hazardous alternatives (i.e. paints, cleaners, detergents).

Indoor Air Quality

The quality of the air at sport facilities is often overlooked, to the detriment of athletes, employees and even spectators. Three principal areas should be addressed in facilities operations: tobacco smoke, chemical contaminants, and inadequate circulation and venting.

Tobacco Smoke

More and more athletic facilities have instituted outright bans on smoking, both inside and outside. The majority of others have restricted smoking to certain areas. Although a total ban on smoking in all indoor facilities and in the playing and viewing areas of outdoor stadiums should be the minimum standard, it may be necessary to allow smoking in certain designated spaces. These should be physically separate from all non-smoking areas and ventilated directly to the outside.

The benefits of a smoke-free environment are several. They include higher quality of air for all and lower air filtration and circulation costs for facilities operators. Also, and significantly to sport facilities, improved athletic performance through lower carboxyhemoglobin levels. Haymes and Wells (1986) reported that exposure to carbon monoxide from tobacco smoke and car exhaust, among other sources, can significantly increase levels of carboxyhemoglobin in the blood, which in turn decreases the amount of oxygen that an athlete's blood can carry.

Chemical Contaminants

Many of us are working and playing in a chemical soup. Our air contains significant quantities of invisible chemical fumes that may have been "off-gassed" by furniture, carpets, cleaners, etc. Facilities managers and purchasers should familiarize themselves with the sources and potential impacts of these chemical contaminants. Techniques for improving the quality of air in sport facilities include: using available guides, looking for products that are certified as "low emission" (i.e. by Green Seal, Environmental Choice, etc.) and placing the onus on suppliers to provide demonstrably superior alternatives.

Apart from reducing or avoiding the sources of indoor air pollution, ways to counter poor air quality include better ventilation (opening windows and/or circulating fresh air more frequently) and the use of indoor plants to filter air.

Factors Influencing Indoor Air Quality (IAQ)

A. From outside the building

Factor	Control	Options
Climate	Air temperature and humidity	Optimize ventilation
Ventilation with and infiltration of outdoor air	Intake air quality	Select location of air intake; reduce non-designed air entry
Infiltration of water	Unwanted moisture entry	Design and maintain waterproof construction; ensure moisture does not form in HVAC systems

B. From the building and HVAC system

Factor	Control	Options
Building design	Natural/mechanical ventilation	Building depth, location and orientation
Structural building materials		
• Adhesives and sealants	Solvents	Choose low-emission products
• Glass	Lamination interlayer and coatings	Impact on IAQ unknown
• Metals, ferrous and non-ferrous	Pre-painting	Impact on IAQ unknown
• Termite control	Physical termite barriers and chemicals	Physical barriers do not affect IAQ; synthetic pyrethroid/ chlorpyrifos mixtures need frequent reapplication and can vcause human toxicity
• Timber preservation	Use of toxic products	Avoid where possible; use durable timbers
• Brick and block	Natural radioactivity	Found to be low in range of products
• Concrete products	Natural radioactivity, additives	Control levels of fly ash, impact of additives unknown
• Wood framing	Volatiles affecting sensitive individuals	Impact on IAQ unknown
• Thermal insulation	Fiber and volatile organic emissions	Product selection
Heating, ventilation and air-conditioning	Generation, transfer and removal of air contaminants	System design and maintenance

C. From the building interior

Factor	Control	Options
Interior design	Pollutant sources, ventilation flow	Material selection; ventilation design

Factor	Control	Options
Interior materials	Odorous or toxic emissions, sinks and reservoirs for pollutants	Material selection
• Plywood/LVL	Formaldehyde and volatile organic emissions	Select low-emission products
• Reconstituted wood-based panels	Formaldehyde and volatile organic emissions	Select low-emission products and overlay adhesives
• Plastic laminates	Volatile organic emissions	Select low-emission adhesives
• Plaster/gypsumboard	Few emissions but sinks for pollutants	
• ceramic tiles	Emissions from adhesives/grout	Select low-emission materials
Interior surface finishes		
• wallpaper	Formaldehyde and volatile organic emissions	Low-emission products; delay occupancy
• Paints	Solvent and additive vapors during and after application	Low-emission products; delay occupancy
Floor coverings		
• Carpet	Odor and volatile organic emissions; accumulation of contaminants	Low-emission adhesives; cleaning methods; walk-off mats
• Linoleum	Volatile organic emissions from adhesives	Low-emission products
• Vinyl	Long-term emission of volatiles and plasticisers	Low-emission products
Furnishings and furniture	Formaldehyde and volatile organic emissions from components and surface treatments	Low-emission products
Equipment and appliances	Volatile organics and ozone from photocopiers and printers; combustion products from gas and fuel appliances	Low-emission products; exhaust flues
Organic bio-effluence	Odors; skin flakes	Ventilation to Standards
Occupant activities	Smoking; cooking; hobbies; cleaning	Smoking prohibition; range hoods; cleaning practice
Consumer products	Volatile organics from "wet" products; dry-cleaned clothing; printed material	Quantity of products
Pest management	Pesticide residues, indoor and outdoor	Product usage
Cleaning	Volatile organic emissions from products; dust disturbances	Low emission products; high-efficiency vacuum cleaners
Interior renovation	Volatile organic emissions from new products; pollutant transfer through building	Low-emission products; isolation of area

(Immig, J., Rish, S. and S.K. Brown, 1997; reprinted with permission of CSIRO)

Steps to improve air quality at sport facilities

- Monitor for key indoor air pollutants on an on-going basis: i.e. carbon monoxide, nitrogen dioxide, radon gas.

- Select building materials which "off-gas" as little as possible, including insulation, composite woods, glues, caulking, paints, solvents and non-natural carpets.

- When renovating and redecorating, arrange for glues and paints to be applied on weekends and ensure that ventilation is adequate.

- Avoid furniture and carpets which contain volatile organic compounds (VOCs) such as formaldehyde.

- If possible, avoid carpets entirely. Dust mites, molds and other substances which can trigger allergic reactions often make their homes in carpets.

- Ventilate new buildings for at least several weeks before occupancy.

- Add natural plants such as spider plants, philodendrons, potted mums and ivy, which help to reduce concentrations of many indoor air pollutants. One or two houseplants per office can make a significant difference to the air (and the working atmosphere!).

- Have outside experts test air quality on at least an annual basis.

- Register and respond to complaints from staff and facility users.

Inadequate Circulation and Venting

The development of better insulation and "sealed" buildings may have been tremendous for saving energy, but they can indeed cause "sick building syndrome" if not matched by improvements in ventilation. Without adequate ventilation, air becomes stale and harmful compounds can be trapped inside. Increasing the frequency at which indoor air is exchanged with fresh outdoor air can make a big difference. However, if the outdoor air is equally or even more polluted, the only true solution would be to move.

If outdoor air is relatively clean, consider redesigning the ventilation system to increase intake of outdoor air. Allowing employees to open their windows as part of a system redesign may be one part of a solution.

- Distribute a regular supply of fresh air to all areas of a facility

- Locate intake pipes away from traffic and other possible pollutants

- Consider heat exchangers, which can improve ventilation while minimizing heat loss.

Hazardous Materials

For those hazardous materials (chemicals, asbestos, fuels, lubricants, etc.) that are already on site or for which there are no alternatives, it is critical to comply strictly with all regulations and legislation governing the use and disposal of hazardous material. Contact your local regulatory agency for assistance.

The most sustainable approach to dealing with hazardous materials is to avoid them. Though this might not be entirely feasible, the safest and cheapest method by far is to seek non-hazardous alternatives to essential products and to look for others that can be eliminated from your facility. The range of less hazardous products is growing: look for alternative paints, stains, furniture stripper, glues, wood preservative, cleaning products, organic fertilizers, herbicides, pesticides and much more. Use your power as a buyer to insist on the least hazardous materials from your suppliers and write them into you purchasing specifications. Some of the steps for handling hazardous materials overlap with the guidelines for avoiding contamination of water supplies.

Steps for handling essential hazardous materials and maintenance products

◆ Obtain and follow local health and safety regulations.

◆ Clearly label and safely store all unused, partly used or contaminated materials.

◆ Empty containers completely before disposing of them (i.e. paints, stains) or find a recycler for the contents.

◆ Arrange for hazardous materials to be transported safely to appropriate municipal hazardous waste depots.

◆ Do not use private hazardous waste disposal brokers without first carefully checking their credentials with local environmental officials.

Preventing Pollution from Laundry in Park Settings

The conversion to a non-chemical, non-toxic materials in all of the laundry and cleaning processes in the Housekeeping Department of Signal Mountain Lodge in Grand Teton National Park was outlined in a unpublished report by Fahrenkamp and Ferre (1991). This case study demonstrated how any facility can prevent pollution, save money and time and reduce risk to staff without lowering standards of cleanliness. The shift away from hazardous chemicals achieved the following tangible results:

◆ Total elimination of toxic products in cleaning processes, thereby eliminating toxic materials from wastewater emissions and the solid waste stream.

◆ Savings of more than 40% in annual cleaning product costs.

◆ Reduction of 70% in quantity of cleaning products consumed.

◆ Demonstrating to all departments (restaurants, grounds workers etc.) the feasibility of achieving similar results.

Dirty Laundry in the National Park. A Pollution Prevention Project 1991

Powering Remote Locations with Innovative "Renewable" Technology

Sport facilities are sometimes located in remote areas, which are off the electricity grid and not served by natural gas lines. Alpine and cross-country ski lodges are a good example. Portable equipment such as timers and scoreboards also have power needs. The standard way of generating power is to run these facilities or equipment on diesel generators or propane. Of the two, propane is certainly the cleaner and quieter option. Better still, there may be an opportunity to use some innovative, renewable energy technology such as solar electricity or wind energy. Manufacturers or dealers of these technologies may even be interested in lending, leasing, donating or offering a discount on equipment/systems in exchange for publicity.

For remote permanent installations, both photovoltaic solar panels and small wind turbines should be considered as sources of electricity. Although the actual wattage they are capable of producing is limited, it may be sufficient for the needs of the facility, especially if the demand is primarily on weekends — batteries can store energy during the week. For example, mountaintop timing equipment can charge in place when not in use.

Facilities can be sited and designed to make optimum use of sunlight both for passive solar heating and for lighting. Although a propane or diesel system may be needed to provide supplementary light or heat, the sun can provide the bulk of energy.

Geothermal energy may be an ideal solution for heating and cooling water and buildings in areas where it is feasible. Japanese hot spring spas use geothermally heated water for bathing, to pre-heat other water and to heat buildings. A growing number of sport facilities that require both heating and cooling (pools, arena, etc.) are finding geothermal heat pumps to be a safe, effective and cost-efficient technology. Geothermal systems can be installed in most existing as well as new facilities.

Responsible Facility Operation in a National Park

Cross-Country Ski Canada's training facility at Haig Glacier inside Banff National Park has gone to great lengths to limit its environmental impact. Forced by public concern and the limitations of operating within a park, the managers at the Haig Glacier center have put to the test a number of innovative technologies and systems. The center serves approximately 175 athletes per year. Groups of 10-20 at a time must hike the 18 km to the center, whose location was selected so as to be as invisible as possible. The skiers train, eat and sleep at the center. Following are some of the principal initiatives taken to limit environmental impact on the Glacier and park:

- Various toilet systems were tested which would not require transporting raw sewage by helicopter. On-site incinerating toilets are currently in use.
- Solar energy provides the bulk of electricity needs.
- A snow-grooming machine was switched to propane, which burns more cleanly. The sealed tanks eliminate fuel leaks.
- Water is hauled in by bucket from streams.
- A gray water filtration system (sand, chlorine and activated carbon) is used.
- Food leftovers and "black" water are incinerated.
- A back-up propane generator is used in peak periods.

Noise and Light Issues

Like aesthetics, noise and light disturbances receive relatively little attention, perhaps due to a lack of awareness. We tend not to think about the effects of noise and light pollution, perhaps because they are so localized. If we don't live right next to a noisy or floodlit facility we may never notice that a problem exists. However, facilities users, employees and neighbors are all potential complainants. Managers should react swiftly to deal with complaints by rectifying obvious problems. It pays to keep annoyance from escalating into on-going disputes and ill will, fines or even court summons.

Psychological tests have shown that one of the greatest sources of stress in humans and other animals is noise. Noise problems are often a question of timing. People are especially bothered by noise in the evenings and on rest days (Sundays, holidays or religious days). Noise curfews should be imposed.

Facilities should be designed to contain noise. Limitations should be placed on loudspeaker systems and speakers should be placed and directed so as to be audible to those within the facility, not without. Placing more speakers in the right spots allows you to turn down the volume without affecting service.

Sport facilities generate noise from a number of sources: loudspeakers, cheering crowds, amplified music, generators and traffic. The majority of noise problems can be reduced by taking a few simple (and mostly free) steps:

Steps to reduce noise

- As you plan events, think about the noise that will be generated by your facility.

- Add baffles to shelter the nearest communities.

- Monitor decibel levels to keep noise within the limits of local bylaws.

- Limit generator use as much as possible (see alternative technologies); it should be muffled.

- Good traffic flow systems and public transit will limit traffic noise.

- Apply and enforce a "No Idling" policy for stationary vehicles, especially tour buses and trucks.

Dealing with light pollution (and waste through light spillage) is equally a question of practice and technology. More efficient and effective lights may be half of the solution; turning lights down during maintenance periods or when events are not televised , or off when the facility is not in use may be the other half. For new facilities and when upgrading or retrofitting, seek systems which are better directed toward the playing area. Light that falls outside this area is money wasted. Technical improvements have greatly reduced stray light. Develop a lighting policy in consultation with neighbors. Once the policy is determined, stick to it.

Steps to limit light pollution

◆ Audit your current lighting to see if light is being wasted or could be more effectively targeted, upgraded or down-sized; monitor lighting regularly as part of regular maintenance.

◆ Place strict curfews on outdoor floodlighting.

◆ Enforce your organization's lighting policy.

In their relations with neighbors, sport facilities often suffer from the "airport syndrome": People move into the neighborhood knowing that the facility exists and benefit from lower land prices as a result. Once settled, however, they may begin to complain about the facility. While the facility operator can do little about human nature, he/she can listen to the concerns of neighbors and take steps to reduce noise and light pollution.

Equipment Maintenance

You gain efficiency and extend the life of any vehicle or piece of equipment through regular cleaning and maintenance. Maintenance should also be done responsibly. This entails proper handling of all hazardous materials and the choice of less hazardous alternatives.

Steps for sustainable equipment maintenance

◆ Carefully remove fluids and parts, store them safely and dispose of them appropriately (as above).

◆ Use re-refined motor oils and send used oil for re-refinement.

◆ Send vehicle batteries to a recycling company.

◆ For vehicles with air conditioning, ensure that these are carefully serviced, with no CFC coolants allowed to escape to the atmosphere.

◆ In summer, use water or non-toxic windshield cleaning fluid.

◆ In winter, refill windshield fluid at bulk dispensers.

◆ For washing vehicles, use biodegradable soap and limit water use.

The Eco-Efficient Office

The most effective anchor for creating a more sustainable organization is the eco-efficient office. More than just a nice place to work, the eco-efficient office is a concept. An eco-efficient program is one that promotes use of the most appropriate materials, equipment and routines in every conceivable situation and savings both to the environment and budget. It includes everything from choice of paper and office equipment, to cafeterias, washrooms and responsible waste management. It extends into every task performed by office workers. Though many of these same issues and practices arise in other situations, the office is truly a place where many environmental issues converge and can be positively addressed.

The goal is to make the most efficient use of resources and to reduce waste so as to limit environmental impact. Both measures generally translate into long-term savings, even if some initial investment is required.

Paper and Supplies

Contrary to the "paperless office," forecast in the 1970s, consumption of paper products has actually increased with the addition of each new piece of electronic equipment. Photocopiers and laser printers seem to have bred an even greater demand for paper-based information. Try cutting back through a three-prong approach: (1) reduce the amount of paper being used; (2) ensure that the right kind is being used; and (3) limit paper entering the waste stream.

More than half of the waste created by a typical office is paper. By placing a special emphasis on reducing the amount of paper being used, by encouraging reuse techniques like double-sided copying, and by ensuring that paper is ultimately recycled, a number of savings can be achieved. Also, by ensuring that the paper that is used contains a high post-consumer recycled fiber content and is as chlorine-free as possible, an office helps create a market for paper that is produced in a less harmful manner; minimizes the amount of chlorine, dioxins and furans entering the ecosystem; and reduces the demand for virgin pulp from old-growth forests.

Paper consumption by Sydney 2000 organizers in their offices and during the Games (primarily providing results to officials and media) was reduced from the 45 million sheets used at the 1996 Atlanta Olympics to 29 million sheets — a savings of 16 million sheets (approximately 90 tonnes) and hundreds of thousands of dollars.

Similar steps to limit the consumption of non-paper office supplies and keep hazardous materials out of the waste stream can generate comparable savings and limit environmental impact. Refilling toner cartridges saves money and cuts down the amount of plastic, packaging and hazardous chemicals entering the waste stream.

By stocking office supplies that are durable and which have high recycled material content, you help to "complete the loop": recycled materials are turned into new products which are in turn used in the office.

Equipment

Not all photocopiers are the same. Nor for that matter are computers, printers or fax machines. Some have features that greatly reduce their operating expenses, energy consumption and other forms of environmental impact. A photocopier with a power-saver or standby function can cut electricity consumption by as much as 60 percent. A desktop computer with color screen and laser printer uses 30 times more energy than does a laptop computer with an ink-jet printer. Annual energy costs for the two are $61 as opposed to $2, according to the calculations of a major utility.

Smart equipment practices are about more than just energy savings. Many fax machines now use ordinary paper instead of rolls of thermal paper. Thermal paper is non-recycled, has a limited lifetime, and costs more.

Reduce, Reuse, Recycle

The eco-efficient office takes a "3R" approach to all materials, equipment and resources. Keeping in mind, however, that there is a hierarchy to the 3 Rs — first reduce, then reuse and then recycle — the emphasis must be on modifying processes and behavior so as to encourage reduction above all else. It is when an organization requires less of something that it makes its biggest savings impact. By eliminating the use of disposable single-serving coffee cream containers in one cafeteria and replacing them with bulk dispensers, one hotel saved more than $6,000.

Planning and Design for Publishing

The first step in responsible publishing and printing is to determine whether the same information can be distributed effectively via an electronic format. Enormous strides have been made in this area recently, with most sport events now providing results via some form of networked information system. Major events, and even regional events, typically post schedules, information and results on some form of intranet for the use of officials, the media, coaches and athletes as well as via the internet for the general public. For the media alone, this has helped to reduce the number of full packages of information that would normally be photocopied and distributed to all journalists. Potential information uses can now choose what if anything they want to print out.

The second step in the preparation of printed material is to determine what the finished product should consist of: its content, appearance and method of printing. For guidance, remember the rule of "reduce." Though nobody wants a dull, gray document, fortunately a lively and even color-filled publication need not be at all incompatible with reducing waste. Design sense combined with modern techniques and materials can produce an attractive and informative document that costs less and wastes less.

Where printed material is necessary, you can ensure that members of your organization reduce environmental impact as well as costs. (See the Sustainable Publications Checklist on page 142.)

Distributing and Packaging Information

Sport events often deal with not just one publication but packages of printed materials: registration forms, directions, tourism and accommodation material, media background booklets, etc. For ease of preparation, packages tend to come in one format only: all the materials are sent to each recipient. This process can be greatly refined by instead using a two-step process:

1. People responding to initial publicity for the event — brochures, posters and announcements via print and electronic media — are asked to complete a registration form (ideally via a web site) or to phone a dedicated number. On the form or by the phone receptionist, they are asked what additional information they would like sent with their registration package.

2. Packages are prepared and e-mailed (or mailed if necessary) containing only those documents requested.

Such a two-step system avoids needless printing and mailing costs. The same guidelines should be applied to internal reports as well as documents for public distribution. They should also be implemented during the course of an event. Daily press releases and results should be distributed in electronic form wherever possible and otherwise follow the appropriate steps for printing and minimizing hard copies.

Sustainable Publications Checklist

Planning and Design

- Determine if a publication is required at all.

- Provide information electronically if possible.

If printed material is necessary:

- Use both sides of the paper.

- Use paper with a high recycled-fiber content (at least 50 percent post-consumer waste) that is not chlorine-bleached.

- Use as light a weight of paper as is practical.

- Use a standard paper size, to cut down on waste from trimming.

- Use white space efficiently (i.e. narrower margins and single-spacing) and select typeface sizes to reduce the overall size and length.

- Limit the number of colors used to save energy consumption and costs.

- Avoid dark blues, reds and purples which are difficult to remove for recycling.

- Avoid solid areas of ink to facilitate de-inking. Consider screened tones instead.

- Avoid "bleeds" to the edge of the page, which waste ink, paper and energy.

Production

- Avoid glosses, varnishes and coatings, which hinder recycling.

- Use vegetable-based inks in printing; avoid metallic and petroleum-based inks.

- Avoid laser printing where possible. Ink is burned onto paper and is hard to recycle.

- When binding is necessary, use staple or wire bindings that can be easily removed in the recycling process, or cerlox reusable plastic bindings. Avoid all glues in binding.

- Avoid bilingual or multilingual documents. Print separate versions to reduce paper and energy consumption and mailing costs.

Distribution and Packaging

- Ensure that quantity requirements are accurately estimated. Consider producing additional copies later, on demand.

- Keep distribution lists up to date and well targeted.

- Recommend that recipients circulate or share their copies of a document.

- Ensure the packaging specified is environmentally appropriate and minimal.

Eco-Efficient Office Checklist

Some ideas for making the most efficient use of resources and reducing waste

General

- Produce only double-sided documents.
- Collect paper that has been used on one side only, and reuse it for: fax cover sheets, draft documents and notepaper. Stroke out the used side to avoid confusion.
- Circulate documents and post memos rather than distributing copies to all individuals.
- Edit documents on-screen rather than printing unnecessary drafts.
- Ensure that all publications meet environmentally responsible printing standards.
- Use electronic mail instead of hard copies, and print messages only if essential.
- Refill laser printer and inkjet cartridges.
- Dispose appropriately of any hazardous products whose use cannot be eliminated.
- Regularly update subscription and mailing lists to ensure accuracy.
- Reduce fax-related paper waste at both ends by using a cover sheet that is:
  - printed on the flip side of a used piece of paper;
  - designed with space to list multiple recipients and with space for a message; and
  - on only a partial page.
- Send longer documents by e-mail or mail unless it is essential that they be faxed.
- Establish a routine for turning off all lights, computers and non-essential equipment.
- Return plastic cerlox bindings, binders and other folders to the print shop for reuse.

Food

- Use reusable cloth or stainless steel coffee filters in all office coffee machines.
- Use personal mugs for coffee/tea; keep extras on hand for visitors.
- Encourage in all cafeterias the elimination of disposables and excess packaging.

3Rs

- Follow letter/memo formats that minimize unused space.
- Recycle fine paper that cannot be reused.
- Recycle glass, cans, newspapers, and corrugated cardboard.

Purchasing supplies

When purchasing give preference to:

- reusable and durable supplies and materials;
- products with maximum recycled content available;
- products that meet national environmental standards;
- products with minimal packaging; and
- For paper products: unbleached and not de-inked, with a high recycled content.

Equipment and facilities

Equip offices with:

- fax machines which use bond paper instead of thermal rolls;

- photocopiers with automatic double-sided capabilities and stand-by features;

- computer systems appropriate to office needs and with energy-saving features;

- printers with double-sided capabilities; and

- an accessible area for used supplies such as binders, file folders and envelopes.

Transportation

- Use alternative fuels to reduce costs and emissions.

- Have servicing done at a garage, which recycles oil, batteries and recovers CFCs.

- Encourage car-pooling, public transit and human-powered commuting.

- Instruct drivers in fuel-saving driving habits.

- Ban idling near any buildings.

What You Can Do

Summary of Recommendations for Facilities Operation and Maintenance

- Perform an audit of your facility's energy use.

- Develop an action plan to save energy and money, based on the audit.

- Investigate financing options including government and utility subsidies and energy service company (ESCo) financing.

- Perform an audit of your facility's water consumption.

- Develop an action plan to save water and money, based on the audit.

- Take steps to reduce/eliminate water pollution emanating from your facility, by substituting non-toxic, biodegradable cleaners, etc. and keeping all harmful compounds out of your wastewater.

- Where necessary, treat all discharged water and rehabilitate polluted or altered landscapes.

- Perform an audit of indoor air quality and monitor for key pollutants regularly.

- Develop an action plan to improve air quality through better venting and circulation and replacement or minimization of polluting materials and supplies.

- Perform an audit of noise and light pollution at your facility.

- Develop and implement an action plan to address noise and light issues.

- Seek alternatives to any hazardous materials currently used.

- Carefully handle and dispose of all hazardous materials.

- Implement eco-efficient office practices throughout your organization.

What to Use

Helpful resources

Bearg, D. *Indoor air quality and HVAC systems.*

Immig, J., S. Rish, and S. Brown. 1997. *Indoor air quality guidelines for Sydney Olympic facilities.*

Olympic Co-ordination Authority (OCA). 1996. *Environmental tender specifications: A guide for specification, brief and contract writers.*

Ludwig A. 1997. *Builder's graywater guide: Installation of graywater systems in new construction and remodelling.*

Suozzo, M., et al. 1997. *Guide to energy-efficient commercial equipment.*

Vickers, A. 1998. *Handbook of water use and conservation.*

Whom to Consult

For Energy and Water

Contact your local utilities, and state/national energy agencies.

For Indoor Air Quality:

Contact your local/regional/national health authority.

For alternative refrigeration

Greenchill Technology Association: **www.greenchill.org**

Chapter

Specialized Facilities

This chapter focuses on specialized types of sport facilities and venues with an eye to identifying where opportunities exist to make them more sustainable: that is, to reduce the costs of operating and maintaining them and minimize their environmental impact and related costs. This is intended as an overview of those common areas where administrators, operators and managers could be looking to make helpful changes. For more precise information, technical advice and assistance with implementing changes, however, the reader should turn to professionals in the field. This chapter is intended to equip managers and decision-makers to ask the right questions — of their colleagues, of their staff and of experts.

When looking for the help of professional consultants, it is essential to keep in mind that many such experts turn to established and time-proven solutions to today's problems. What may be needed, however, is someone who can offer insight into what the future looks like, as opposed to only a firm grasp of the past. There are, in increasing numbers, people who have made a point of supplementing their knowledge of traditional solutions, sometimes with cutting-edge technology and occasionally by reviving older but often forgotten methods. People who view today's challenges from the sort of holistic perspective that characterizes sustainable thinking are the most likely to have innovative solutions.

You can find such innovative professionals in several ways:

♦ **Surveying recent projects:** Look through recent sport and recreation industry trade journals for articles profiling recent innovative projects. Ask your colleagues and competitors if they know of any exciting new facilities projects. Contact trade and professional associations (architects, developers, engineers) and ask who has been behind the development or redevelopment of sport facilities that exhibit innovative thinking and features. Specifically, ask about energy and water conservation, waste reduction, use of recycled materials, indoor air quality, wetlands protection, or whatever issue is of greatest importance to you and your community.

◆ **Contacting local/regional environmental authorities and utilities.** Environmental protection authorities, departments responsible for energy and land management and both public and private utility operators (energy/water) should be able to direct you to projects which they deem to be success stories. Find out who were the real brains behind any exciting elements of these projects.

◆ **Asking probing questions.** At the pre-tendering stage, ask your potential developers/designers/consultants probing questions about critical environmental issues. What do they know about designing/building/renovating a more sustainable facility? What have they done before? What recognition have they received? What can they do for you? At the tendering stage, ask specifically how their proposal will achieve a more sustainable outcome in the areas you identify. Leave them as much freedom as possible to propose an innovative and yet achievable and cost-effective (long-term) solution.

Operators and managers should take steps to ensure that their associations and other resource bodies adopt sustainability as a primary objective. By collaborating with others who regularly face similar situations and challenges, facilities managers can help one another to identify and implement appropriate solutions.

What follows is a selection of many of the principal types of facilities where different forms of sport and recreation are practiced. Each of these facilities can be designed, renovated or retrofitted to improve its sustainability. Under each facility heading, some of the primary current opportunities are listed. Every facility operator/manager will be in a unique situation and will be best placed to decide, upon review of these options, whether any or all of them are applicable.

Golf Courses

The significant amount of work on environmental issues already carried out by the golf industry provides a rich source of material for any sport organization or facility designer/operator. For this reason, this chapter devotes a disproportionate amount of space to this one sport. Much of what is related below for golf, however, will be instructive for managers of other sport facilities and governing bodies.

Golf originated on natural coastal sand dune systems and has always had a strong association with the natural environment. Curiously, for a sport that is so integrally dependent on natural quality, golf has been a focus for strong criticism from environmental pressure groups. Instead of a traditional, comfortable image of harmony with nature, the game has increasingly been viewed as ecologically damaging. Opponents have objected to the large areas of land required, the modification of terrain and impacts on wildlife, water and communities.

Many of these problems can be attributed to the game's growth in popularity. First came the spread of televised golf tournaments in the 1950s and 1960s, which both created a false image of the 'perfect' golfing environment and fuelled an unprecedented boom on the construction of new facilities. In parallel with this came the rapid growth in tourism and golf resort development.

Environmental Outcome Table

One way to prompt design consultants to achieve better environmental results is to specify the "environmental outcome" you wish to achieve, rather than a specific performance level, technology or product. This leaves your professional advisers maximum flexibility to seek cost-effective ways to fulfill your expectations. The Olympic Co-ordination Authority (OCA) for Sydney 2000 provided tendering consortia with the following guidance.

OCA Environmental Performance Outcomes

Key General Performance Area	Specific Performance Area	Desired Environmental Outcome
Conservation of Species	Flora and Fauna (ecosystems)	The remaining natural ecosystems of OCA sites are enhanced during development and protected throughout ongoing use of the sites.
	People (their environment)	After redevelopment, OCA sites will offer a high quality of life to those who live or work at the sites, and are highly desirable recreation destinations.
Conservation of Resources	Water	Developments will minimize the demand for potable water from Sydney's main supply.
	Energy	OCA developments will minimize, as compared with contemporary development, the use of energy from sources which are nonrenewable or which emit greenhouse gases in energy generation or consumption.
	Construction Materials	OCA developments will minimize the use of materials that deplete natural resources or create toxic pollution in their manufacture, use or disposal.
	Open space	OCA developments will preserve significant areas of open space as a resource for generations to come.
	Topsoil	OCA developments will minimize the importation of topsoil.
Pollution Control	Air	OCA developments will minimize negative impacts on Sydney's air quality and avoid ozone-depleting substances.
	Noise	Measures are taken to minimize the impact of noise at OCA sites.
	Light	OCA developments will minimize the impact of night lighting on environmental conservation and residential areas.
	Water	OCA developments result in improvement in the quality of water entering adjacent waterways.
	Soil	OCA remediates the results of past polluting activities on its sites and ensures protection of soil and sediments within the developed area.
	Waste Management	All development and ongoing management of activities at OCA sites reduces waste generation and maximizes the appropriate use of recycled or recyclable materials.

Adapted with permission, Olympic Co-ordination Authority 1996b

Today there are well over 30,000 golf courses worldwide, with nearly 17,000 in the USA and over 5,000 in Europe (Source: Golf Research Group).

While some in the golf industry regard environmental opponents merely as politically motivated "tree huggers", the mainstream opinion has been that this is an issue to be taken seriously. In this respect, the golf authorities are way ahead of all other sports bodies in committing effort and resources to addressing environmental issues. Moreover, this has been treated in a professional, technical way, not as a public relations exercise.

The most significant contribution has been from the United States Golf Association (USGA), which in the period 1983 — 2002 will have contributed $22,000,000 to its Turfgrass and Environmental Research Program. This has looked at breeding programs for new varieties of turfgrass to be less water demanding and more disease resistant, it has researched into the fate of nutrients and pesticides applied to turfgrass, and promoted Best Management Practices and alternative pest management strategies. All projects have been university based, independent research, published in peer-review scientific journals.

The USGA has also funded the Audubon Cooperative Sanctuary Program (an education and conservation initiative for golf courses) since 1991 to the tune of $100,000 annually. More recently the research program has established *Wildlife Links* in partnership with the US Fish and Wildlife Foundation. This specifically supports ecological research, trying to find ways of better integrating wildlife management and promoting biodiversity on golf courses.

A different, but equally credible approach has been taken in Europe. In 1994 the Royal and Ancient Golf Club of St Andrews (the global governing body of golf outside USA and Mexico), PGA European Tour and European Golf Association joined forces to establish a specialist Ecology Unit. Its mandate was to establish a clearinghouse for technical information on golf-environment topics and to develop a strategy for encouraging responsible environmental management of golf courses. The Ecology Unit was also a vehicle for building dialogue with public authorities and major environmental NGOs.

A particular achievement of the Ecology Unit was in developing good relations with the environmental community. This transformed an almost universally hostile attitude to golf among NGOs, into one of recognition by many that cooperation with the golf authorities could achieve tangible environmental benefits.

One factor in particular stood out. Golf clubs had been identified at a UNEP-hosted workshop as one of the best focal points for raising environmental awareness among decision makers and business leaders, especially from small and medium enterprises. Thus, instead of blindly resisting the expansion of golf, some environmentalists began to see the opportunity to work with the golf industry, both to achieve mutually beneficial outcomes, and to spread a positive message to a large and influential audience.

This point was eagerly grasped by the European Commission, which supported and encouraged the work of the golf Ecology Unit in the development of an Environmental Management Program for golf courses. This was developed on the basis of Environmental Management Systems

The Valderrama Declaration

Golf is a game rich in tradition and heritage, which owes its origin to nature. The first golf courses were formed entirely by natural elements and the game evolved to fit what nature provided.

However, like in many other sports, the pressures of modern life have tended to move the game away from its natural origins, as courses have increasingly become concentrated near to large population centers. Moreover, the growth of the game has spread golf far beyond its original climatic region, which has led to the need to confront new challenges in the field of course design and construction, and the management of turfgrass and water resources. The television image of manicured perfection reinforces the risk of golf becoming more and more disconnected from its natural environment. This is having a fundamental effect on how the game is played and perceived.

Golf has an enormous global following. It has the capacity to motivate and inspire. At the same time, when pursued without the limitations of a guiding environmental ethic, it can impact severely on ecosystems and communities. Golf is both influenced by, and exerts an influence on, the society and the natural environment in which it takes place. By drawing on its traditions and values, golf has therefore a remarkable opportunity, and a responsibility, to play a positive role in molding the attitudes and goals of the world in which we live and to set an example in environmental stewardship.

Over recent years the golfing bodies in the USA and Europe have achieved a greater understanding of the environmental aspects of golf course construction and management. By using science as a foundation for research and education programs in the areas of turfgrass management, sustainable development and environmental protection, it has been possible to develop initiatives and partnerships for the benefit of golf, the environment and people.

These actions represent long-term commitments, embodied in the philosophy of a "Green Games" ethic: a combination of environmental stewardship, economic efficiency and social responsibility, which together form the cornerstones of the international sporting community's Agenda 21. By subscribing to this ethic, and by continuing to support the principles and practices of the *Audubon Cooperative Sanctuary Program* and *Committed to Green*, the golf community declares its commitment to sustainability and respect for its natural heritage.

This declaration issued on Monday 8 November 1999 has been signed by:

F Morgan Taylor (President, United States Golf Association)

Peter Dawson (Secretary, Royal & Ancient Golf Club of St Andrews)

Dieter Usner (President, European Golf Association)

Pál Schmitt (Chairman of International Olympic Committee Sport and Environment Commission)

Claude Martin (Director General, World Wide Fund for Nature International)

Jacqueline Aloisi de Larderel (Director, Technology, Industry and Economics Division, United Nations Environment Programme)

James Currie (Director General Environment, European Commission)

Additional endorsements have been received from the **European Tour**, the **Professional Golfers Association** and the **Golf Course Superintendents Association of America**.

(see Chapter 4) but tailored to the specific issues and scale of the golf market. The project was branded *Committed to Green* and was launched during the Ryder Cup matches in Spain, in September 1997.

In November 1999, the Audubon Program and Committed to Green came together to organize a special golf-environment summit. The highlight was the issuing of a special declaration on golf, environment and sustainability. For the first time this brought together top officials from the game of golf alongside world authorities in environmental protection, to agree on a common agenda. Not only does the Valderrama Declaration set out the principles for a joint approach on environmental issues but it also specifies direct long-term support for practical programs.

Shortly afterwards, responsibility for the management of Committed to Green was handed over to the Committed to Green Foundation, a newly created, independent, charitable Trust. This superseded the former Ecology Unit but retained much of the original mission to raise awareness and to serve as an information center on environmental aspects of golf, as well as to broaden the remit to sport generally.

In Canada, the GreenLinks program was launched in 1997 with a slightly different approach to encouraging more sustainable golf course management. The GreenLinks Eco-Efficiency Service evaluates golf courses/clubs, awards them an "eco-rating" on a scale of 1 to 5, and provides various vehicles for promoting their achievements. GreenLinks examines all aspects of course/club management and operations, focusing on actual achievements as a business operation. In addition to issues related to the natural environment, GreenLinks applicants are evaluated on energy, water and materials use in all areas of operation — from the pro shop to the locker room, from the equipment maintenance yard to the restaurant. The GreenLinks program is also closely tied into tourism, having formed partnerships with a number of provincial and national tourism promotion bodies looking to attract environment-minded golfing tourists.

Key performance areas for golf courses

The Committed to Green program for golf courses lists nine principal management categories that have to be addressed by clubs seeking full recognition. These are:

Environmental management planning

- ◆ Communications and public awareness

- ◆ Education and the working environment

- ◆ Nature conservation

- ◆ Landscape and cultural heritage

- ◆ Water resource management

- ◆ Turfgrass management (pollution control)

- ◆ Waste management

- ◆ Energy efficiency and purchasing policies

These cover the full range of environmental subject areas relevant to golf course operation. The program is designed to provide a holistic approach to golf course management, rather than treating environmental issues as separate entities. Another way of considering the environmental load of a golf course is to examine potential environmental impacts — see table below.

Activity Categories, Environmental Aspects and Potential Impacts (Koch 1998)

Activity Category	Environmental Aspects (Single activity that interacts with the environment)	Potential Environmental Impacts (Environmental changes resulting from an activity)
1. Turfgrass Management	Mowing grass	• Ecosystem disturbance • Organic waste generation (grass clippings) • Eutrophication of water bodies
	Applying fertiliser	• Eutrophication Water and soil contamination
	Applying pesticides	• Water and soil contamination • Hazardous waste (empty containers) • Human health risks (to applicators, golfers, others)
	Treating soil mechanically (e.g., aerating)	• Ecosystem disturbance • Noise pollution
	Draining soil	• Hydrological disturbance
	Irrigating/pumping water	• Water resource depletion • Energy resource consumption
	Storing chemical	• Human health risks • Soil/water contamination
2. Equipment Maintenance	Cleaning equipment	• Water resource depletion • Water contamination • Solid waste pollution
	Repairing machinery	• Soil pollution • Noise pollution
3. Course Redesign	Moving soil	• Ecosystem disturbance
4. Transport/ Machinery Operations	Operating machinery (mowers, tractors, etc.)	• Air pollution • Non renewable resource depletion • Renewable resource consumption • Soil contamination • Hazardous waste generation
	Running (fuel driven) golf cars	• Air pollution • Non renewable resource depletion • Noise pollution
	Running electric golf cars	• Energy resource consumption

The management categories set out in the Committed to Green program, or the similar Audubon Cooperative Sanctuary Program, would broadly apply to many other outdoor sports facilities. For golf, however, three technical subjects deserve particular attention:

◆ Nature conservation

◆ Water resource management

◆ Turfgrass management using Integrated Pest Management

Nature conservation

There are many ways of encouraging wildlife on golf courses. Quite often this is best done through relaxing management on certain areas, rather than engaging in complex intervention measures. Regeneration and succession are natural processes. They do not need to be designed or forced, they will occur according to the prevailing conditions. The best general conservation policy is to think first in terms of managing people rather than wildlife. Only when you have a more detailed understanding of the ecology of your golf course, should you contemplate more direct actions, such as creating new habitats, or modifying existing ones.

Wildlife sanctuaries: Identify suitable out-of-play areas that can be designated as wildlife sanctuaries. These core undisturbed areas will provide valuable sources of cover, food and nesting habitat. The priority management should be to ensure that the habitats are adequately protected from disturbance, fire or rubbish dumping. It may also be necessary to control the spread of invasive, non-native plants if they threaten to smother the natural vegetation.

Corridors: Most of the mobile species inhabiting sanctuary areas will also utilize the golf course proper, as well as habitats on neighboring properties. Sanctuaries are not self-contained islands. Their effectiveness can be considerably enhanced by 'support' habitats in the form of interconnecting corridors: e.g. a tree line, hedgerow, ditch, or strip of uncut grass. It may not be practicable to establish continuous corridors but a series of small habitat 'stepping stones' can serve a useful function.

Buffer zones: The effectiveness of wildlife sanctuaries and other habitat features, such as lakes and ponds, will be improved by a protecting buffer zone. This is an intermediate area which is not of high ecological interest in itself, but is less intensively managed than the in-play areas. Buffer zones help to cushion the core area from disturbance, or in the case of rough grass strips around lake margins, they help prevent chemical run-off into water bodies.

Wetlands: Water bodies on golf courses are often among the most important habitat features. Their effectiveness can be greatly improved by providing shallow, sloping edges and allowing a band of marginal vegetation to grow. If this is not suitable for the entire water's edge, because a water body comes into play, try to leave at least part of the pond or lake edge in a more natural condition. It should at least be possible to establish some floating-leaved and submerged aquatic plants.

Nest-boxes: On golf courses where there are relatively few natural nesting sites, nest-boxes can be a considerable benefit to several small bird species — and bats. But even on courses where more suitable habitat exists, nest-boxes can serve a useful purpose in building awareness of your conservation program among members and visitors. A few sited close to the clubhouse, perhaps complemented in winter with a feeding station, can be a point of added interest. Checking the numbers and species using nest-boxes is a simple and effective means of monitoring your conservation program over the years.

Water resource management

The use of water is the most critical environmental issue facing golf today. This applies equally to the consumption of scarce freshwater resources and to the issue of protecting water quality.

To have an effective water management program should be the priority goal for all golf clubs. For most it is a question of conserving water resources and reducing quantities used. Not only is this a responsible approach to an issue of major public concern, it is also the most sensible economically and for the golf course itself.

Inefficient irrigation, especially over-watering, is probably the primary cause of poor turf management on golf courses. Invasive weeds, disease problems and then reliance on chemical treatments, often stem from bad irrigation management. This can lead to risks of surface or ground water contamination and potentially regulatory infringements. Where water supply is not a problem, drainage often is. To manage water correctly is, therefore, vital to successful golf course management and environmental protection.

Water conservation: The first step should be to know how an irrigation system is set up and exactly how much water is used. Although there will be variations from year to year depending on weather, one should have enough data to establish normal levels of use. This will be the base line for checking future progress. The following points should be considered:

- Are you using the best-adapted turf cultivars for the climatic region in which your golf course is situated? Advances in turfgrass breeding are producing many more drought-resistant cultivars suitable for golf courses.

- Is irrigation confined only to crucial playing areas? Set water priority areas, to identify those requiring little or no supplementary irrigation.

- Introduce a regular checking and repair system for leaks, faulty sprinkler heads, etc.

- Assess opportunities for using alternative water sources that have the least impact on local water supplies and water quality.

- Investigate possibilities for increasing water storage provision.

- Fine tune irrigation practices to maximize efficiency: Regularly monitor soil moisture levels, avoid irrigating in windy conditions or during day time, check pump performance, use half-circle sprinklers where applicable and ensure that configuration of sprinkler heads and nozzle sizes provide uniform coverage.

- Check that products and irrigation systems are suited to the locality and soil type.

- Ensure that appropriate personnel are properly trained to operate your irrigation system.

◆ Seek advice from professional, independent irrigation and drainage specialists.

◆ Use evapo-transpiration rates and weather data to adjust irrigation programs.

◆ Hand water small dry areas to prevent over-watering adjacent areas.

◆ Use drought-tolerant plants and mulch in landscaping areas.

◆ Create screens and windbreaks in exposed places to reduce evaporation losses.

Water quality management: It is quite common to see turbid and algae-choked water bodies on golf courses. However, with careful management these problems can be avoided and high water purity levels achieved. This is good aesthetically, for wildlife and for the wider environment. A key principle is to aim to minimize nutrient input to aquatic systems. Points to consider include:

◆ Create vegetative buffers around water bodies to filter run-off and reduce erosion.

◆ Determine no-spray zones around water bodies.

◆ If mowing close to water's edge, ensure clippings do not spill onto the water body — this is a frequent, unnecessary source of additional nutrient input.

◆ Ensure that water outflow is filtered before entering off-site water courses.

◆ Set up a regular monitoring system for surface water and groundwater. This should consider sampling methods, frequency, locations and variables to be tested.

◆ Monitor populations of aquatic invertebrates and amphibians inhabiting the water bodies — these serve as bio-indicators of water quality.

Turfgrass Management Using Integrated Pest Management

The essentials of turfgrass management are to maintain minimum but adequate soil fertility, apply plenty of mechanical treatments and to control soil moisture levels through good drainage, adequate irrigation and appropriate top dressing. Integrated Pest Management (IPM) is an ecologically based program to prevent, or to limit, unacceptable levels of pest damage, using a combination of cultural, biological and chemical controls. IPM first takes a preventative approach, using sound cultural practices, regular scouting and monitoring of turf and environmental conditions, and the setting of damage thresholds. Chemical management practices are normally then used on a curative basis, and only where necessary.

Turfgrass varieties:

◆ Select turf species appropriate for the climate and soils, and which are least demanding for water.

Cultural practices:

◆ Employ cultural practices to increase turf health and deal with underlying problems or conditions.

◆ Reduce turf stress by traffic management and correct mowing heights.

Turfgrass nutrition:

♦ Use slow release or natural-organic fertilizers.

Pest monitoring and management:

♦ Identify local disease, insect and weed problems.

♦ Establish a regular scouting and monitoring program to check turf quality, moisture levels, soil fertility and for signs of pests and diseases.

♦ Set threshold levels .

♦ Keep written records of monitoring activities, control measures used and results.

Choose least toxic pest controls:

♦ Limit pesticide applications by treating affected areas only; spot treatment rather than spraying and using non-chemical methods whenever possible.

Environmental Performance Indicators

One of the key challenges facing all current environmental programs in the sport sector, is the question of measuring environmental performance to establish meaningful benchmarks. Some work has been done on this topic in relation to golf courses participating in the Committed to Green program (Koch 1998 and Sanchez 1998).

Ivanhoe Club a Leader

Peter Leuzinger (1998) was the superintendent of the first golf course in the USA to be certified by the Audubon Cooperative Sanctuary Program. Now he supervises the Ivanhoe Club in Illinois and has transferred his innovative management strategies to this award-winning club. He is championing the "Stewardship Campaign" which addresses environmental quality in all aspects of the course maintenance.

This campaign is a multifaceted plan that includes; biweekly staff training, nature walks, a trial garden, and a waste treatment system that takes the effluent from the clubhouse and community and reuses it on the greens. The course attracts many wild birds because of the various nest boxes and the maintenance of natural terrain. The Ivanhoe grounds include 15 bodies of water and wide buffer zones were created to protect these aquatic habitats.

Luezinger works with a sophisticated integrated pest management system in order to minimize the need for pesticides and herbicides. A close monitoring and scouting practice allows for specific applications of agents only where necessary. Also, he carefully times the applications during the year in order to get the most effect from the least amount of chemicals.

Golfers have expressed their appreciation for the increase in wildlife and aesthetic value that has come with letting the grounds revert to a more natural and wild state. They have also been galvanized by the nest box program to volunteer in bird watching programs and other environmental initiatives.

Many environmental attributes of golf courses are difficult to quantify in a way that provides any useful form of comparison. For example, species surveys may show a certain number of breeding birds on the course. However, it would be unfair to compare such data between different courses. Even within a single site, although numbers of breeding birds could be monitored over the years in a comparative way, in many cases it would be difficult to relate any changes with management actions undertaken by the club.

The following table illustrates some simple Environmental Performance Indicators that relate primarily to resource consumption and are calibrated to either the size of the site (number of holes or area), or its usage (i.e. number of members or rounds of golf played). These may not be precise measures but they do offer potential comparability and provide a basic framework for benchmarking. Further work is needed on these, both in respect of golf and for adapting to other sports.

Proposed Indicators to Evaluate Environmental Performance within European Golf Clubs (adapted from Koch, 1998)

Environmental Impact Category	Proposed Environmental Performance Indicators (EPIs)	Reference Parameter	Unit
Water resource consumption	Total water consumed/year	• Area of greens, tees and fairways • Member, or rounds played	m^3/ha m^3/member m^3/round
Water pollution/ eutrophication	Fertiliser applied/year Pesticides applied/year	• Area of greens, tees and fairways	kg/ha
Soil contamination	Lubricants and hydraulic oils consumed/year	• Area of greens, tees and fairways	l/ha
Solid and hazardous waste	Solid waste generated/year Hazardous waste generated/year	• Area of greens, tees and fairways • Member or rounds played	kg/ha kg/member kg/round
Energy resource consumption	Energy consumed/year	• Area of greens, tees and fairways • Member or rounds played	kWh/ha kWh/member kWh/round
Noise pollution	Mowed area/week	• No of golf holes	ha/hole
Air pollution	Fossil fuel consumed/year	• Greens, tees and fairways	l/ha
Ecosystem disturbance/ biodiversity	Out-of-play areas managed with the aim of nature conservation	• Total area of the property	ha/ha

Playing Fields

Many of the recommendations for golf courses hold true for playing fields (land preservation, naturalization, user education). The groundskeeper for playing fields is primarily concerned with turf management and its associated issues. Members of the turfgrass industry and professional turfgrass associations have either developed their own guidance resources or use those produced for both golf and other playing fields. Sport field managers interested in pursuing more sustainable practices should look beyond just the turfgrass, however.

Especially important are:

Water conservation

Limit irrigation demands by using more native turf grasses, reducing watering during dry seasons and scheduling watering for appropriate times of the day. Explore means of capturing rainwater and reusing gray water for irrigation.

Chemical treatment

Eliminate the use of harmful chemicals through natural turf management practices such as Integrated Pest Management, appropriate grass selection and encouraging greater tolerance for certain "weeds."

Lighting

Look to upgrade or replace lighting systems with more energy efficient bulbs, more accurate reflectors (less light spillage to adjacent areas and residential homes!) and computerized energy management systems.

Using Compost Makes Better Fields

Ward Associates, a firm of landscape architects and engineers from Bohemia, New York, use compost in topsoil mixtures for athletic fields for many good reasons. It seems that recycled organic waste is beneficial for more than your average garden or farm.

Norman Hummel (1998) of Hummel and Company, a soil-testing laboratory in Trumansburg, New York, has determined that mixing 20 to 30% organic content into the topsoil improves the drainage. He explains that the compost helps vertical draining because it contains more air pockets for better aeration. In addition, adding compost to the topsoil mixture, most of which is sand, encourages better root migration from the sod to the soil because it contains necessary nutrients. Furthermore, Hummel says that in some cases it is significantly less expensive to use compost over other material such as peat moss.

Ice Arenas

Ice arenas and multi-purpose arenas with ice surfaces have many environmental management issues to consider. Ice arenas are major consumers of energy (heating and cooling, lighting) and water, and users of hazardous chemicals. They also, along with pools, head the list of facilities with air quality concerns. A sustainable sport manager can take a number of steps to address these issues.

Lighting

Better-quality lighting can be installed which by virtue of its energy efficiency will quickly pay back capital installation costs. Natural lighting should be admitted wherever this can be done without excessive heat transfer.

Water conservation

Ice-making systems can be installed which use closed-loop systems to save water and reduce contamination and demand on the sewage system. Water from ice shavings can be captured, melted, filtered and reused for ice making. Alternatively, melted ice can be fed into a graywater system that, along with shower water, can be used for toilet flushing.

Energy saving

In addition to lighting, recent advancements in a number of areas can slash energy consumption by 30% to 50%. These include:

- efficient pumping systems and motors (variable-speed pumps);
- brine pumps;
- ice surfacing machines (cleaner and more efficient);
- heat reflectors and low emissivity ceilings; and
- heat exchange systems (for air and water) including geothermal pumps.

Refrigerants

The use of Chlorofluorocarbon (CFC) cooling systems requires careful handling of these chemicals to prevent leaks. As the Montreal Protocol has effectively banned production of CFCs, all arenas should be moving to a non-CFC system. These include substitutes such as hydro chlorofluorocarbons (HCFCs) that have a lesser, but still significant effect on depleting the ozone layer. However, ammonia-based systems may ultimately prove more cost effective as well as having no effect on the ozone layer. New arenas can avoid the costs and headaches of phasing out ozone depleting substances in the future by installing systems which use alternatives. R717 (ammonia) refrigeration machinery is generally less expensive to operate and the refrigerant costs less (Louria 1996).

Air quality

Air quality in ice arenas is of growing concern for workers and users. The chief pollutants are the gases carbon monoxide and nitrogen dioxide both of which are produced by the internal combustion equipment used to maintain the ice surfaces. Above certain concentrations exposure to carbon monoxide causes dizziness, and nausea and nitrogen dioxide causes lung irritation, bronchitis and pneumonia. Building materials, cleaning supplies, paints, and cigarette smoke are also culprits.

Etobicoke's 4-Step Cost-Saving Measures

Step # 1 — The Energy Database

The energy database is an essential baseline for identifying opportunities, charting progress, making comparisons and proving success. Steps to develop such a database include:

- create a database of energy used;
- analyze energy consumption accounting for weather and use patterns; and
- use the database as a sales tool — proof for the decision-makers.

Step # 2 — Zero-Cost Measures

Many initial and highly effective measures come at no cost and can be implemented immediately. They include:

- manual shut-off and lowering of thermostats for heating;
- turning off unnecessary lights;
- reducing hot water temperatures (pools, arenas, showers, etc.);
- less frequent pool water and arena ice changes;
- removal of arena stand heaters; and
- "de-lamping" excessively lit areas.

Step #3 — Minimal Cost Measures

Lower-cost measures which can bring significant energy and cost savings, while improving the environment of a facility include:

- air-sealing doors, windows, roof-to-wall joints, service openings;
- night set-back controllers for both heating and cooling systems;
- replacing standard fluorescent lamps and incandescent bulbs; and
- instantaneous water heaters for low-volume areas.

Step # 4 — Capital Cost Measures

Etobicoke committed substantial effort and capital to implementing capital cost measures, of which more than 100 had a payback period of 5 years or less. Types of measures include:

- **Low Emissivity Ceilings for ice arenas**
  Average Cost . . . .$22,000 per ceiling
  Payback period . . . . .4.9 years

- **Heat Reclaim Systems for capturing heat from hot water**
  Cost for Centennial Arena $40,000
  Payback period . . . . .4.7 years

- **Redesigned lighting systems**
  Cost for Centennial Stadium $52,000
  Payback period . . . . .4.0 years

- **Thermal pool covers/heat set-back systems**
  Average cost $9,000
  Payback period . . . .< 1 year — 1.2 years

- **Co-generation system**
  Cost for Etobicoke Olympium $90,000
  Payback period . . . . .2.7 years

(Based on a speech by David Jones, Supervisor of Energy and Building Systems for Etobicoke Parks and Recreation Services, 1994)

The U.S. Environmental Protection Agency (EPA) suggests the following measures for rink operators in order to maintain safe air quality:

◆ Substitute electric (battery or direct) engines in resurfacers whenever possible.

◆ Equip internal combustion ice resurfacers with catalytic converters.

◆ Frequently maintain all combustion equipment such as resurfacers, edgers, forklifts, water pumps and auxiliary generators.

◆ Provide adequate mechanical ventilation. At a minimum. ASHRAE Standard 62-1989, *Ventilation for Acceptable Indoor Air Quality*, for the playing area of ice arena should be followed.

◆ Ensure that the fresh air intake is not affected by exhaust from loading areas and outside vehicles and that the intake is not blocked.

◆ Warm up resurfacing equipment in a well ventilated room or a room equipped with a local exhaust, such as powered drop-hose attached to the vehicle exhaust.

◆ Use ice edgers only when the ventilation system can adequately exhaust the emissions.

◆ Keep arena gates open during resurfacing to allow for better air circulation.

◆ Extend vehicle exhaust pipes up to at least one foot above the top of the rink safety barrier to enable better capture with ventilation system.

◆ Monitor the area for carbon monoxide and nitrogen dioxide using permanent sensors to ensure that these recommendations are working to provide healthy indoor air quality. Have professionals recommend locations for the sensors.

Ice painting

By using safer paints or substituting paper lines for paint and eliminating ice-brightening paints, costs can be reduced and water contamination minimized.

Swimming Pools

Recreation facilities, already among the highest energy users in the United States, spend about one-third of their energy costs to heat and maintain swimming pools. Other significant costs and challenges can be found in the areas of water conservation, chemical use and disposal, and indoor air quality. Many low-cost and even no-cost measures are available to facility owners and operators.

Energy

Examine the efficiency of all appliances, lighting and building heating systems. Opportunities for conserving include:

- heat pumps and exchangers;

- water heating systems;

- more efficient pumps (also quieter);

- heat blankets, which retain heat and limit evaporation of water and chemicals; and

- energy management systems that can easily boost or lower output according to fluctuating demand.

Water conservation

Pool blankets are the most effective method of conserving water through the suppression of evaporation (see pool blanket tip opposite). Within the limits of water quality regulations, water can also be conserved within a closed-loop system.

The Heat is On: Energy Saving Tips

Here are some pointers on how to save money, and reduce energy consumption in your pool (Smith 1998):

Heating and Ventilation
- Don't turn down thermostats over night because reheating costs are just as expensive as maintaining the same temperature over night.
- Don't turn off the humidistat as the cost of damages due to humidity outweigh the cost of keeping the dehumidifying mechanisms running
- Install dehumidifying equipment which is more energy efficient than paying to heat cold dry air brought in from outside.
- Install an air-to-air heating system, which uses the heat from outgoing humid air to heat the incoming cold outside air.
- Install ceiling fans that deflect the hotter air down to pool deck level.
- Use a pool cover to reduce the evaporation of water and loss of heat

Lighting
- Set your lights on various circuits so that every second or every third light can be turned off if not needed
- Turn off underwater lights when not necessary
- Use metal halide fixtures for overhead lights
- Review which areas in the facility need to be lighted at certain times in the day

Good architecture and design go along way to creating energy efficiency, but proper procedures and employee awareness are also necessary to cut costs and reduce energy consumption.

Hazardous chemicals

Many pool operators are moving away from chlorine gas. Non-chlorine substitutes should be explored and evaluated for effectiveness and cost. Many municipal pools and competitive pools are using various ozone and bromine water purification systems, effectively and at reduced cost. By electrically generating bromine continuously through the water circulation loop, the pool filtration system can potentially use 60% less chemicals than a standard sanitizer, and water will need to be replaced less often.

Nederland Pool Slashes Operation and Maintenance Demands

A health and fitness center in Nederland, Colorado, switched to a bromine system. They now replace less than one-third of their spa water every time they backwash the filter, every two to three weeks. They have saved $675 per year in water heat, and use only $25 worth of chemicals each month. The non-corrosive bromine salts have also reduced the amount of equipment maintenance throughout the facility, lowering staff time and maintenance budget demands.

Low-Tech Tip: Use Pool Blankets

By using pool blankets/covers you can limit evaporation and reduce the need for water heating and dehumidifying at the same time. An 18x36 ft. pool that is uncovered when not in use can lose 900-3000 gallons of water per month through evaporation. A pool cover can prevent about 90% of the loss. Covers are the most cost effective energy conservation measure and their pay back period ranges from six months to three years, depending on their size, type and frequency of use. The trick to effective use of pool blankets is a quick and simple method of deploying (unrolling and re-rolling) them. Cumbersome methods of deploying blankets will lose staff time and act as a disincentive to their regular use.

Alpine Ski Resorts

Alpine ski facilities must take great care to avoid harming what are among the most fragile of all geographical sites. Mountain slopes and valleys not only have short growing seasons, they can be prone to erosion, avalanche and landslide. Slopes which have been cleared of most or all of their tree and plant cover become especially prone to erosion during the spring thaw, when there are few plants or roots to provide stability. Furthermore, artificial snowmaking and chemicals that help retain snow as long as possible into spring can reduce the length of the alpine growth season as well as increasing the effects of soil compaction.

Habitat destruction

The number of undeveloped alpine locations has shrunk dramatically since the popularization of alpine skiing this century. To preserve what remains, existing resorts must limit their future growth and conservation authorities should implement strict measures for both existing and planned developments. In many regions, a freeze on additional development is the only solution.

Flora and fauna

The impact on flora and fauna can be reduced only through great care in the siting of resorts, ski runs, lifts and other facilities and equipment. Machine operation practices, as well as skiers' habits, should be reviewed with an eye to restricting damaging behavior.

Water conservation

Consumption of water both by resorts (accommodation, day facilities and restaurants) and especially snowmaking equipment typically exceeds the local supply. To avoid draining water tables and placing too great a demand on surface water sources (lakes and streams):

◆ select snow-making machinery which uses as little as one-fifth the water as earlier versions;

◆ limit the amount of snow-making during dry seasons;

◆ install water conservation devices within all resort facilities; and

◆ recycle "gray" water for suitable uses such as toilet flushing (for explanation see Killington Ski Resort example on page 130).

Ski Areas Strive for Sustainable Slopes

Because "the environment is a ski area's number one asset" the National Ski Areas Association has developed *Sustainable Slopes: the Environmental Charter for Ski Areas*, launched in the year 2000. According to the NSAA, it has many reasons to demonstrate environmental stewardship. Primarily, since many people who ski have a lot of respect for the natural setting, ski area owners/operators want to align themselves with the values of their guests. Also, they are looking to the future and want to make sure that present day activities do not spoil the opportunity for enjoyment by future generations.

The Environmental Charter is a brief document that provides guidance in environmental stewardship primarily for ski area operators but also tips for users. The handbook outlines environmental principles for planning, design and construction, operations, and education and outreach. A range of options accompanies each principle so that operators can choose which actions are most realistic and useful for their situation. The booklet also includes a section on "Next Steps for Ski Areas" which suggests how operators can start acting on the principles. For skiers and other guests the NSAA has also created an Environmental Code of the Slopes, which outlines how they can contribute. The NSAA Environmental Charter is available on their website at **www.nsaa.org**

For an independent evaluation of many North American ski areas, the Ski Areas Citizens Coalition operates a web site (**www.skiareacitizens.com**) that grades ski resorts on their environmental behavior, allowing skiers to patronize resorts that reflect their values. According to the Coalition, "by choosing environmentally friendly ski areas as recognized by the Ski Area Citizens Coalition, you will encourage ski resorts to improve their environmental grade in the future." The web-based scorecard is prepared by regional non-profit conservation organizations. Most volunteers and staff of participating organizations are themselves skiers, and recognize skiing as a valid use of public lands. "We also recognize that not all ski areas are the same when it comes to environmental protection," states the Coalition.

Water quality

Minimize water pollution through careful choice of cleaning products and other chemicals, emphasizing less-harmful alternatives and the appropriate disposal of hazardous materials. Also, ensure that machine maintenance follows strict guidelines for avoiding spills.

Chemicals

Eliminate the use of harmful or bio-accumulative snow-hardening chemicals. These pollute soil and water, and inhibit recovery for vegetation on some slopes by retaining snow long into the spring. The subsequent death of vegetation will increase the likelihood of erosion and even landslides.

Noise

Limit the use of amplified sound systems and operate snow-guns for as brief a period as possible. Operators of Calgary's Canada Olympic Park have bought up a significant amount of adjacent land to act as a buffer zone between the sport park and encroaching suburban development. By leaving this buffer land in its natural state, neighbors will be protected from noise and light pollution.

Wind Power Gives Aspen Skiers a Lift

The Aspen Skiing Company chose wind energy to power its newest Cirque lift. The first of its kind, the lift operates solely on clean, renewable wind power purchased from the Ponnequin Wind Farm in Northern Colorado. The company chose the lift to be a simple platter pull rather than a multi-passenger high-speed lift, thus ensuring a limited number of users and minimum impact on the mountain.

In keeping with the company's environmental program, the lift was built in a manner that would avoid harming the fragile tundra on which it was constructed while preserving the wildlife habitat of the area. Construction took place over a period of several months, scheduled around times when mechanized equipment could move over the snow without harming the land or disturbing mating or nesting animals. Holes were dug using backhoes while snow was on the mountain, then covered and left for 3 months. The excavated soil was piled on platforms, then later hauled off the mountain. During this period, the mating and nesting season took place for ptarmigan, elk, bighorn sheep, mountain goats and other wildlife. Once the season was over and the snow melted, work crews hauled supplies on foot, making as many as 7 trips per day carrying 50lbs of equipment up the 750 vertical feet of the mountain. They planned each trek carefully to ensure that they never walked up the same terrain, thereby avoiding making trails that would compact the soil and destroy vegetation. All of the discarded materials from the construction were carried off the mountain in the same manner, while excavated rocks were piled at the foot of the poles to help prevent erosion. Heavier construction items such as poles and concrete were flown in by helicopter.

The Cirque lift is a model for ski lift development that is more sustainable both in construction and operation. The Aspen Skiing Company has many remarkable environmental achievements to its name and can be proud of its wind-powered lift, which could easily be replicated by other resort developers.

Energy consumption

Examine the possibilities for reducing energy demand through better insulation and heating systems, more efficient appliances, machinery and lighting, and improved snowmaking equipment.

Light pollution from illuminated night skiing

Select systems that minimize wasted light, redirect lighting, dim lights during maintenance periods and extinguish lights when runs are not in use.

Marketing of eco-tourism

Resorts that have made legitimate strides to manage their operations responsibly should capitalize on this fact by designing and marketing eco-tourism ski packages to target groups.

Road Races

Short races (walking and running a 5k or 10k route) and marathons have become ever more popular. Many communities use these as fund-raisers for nonprofit causes. Competitions held on roads, such as wheelchair, running and cycling races, should address several environmental issues.

Traffic congestion

Keep non-official vehicles (those of participants and spectators) away from the race area by limiting access and parking in the immediate vicinity, and encouraging and facilitating the use of public transportation and active transport.

Air pollution

Limiting traffic congestion in itself will reduce air pollution. You can help also by selecting venues and times of day with low air-pollution levels (i.e. weekends and early morning), and by using low-emission vehicles or electric vehicles on or near the race course. Pace cars, on-course official vehicles and media cars should be electric, wherever possible. Ban idling of vehicles near the start and finish lines and, where possible, the course itself.

Noise

Limit the use of amplified sound and generators. Discourage observers with boom boxes.

Bobsled and Luge Tracks

Much criticism has been aimed at bobsled and luge tracks, as costly, single-purpose facilities which require considerable terrain and construction materials (typically concrete), and which use potentially harmful refrigerants (ozone-depleting chlorofluorocarbons or hazardous ammonia). Recent tracks built for the Olympic Games in Lillehammer and Nagano, however, have showcased less intrusive building techniques and high-efficiency coolant systems. One solution, which may be feasible in certain climates, is to return to all-natural runs built from snow and water.

Coolants

Cooling systems must be carefully designed to prevent any possible leak into the atmosphere of either ammonia or CFCs. Ammonia, despite its short-term risk, remains the preferred coolant — at least until such time as non-ozone depleting alternatives to CFCs/HCFCs are available. The Nagano Olympic track uses ammonia, but a mere one-sixtieth of the amount required by the already-efficient Lillehammer track. An ammonia system has the added advantage of being the most energy efficient.

Energy efficiency

Tracks should be kept cooled only when demand is sufficient. Summer use should be avoided unless demand is so high as to merit off-season operation. Screens shading the track from the sun should be used wherever a demonstrable energy savings will result..

Design

Tracks should follow the existing terrain and be partially underground wherever possible for reasons of energy efficiency, aesthetics and reducing demand for building materials. Where feasible, the use of all-natural tracks should be considered. The all-natural Cresta Run in St. Moritz is considered by competitors and officials to be as safe and as technically challenging as the more common artificial tracks.

Trails

Trails (cross-country skiing/running/hiking/mountain biking/equestrian, etc.) that run over natural terrain are of themselves prone to erosion over time. Trails that are shared by various users can also become a "battleground" over issues of trail use etiquette, where one group (frequently hikers) blames the others (mountain bikers, horseback riders) for trail damage. Trail designers and operators can take a number of steps to reduce damage.

Erosion

To prevent erosion, trails should avoid fragile areas, such as wet depressions and those where tree roots are close to the surface. Study and test various techniques for diverting water runoff without substantially altering the local ecosystem. Rebuild and reinforce those trails where erosion has already occurred. Activities such as horseback riding and mountain biking should be kept to firmer trails. All trail users should be educated in proper trail-use etiquette so as to reduce the amount of damage done during wet periods.

Wildlife habitat

Where trails pass through significant wildlife habitat, they should be directed away from known feeding, nesting and breeding grounds. Users should also be educated to stay on marked trails and not to trample or harm vegetation.

Trail design

Trails should be only as wide as necessary to accommodate users; you want to avoid unintentional damage to vegetation. Wherever running water crosses a trail, proper drainage pipes should pass under the trail.

Parking

By keeping parking as far away from the trail as is feasible, trail users will be spared unnecessary noise and smog disturbances. Avoid paving parking lots in heavy use or wet areas by using less expensive and more porous materials such as crushed stone or even semi-porous paving stones/bricks

Facilities/amenities

Bringing all the trappings of home onto wilderness trails may only encourage people to use the trail as they would a non-wilderness setting. This is typically expensive and considered unnecessary and undesirable by many users. Take a minimalist approach. Where toilets are deemed necessary, use outhouses with pits or, where budget allows it, investigate the use of composting toilets (less odor and no need to frequently dig new holes and move the outhouse). In more remote areas, inform users that no garbage cans are provided, and that they are expected to pack out what they pack in.

Maintenance partnerships

Form partnerships with regular user groups (i.e. hiking or mountain biking clubs) who are willing to accept certain trail maintenance tasks. Many such groups will do so willingly, recognizing that they have a vested interest in seeing their trails maintained and in creating a positive image for their sport. Offer benefits such as recognition plaques and, if necessary, reduced access fees in exchange for work performed.

Water Courses and Venues

Water sports illustrate clearly the two sides of the sport-environment relationship: polluted water can present a significant risk to athletes who spend many hours in it or on it; and water sports need to be particularly sensitive not to pollute the water, damage shorelines or disturb aquatic flora and fauna during training or competition or through construction and operation of facilities.

Sailing, sailboarding

Sites for sailing facilities and competitions should avoid polluted waters, which put all sailors at risk. Potential polluters, both on the shoreline and other marine traffic, should be involved as partners in limiting emissions of sewage, garbage and boat fuels.

Sailors are themselves common contributors to water and shoreline pollution. Sailing clubs should implement a strict code of conduct and governing bodies should ensure that sewage tanks are emptied only in appropriate on-shore disposal tanks. Sailors should recognize that poor waste management practices are harmful to the sport.

Motorboats play a key role in a number of water sports, transporting coaches and officials and performing a variety of logistical functions. Sport that makes regular or occasional use of motor boats, including newer personal water craft (Sea-Doo, Jet Ski, etc.) should ensure that boat users follow good environmental practice in their operation, maintenance and refueling, and in solid and liquid waste management.

Canoe, kayak, rowing

Several issues should be addressed when designing or selecting sites for training and competition:

- current air and water quality and their impact on the health of the athlete;
- preserving natural water courses and water levels;
- management of sewage, garbage and fuel pollution, as above;
- possible erosion of shorelines from increased shoreline traffic and wake created by boating activity; and
- noise, fumes and wake created by the motorized boats of coaches and officials.

> ### Lake Lanier's Floating Grandstands
>
> The rowing venue at Lake Lanier presented a major environmental challenge to the Atlanta Committee for the Olympic Games. How to maximize spectator seating without harming the shoreline or cutting many of the trees that grew along the shoreline?
>
> The solution: a floating platform that required minimal site alterations and which could be removed after the Olympic events.

Whitewater

◆ Competitions should not be held in protected wilderness areas.

◆ The preparation of courses should forbid significant changes to the natural environment.

◆ Designated points for entering and exiting the water should be chosen according to their ability to withstand erosion; instruct users not to stray from these access areas.

Stadiums

Stadium designers and operators should ensure that the following principles (most have been covered in more detail above and in previous chapters) are implemented:

◆ **Energy conservation:** design, equipment and other energy practices; natural ventilation

◆ **Water conservation:** fixtures, landscaping and other water use practices; rooftop rainwater capture systems

◆ **Noise reduction:** design, amplifier direction and other sound practices

◆ **Lighting:** design, system selection, direction and timing

◆ **Transportation:** Reduce congestion and private vehicles; encourage public transportation, foot and bike traffic. Work with public transit authorities to provide incentives to leave the car at home. Develop parking schemes that reduce queuing and idling time.

◆ **Location:** Avoid green space, wilderness and agricultural land.

◆ **Materials:** Select environmentally-preferred building materials and products used in operations and maintenance.

◆ **Life cycle planning:** When designing a facility, give full consideration to demographic trends and changing fashions in order to plan for optimal use during the lifetime of the facility. Consider making any facility multi-purpose and easily adaptable for different activities.

Gymnasiums

As with stadiums, gymnasiums present special concerns for using energy and water wisely, reducing noise, improving lighting usage, planning for judicious transportation, finding an appropriate location, avoiding harmful materials, and planning for the full life cycle of the building. Gymnasium designers and operators will also want to consider some special concerns as well.

Sydney 2000's Showcase Stadiums

Among the many new facilities built for Sydney 2000 that showcased a range of sustainable design and operation features were Stadium Australia and the Sydney SuperDome. The many noteworthy elements of these stadia include:

Stadium Australia

- The Stadium was designed for conversion from a Games-time maximum seating of 110,000 to a post-Games configuration of 80,000 seats.
- Natural ventilation systems are used to cool many internal spaces, using a heat stack effect to draw hot air up and out. This reduces demand for energy and air conditioning.
- On-site gas co-generation plants provide a significant portion of the stadium's energy supply, with excess heat used to provide hot water, saving an estimated 500 tonnes of carbon dioxide emissions per year.
- Energy efficient lighting, fans, motors, and appliances were installed.
- Rainwater is collected from the roof. Up to 3.2 megalitres of rainwater can be stored, supplying all of the stadium's annual irrigation needs.
- A dual water supply system is used. Treated sewage water from the Homebush Bay reclaimed water system provides toilet-flushing water, while drinking water is taken from the Sydney potable water system.
- Seats in the stadium are made of polypropylene, an alternative to more common PVC seats. Alternatives to PVC were also used for piping, concourse flooring and electrical cabling.
- A non-PVC translucent roof material serves also to diffuse light, reducing the need to use stadium lights on sunny days to fill in shaded areas of the field.

Sydney SuperDome

- The SuperDome is an indoor multi-use facility with a seating capacity of 20,000.
- A rooftop solar energy system with an output of 70kW feeds power into the grid. It will avoid the production of 85 tonnes of CO_2 per year.
- A "microclimate" air conditioning system in the arena allows only occupied spaces to be air conditioned, reducing energy consumption.
- Alternatives to PVC materials are used for seats, floor and wall finishes and for hydraulic and storm water pipes.
- "Eco Chart" ratings were used to assess the total environmental impact of material manufacturing, use and disposal, in order to select products and materials with a limited life cycle impact.
- Recycled water is used for toilet flushing and landscaping.
- Finishes and furnishing were selected to maximize indoor air quality.

The SuperDome was awarded the 1999 Banksia Construction Practices award for "valuable contribution to enhancement of the environment in construction and infrastructure development."

Multiple use

Design gymnasia to accommodate many types of sport and levels of users, as well as to adapt to shifting preferences in activities over time. The most sustainably-designed facility will allow for significant flexibility in the types of users and their level (i.e. recreational as well as high school or college championships). Considerable thought should also be given to ways of accommodating several activities simultaneously (i.e. climbing walls in use at the same time as the gym floor) and to ease of conversion or renovation, such as changing or replacing the flooring or lighting as technology advances or materials get worn out.

Indoor air quality

Ensure that indoor air quality is adequate for high-intensity activity. Review carefully the choice of building, furnishing and finishing materials; regular fresh-air ventilation; and the banning of smoking.

Flooring materials

A range of floor material options exists, each with particular performance, cost and environmental attributes. When selecting flooring materials, consider the benefits and impacts of wood, synthetic materials and concrete. A life cycle assessment should be conducted (by you, or for you by competing suppliers), providing you with cost and performance information over the full life of the flooring, as well as such details as:

- the source of the materials (is the wood from a sustainable source?);
- manufacturing processes;
- the need for initial and/or regular treatment with harmful materials;
- offgasing of fumes; and
- eventual methods of disposal (will the flooring be taken back by the supplier? will it be recycled/reused in some form?)

Shooting Ranges: Firearms, Archery

Competitive shooting sports (pistols, skeet, trap, biathlon, etc.) and archery should follow much of the general advice provided for similar indoor or outdoor facilities above, such as: energy and water conservation, transportation, location, materials and indoor air quality. Operators of shooting ranges will also want to consider three other key issues:

Noise reduction

Take steps to reduce noise pollution experienced by neighbors through better insulation, baffling, and enforcement of operating hours.

Habitat protection

Steps to protect wildlife and habitat, especially soil and water, from contamination by bullets and shot. Shooting clubs should encourage the growing movement away from lead shot, seeking a replacement with less serious environmental consequences, such as steel shot.

Bullet retrieval

Use of bullet retrieval systems will allow for the recycling of metals. Many shooting ranges have developed ways of reducing the amount of shot that is lost. Since lead cannot be retrieved using magnets, alternatives such as steel are retrieved more easily.

What to Use
Helpful publications
Golf

Audubon International. 1996. *A guide to environmental stewardship on the golf course.*

Australian Golf Union. 1998. *Environmental strategy for Australian golf courses.*

Balogh, J., and W. Walker, eds. *Golf course management and construction: environmental issues.*

Dodson, R. *Managing wildlife habitat on golf courses.*

Environment Canada, 1996, *Greening your B.C. golf course: A guide to environmental management.*

European Golf Association Ecology Unit. 1995. *Environmental guidelines for golf course development in Europe.*

European Golf Association Ecology Unit. 1997. *The committed to green handbook for golf courses.*

Koch A. 1998. *Development of environmental performance indicators for European golf clubs.*

Royal and Ancient Golf Club of St Andrews. 2000. *On course for change — tackling the challenges facing golf in the first decade of the new millennium.* Conference Report.

Royal and Ancient Golf Club of St. Andrews and the European Golf Association. 1997. *A course for all seasons — A guide to course management.*

Schuman G L, P J Vittum, M L Elliott and P P Cobb. 1997. *IPM handbook for golf courses.*

Scottish Golf Course Wildlife Group. 1997. *Golf's natural heritage: An introduction to environmental stewardship on the golf course (revised edition).*

Scottish Natural Heritage and Scottish Golf Course Wildlife Group. 2000. *Nature conservation and golf course development: best practice advice.*

United States Golf Association. 1994. *Wastewater reuse for golf course irrigation.*

United States Golf Association, et. Al. 1996. *Environmental principles for golf courses in the United States.*

Facilities design

Olympic Co-ordination Authority (OCA). 1996. *Environmental tender specifications: A guide for specification, brief and contract writers.*

Olympic Co-ordination Authority. 1999. *Compendium of ESD initiatives and outcomes. Edition 2.*

Puhalla, Jim et al. 1999. *Sports fields: A manual for design, construction and maintenance of sports fields.*

Cycling trails/routes

Velo Quebec. *Technical handbook of bikeway design.*

International Mountain Biking Association:
Multiple resources available at **www.imba.com**

Whom to Consult

Useful contacts and web sites

Audubon Society of New York State: **www.audubonintl.org**

Committed to Green Foundation: **www.committedtogreen.org**

Golf Course Superintendents Association of America: **www.gcsaa.org**

GreenLinks Eco-Efficiency Services Inc. **www.greenlinks.net**

Sports Turf Research Institute: **www.stri.co.uk**

Turfgrass Information File: **www.lib.msu.edu/tgif**

United States Golf Association's Green Section: **www.usga.org/green**

International Mountain Biking Association (IMBA),
P.O. Box 7578, Boulder, CO 80306-7578: **www.imba.com**

International Cycling Union: **www.uci.ch/english/town/uci_guide.htm**

Aspen Skiing Company: **www.aspensnowmass.com/environment/**

Olympic Coordination Authority: **www.oca.nsw.gov.au/**

US National Ski Areas Association: **www.nsaa.org/environ/index.asp**

Part IV
Planning and Operations

Major Operational and Service Issues for Events and Facilities

It is fantastic that the environment has [been] and will be such an integral element of the planning, construction and staging of the Olympic and Paralympic Games.

— **Louise Sauvage**, multiple Paralympic medallist

As an athlete I know how vital it is to train and compete in a healthy environment.

— **Duncan Armstrong**, gold medal, Seoul Olympic Games

Chapter

10

Materials and Waste Management: Cleaner is Cheaper

Previous chapters have introduced practices, such as facility design and construction materials choices, procurement and printing, that enable an organization to reduce its material needs and its production of waste. This chapter offers a comprehensive strategy for material and waste management.

The Materials and Waste Management Strategy

Using a relatively straightforward method is best to achieve goals. For waste management the method is actually a continuous cycle. It consists of three stages: performing a Waste Audit, developing and implementing an Action Plan, and then performing a Re-audit at regular intervals to determine the strong and weak points of the strategy — information which will in turn allow you to develop a more refined Action Plan.

The goals of such a strategy are to

1.   reduce the amount of materials handled;

2.   minimize the need for waste disposal by making optimum use of all materials;

3.   deal with all waste in a safe and cost-effective manner; and

4.   save money and generate income wherever possible.

Waste Audit

The purpose of the waste audit is to determine what types and quantities of waste are currently being produced, how they are being disposed of and what the costs of existing waste management systems are to the organization. The cost of disposal, whether by landfill, incineration, recycling or composting must be picked up by someone: typically either the facility/event operator, the municipality or both.

A sport organization, like any other, requires certain materials to function and generates various waste streams in the process. The waste produced by an event or facility takes several forms: unused materials that are no longer wanted; used materials that are no longer wanted or useable; or byproducts of the original material which have been transformed into another material or state that is either unusable or can no longer be used by the organization in question.

The most common types of materials that are brought into a sport organization pass through and ultimately emerge as materials/wastes to dispose of might include:

- construction and demolition materials of all types;

- packaging materials, containers and pallets;

- food and beverage containers;

- organic materials (food and beverage, grass clippings, etc.);

- office supplies and equipment;

- appliances, machinery and vehicles;

- merchandise for sale or distribution;

- hazardous wastes; and

- medical wastes.

Performing a comprehensive waste audit allows you to establish "baseline" information and statistics, against which the effectiveness of subsequent initiatives can be measured. It also allows you to identify those areas where effort can best be directed to achieve the most substantial environmental and economic gains. Ultimately, the audit serves as the foundation for developing an Action Plan.

A small organization that performs a fairly limited number of operations and handles a narrow range of materials should be able to perform its own basic waste audit. Guidance material is readily available to help you determine what types and quantities of material you purchase, handle and dispose of over a typical sample period — typically 2-3 days. A larger organization (stadium, golf course, major games organizer, etc.) on the other hand, will likely want to seek outside assistance from a waste management specialist to perform an accurately and useful audit.

Action Plan

The Action Plan is a strategy and a series of concrete steps that will enable the organization to carry out its materials and waste management goals. The principal steps include three key words: reduce, reuse, and recycle. There are several subsequent steps to follow as well.

Reduce

Limit waste generation by curtailing the amount of resources and materials entering the organization, through purchasing practices, working with suppliers to limit packaging, avoiding unnecessary services and production of materials, greening printing practices and building to meet real needs only. A critical aspect of reducing is elimination: not buying or accepting materials, supplies or equipment that are hazardous, wasteful, non-recyclable, or difficult or expensive to recycle or dispose of. These might include Styrofoam, mixed plastics, juice boxes, etc.

SOCOG'S Waste Management Policy

The following guiding principles will be embraced for all waste management activities at the Sydney 2000 Olympic and Paralympic Games (SOCOG 1998).

Reduction

Waste reduction shall be achieved by developing appropriate procurement strategies aimed at reducing — through redesign and research and development — the quantity of waste brought into the Games Venues.

Reuse

Waste reduction shall be further enhanced by the promotion of reusable materials — such as reusable packaging and catering utensils — at all Games venues.

Recycling

Recycling shall be maximized from all Games venues by:

    a)   controlling the design and composition of packaging brought onto the Games venues, giving preference to the use of products made from recyclable materials;

    b)   providing appropriate recycling infrastructure to each Games venue;

    c)   securing markets, in advance of the Games for the sale of recycled material generated at the Games; and

    d)   putting into place procurement strategies to give preference, where practical, to the use of products made from recycled materials.

Landfill Avoidance

Waste reduction to landfill shall be further enhanced be the processing (composting) of non-recyclable materials such as food waste and soiled fiber packaging.

Education

A successful waste minimization program can only be achieved with wide community support. An education and training program aimed at encouraging the involvement of materials and service providers, athletes, visitors and the wider community shall be put in place prior to and during the Games.

You might, for example, stipulate that all suppliers deliver materials and equipment either without packaging or in containers and on pallets which the supplier will take back and, ideally, reuse. Mizuno Corporation has developed a packaging and delivery system for its sporting goods and equipment which eliminates most of the wrapping, boxes and pallets that typically accompany sport retail goods.

Reuse

As discussed in previous chapters, seek to purchase products and supplies which are durable, easily maintained or repaired, upgradable and which do not quickly become obsolete. Avoid gimmicks and cheaply-made items, even if they cost less. It is also critical to develop systems that encourage and facilitate reuse: these include two-sided printing policies, exchange storerooms, price incentives and penalties, and collection days.

Canada Games Reuse of Materials

For more than two decades, the Canada Games Council has been encouraging re-use of materials and equipment from one Games to the next. At the conclusion of one set of Games, organizing committees are required to clean, package and ship whatever can be re-used by the next Canada Games organizer. Items typically shipped include bunk beds and mattresses, signage and pageantry (flag poles, flags, banners, material, etc.). Also common is the staging of a post-Games auction where materials that have not already been earmarked for community groups and charities are auctioned to the general public.

Recycle

Although it should always be portrayed as the "last resort," recycling is a critical part of waste management. It is also becoming a generator of income, especially for fine paper and valuable metals. The goal of any organization is to attempt to recycle in some form whatever equipment or materials are no longer usable in any way. This generally consists of identifying "brokers" for recyclables, ideally ones that pay for the materials you supply them with, as opposed to charging for their service. How much you will receive for material, if anything, will depend on whether recycling facilities exist in the region and on the strength of the market for that particular item. For example, in some regions there is a glut of glass, whereas fine paper is usually in heavy demand. Plastics in particular are notoriously difficult to sell, owing to the ubiquitous supply, the many different types and the relatively undeveloped state of recycling technology. An exception is polyethylene terephthalate or PET (many drink bottles are now made of PET) which is relatively easily recycled, and for which there is now a strong market in most regions. As recycling technology improves, the demand for plastics is expected to increase. In general, there should be a market for fine paper, newsprint, glass, metal cans and cardboard.

Recycling at Ski Resorts

Ski resorts, such as Hunter Mountain in New York and Aspen, Colorado, recognized in the late eighties that the growing cost of handling waste could soon outstrip revenues. To deal with this threat, they instituted comprehensive waste management programs to reduce, reuse, recycle and minimize the dangers and costs of handling hazardous wastes.

The Aspen Skiing Company banned polystyrene foam at its hotels and offices and asked its on-mountain restaurant operators to avoid tin and plastics. The restaurants instituted sorting and recycling schemes that involve customers in the process. Reaction among staff and customers has been very positive.

When The Aspen Skiing Company needed to tear down the Snowmass Lodge and Club, they decided to put their environmental policies into practice. Alpine Demolition, which was sub-contracted to do the job, achieved an impressive recycle/reused rate of 88% on the project. Jim Gochis, from Alpine Demolition, said the key was convincing the managers to carefully deconstruct the building instead of demolishing it. Although this is a more time consuming process and therefore more expensive, the decision saved the company about $80,000 in tipping fees and even generated revenues from the sale of the salvaged items.

A total of 6,000 cubic yards of material were diverted from the landfill. The key to the success of the recycling program was crushing several of the materials so that they could be used for other purposes. For example, 4, 251 cubic yards of wood were turned to mulch and used for compost. In addition, concrete was crushed on site and used for fill. Even if some of the materials could not be used their volume was greatly reduced by the grinding process and therefore needed fewer loads to transport to the landfill.

Reusing materials on site or selling them also contributed to the high waste reduction figure. The construction company was able to reuse the copper and aluminum pipes, wire and steel in the new building. Old doors, window, carpeting and other fixtures were all sold at a successful salvage sale.

Compost

Organic waste (food, grass clippings, leaves, wood chips, etc.) constitutes up to 45 percent of municipal waste and around 70-80 percent of waste from a sporting event. Food waste from cafeterias, restaurants and even individual meals is generally compostable and represents a significant opportunity for waste reduction. Compostable food represents the second highest percentage of waste by weight in most institutional settings, after paper. Compostables are also a valuable organic resource which should not be sent to landfill or incinerated. Food waste can be composted on site, for use in landscaping or, where facilities exist, sent to municipal composters.

On-site composting of some food scraps, such as meat and dairy products, may be regulated for health reasons. This will depend on the type

SOCOG Has Worms

The Sydney Organizing Committee for the Olympic Games (SOCOG) established a worm colony in the basement of its offices. SOCOG employed a colony of 400,000 earthworms to compost the food waste from its staff cafeteria, which serviced more than 1000 employees. The worm composting, an initiative being tested by a composting service company, is an example of SOCOG's commitment to environmentally sound waste management practices.

Composting Challenges at 1999 Canada Winter Games

The environmental committee of the 1999 Canada Winter Games, held in Corner Brook Newfoundland, had planned an ambitious composting program in the cafeteria of the athletes' village. They had an arrangement with a composting company to manage the food wastes for free and an agreement with the Municipality to transport the food wastes to the compost center located near the town landfill. All that needed to happen was to place the food scraps in the large garbage container that had been placed outside the kitchen. In addition, the Host Society tendered out the food services contract to a company that created an entirely compostable menu. They also required that wherever possible the condiments be served in bulk so that, in theory, all food scraps on the plates could have been composted.

However, some condiments, such as jams, were purchased in plastic and tin single serving packets and therefore separation of waste streams became necessary in the kitchens. Unfortunately, there were not enough volunteers in the kitchen to manage the separation of the non-compostable items from the high volume of food waste. The composting program had to be abandoned due to contamination and a great opportunity was lost.

of composting system (the composted material must become hot enough over a long period to eliminate the possibility of spreading disease). Professional advice should be sought from composting experts and local health authorities. Where composting is not an option (i.e. lack of space or appropriate location), selling food scraps for animal feed should be explored. Any organization that is frequently left with edible food (from cafeterias and catering) should explore possibilities for donating acceptable items to local soup kitchens and food banks.

Composting can be a highly cost-effective element of your waste strategy. Not only will composting food and yard materials on site reduce waste collection costs, it may also produce a valuable resource that can be either sold, generating revenue, or used on site for turf management or landscaping (an effective and natural alternative to chemical soil amendments or fertilizers).

Remove

As an incentive to waste reduction and recycling, wastebaskets should be removed from individual desks in offices and at other applicable locations. They should be replaced by clearly marked recycling containers/stations, which should be regularly emptied. Such a move must be preceded by sufficient notice and explanation.

Install

In tandem with removing wastebaskets, each area should receive individual, clearly marked recycling containers. In central areas, clearly marked bins for true unrecyclable garbage should be installed. In public areas, garbage and recycling systems should be placed side by side, so as to limit the likelihood of contamination by people unwilling to walk as far as the appropriate container. Again, clear marking is absolutely essential.

Dispose of safely

Even with the best efforts to reduce the amount of hazardous materials in use, there will inevitably be some products, liquid and solid, which should not be disposed of with the ordinary garbage. These will require special attention in order to be safely disposed of, in keeping with local regulations. All efforts should be made to encourage the supplier to take responsibility for their collection. If this is not feasible, the sport organization must ensure that hazardous substances are properly stored and disposed of.

Sell or donate

Materials, supplies and equipment that can still be used, but are no longer of use to the sport organization, can usually be sold or donated to another organization to which they are of value. Obsolete equipment which has been replaced, such as computers, ice-resurfacing machines, or golf carts, can generally be put to good use by other groups with different needs or lower demands. Charitable groups, schools and community centers, for example, are often in need of computers and office equipment. Construction leftovers and materials removed during renovation can often be sent to vendors of used building supplies.

Education and communication

Education and communication are essential to the success of material and waste management programs. Cooperative and enthusiastic staff and volunteers are critical to designing a good Action Plan and to implementing it fully. It is essential that they be fully involved at all stages. Changes should only be introduced after people have been advised and offered a chance to comment. Many of these same points hold true for the general public: facility users, spectators, etc. To encourage cooperation and participation in waste reduction and management, clear and innovative communication is indispensable.

Sport events and facilities should develop awareness/education programs for participants and spectators. This can include providing clear explanations (on tickets, in programs, at the point of sale of materials that are recyclable) about why recycling is important and about how to find and use the right containers. To identify recycling facilities, provide clear signage. Use color schemes and symbols that are consistent throughout the facility/event.

Lahti Ski Games

In 1996, the Lahti Ski Games, an annual event in Finland drawing close to 100,000 spectators per day, launched an environmental program. One of the first initiatives was a comprehensive waste recycling program. Students helped the audience and officials to deposit their litter into the right containers. An intense information campaign was organized using local newspapers and radio to inform the public about what recycling measures they should expect to find. At the main sport venue a "waste song" was played from loudspeakers between announcements. An audience questionnaire indicated that 90% of respondents regarded waste separation at a major event to be very important.

Re-audit and revise action plan

One of the greatest failings of change-oriented Action Plans of any type is the absence of follow-up. How successful was the Action Plan? Which initiatives worked and which didn't? How can the failures be turned into successes? How can successes be improved upon further? These are the questions that should be asked in a follow-up or "Re-audit." For example, six months after the launch of the Action Plan, a smaller audit should be carried out to determine whether specific objectives were met, and a revised Action Plan should be developed. Though subsequent audits and Action Plans will not be as extensive as the initial one, they are crucial to targeting both problem areas and areas of high priority. An audit should be carried out annually to judge where progress is being made and whether or not there has been any slippage. The annual audit might focus on a particular area of concern, with that year's Action Plan setting out fine-tuned steps to address it.

Looking for Innovative Ideas

Most of the components of a Material and Waste Management Strategy are fairly basic, allowing an organization to address the majority of concerns. Each sport organization will also want to develop some innovative ideas and approaches to take into account its unique challenges.

Major sporting events, as a result of both their scale and their temporary nature, create some very specific demands. Apart from the general office and administrative waste, the generation of printed materials and waste associated with food can be staggering.

- A typical professional sport event will generate close to 2 kilograms of food and beverage-related waste per spectator.

- Activities during the 1995 NFL Super Bowl Week, involving approximately 225,000 participants, generated 313 tons of waste. 127 tons (40%) was recycled.

- The 1994 Lillehammer Olympics implemented strict green printing standards, as well as recovering and recycling as much paper as possible. Wherever possible, washable tableware was used, and where this was not possible food was served on compostable potato starch-based plates. Overall, 900,000 of these plates were used. When the supply ran out, recycled and compostable paper plates were substituted.

- The Atlanta Olympic organizers succeeded in diverting 3,900 tonnes of waste over the 17 days of the Games — a diversion rate of about 50 percent.

- The 1996 Lahti (Finland) Ski Games sent 5,000 kilograms of waste to landfill. This included biowaste, paper, cardboard, cardboard drink containers, glass and metal.

Novel solutions are clearly required to reduce, not just recycle, the amount of food-related packaging waste at any event or facility. The use of a durable mug by athletes and spectators has been successfully encouraged at smaller community events, but major suppliers and event organizers have been slow to develop the idea. Drink sponsors have a golden opportunity to sell or distribute reusable mugs, made of recycled plastic, emblazoned with their logo and/or that of a particular event or home team.

The whole area of refreshment containers and packaging is ripe with opportunity for inventive waste reduction solutions. Although there is rarely much money to be made in recycling most materials, except perhaps metal cans, there are savings to be had: Concession operators can reduce the cost of buying and storing disposable containers if reusable ones become common; event and facility operators can cut their clean-up and disposal costs if packaging is reduced, reused, recycled and deposited in the appropriate containers; and municipalities can delay the development of new landfill sites by keeping out sport-related waste.

Sport events frequently overproduce souvenir items such as T-shirts and programs, which can quickly become obsolete and unmarketable. In addition to fine-tuning their demand forecasts, these organizations should design material to be reusable at subsequent events, wherever applicable. Otherwise, they should seek worthy recipients of these and other unused materials, such as charities.

Tips for Reducing Promotional Waste

Participatory events such as marathons and other races frequently include T-shirts as part of the race package. While some participants covet these souvenirs, others could do well without their fiftieth T-shirt. It should be common practice to request on entry forms if items such as a T-shirt are desired. If not, the price of entry should be discounted.

A common form of promotion for sponsors is to hand out freebies to athletes and spectators: cheap visors, T-shirts, pens, bags, etc. These disposable, non-durable items soon find their way into landfills. From the sponsors' point of view, they are generally a waste of money, gaining only short-lived exposure, itself minimized by the clutter of items competing for public attention. The opportunity for sponsors and companies that specialize in these marketing gimmicks is to reduce the amount of freebies and create less wasteful ways of promotion. Organizers should work with sponsors to help develop ways of recognizing their contributions without adding to the waste problem. Where freebies remain the gimmick of choice, these should be as useful and durable as possible, and ultimately recyclable.

Signs are items that, although indispensable for getting people to the right places, are a significant source of waste by volume at a sport event. Like cups, the question of signs is crying out for innovative solutions. Though Lillehammer did recycle close to 20,000 signs into making cardboard boxes, there are surely ways to reduce and reuse signs. They can be made as generic as possible, and used over and over again, either at the same event or by selling or donating them to other events/facilities. Sturdy plasticized signboards with removable printed markings can be reused and the lettering and symbols updated several times over.

What You Can Do

Summary of Recommendations for Waste Management

- Implement a comprehensive strategy for material and waste management.
- Conduct a waste audit and regular follow-up audits.
- Focus your Action Plan on the hierarchy of reduce, reuse and recycle.
- Use refined subsequent Action Plans to address priority areas.
- Stress communication with and education of staff, volunteers and the public.
- Look for innovative ideas relevant to your particular needs.
- Choose products according to cost/performance over the length of their life.

Whom to Consult

Local government waste management authority.

Consultants specializing in waste audits and waste management planning.

What to Use

Helpful publications

Federation of Canadian Municipalities. 1993. *The packaging waste reduction guide: Minimizing solid waste through efficient procurement practices.*

Ciambrone, David F., 1995. *Waste minimization as a strategic weapon.* CRC Press.

Creighton, Sarah Hammond. 1998. *Greening the ivory tower: Improving the environmental track record of universities, colleges, and other institutions.*

SOCOG. 1998. *The Sydney 2000 Olympic Games integrated waste management solution.*

Useful web sites

The Aspen Skiing Company: **www.skiaspen.com/environment/index.htm**

Olympic Co-ordination Authority: **www.oca.nsw.gov.au**

Solid Waste Management Associations and Links:

- Solid Waste Association of North America: **www.swana.org/**
- International Solid Waste Association: **www.iswa.org/**
- US EPA: **www.epa.gov/epaoswer/non-hw/muncpl/index.htm**

Recycling and Waste Reduction links:

- NAPCOR's iPET Recycling Toolkit, is a guide for starting or expanding individual-sized PET (iPET) plastic beverage container recycling programs at major venues. **www.napcor.com/iPET_tool.html**

- Recycling Council of Ontario: **www.rco.on.ca**

Waste Audit Guides

- **www.rrfb.com/Auditguide.pdf**

- **www.opala.org/wastaudt.html**

- **www.pcnjwaste.com/comaudit.htm**

Green Procurement

- US EPA: **www.epa.gov/epaoswer/non-hw/procure/index.htm**

- IISD: **iisd1.iisd.ca/business/trancon.htm**

- Buy recycled guide: **www.wastecap.org/alliance/**

- Environment Canada: **www.ec.gc.ca/eog-oeg/greener_procurement/Greener_Procurement.htm**

Case Study:

Waste Management Accomplishments at Sydney 2000

The efforts of Sydney 2000 organizers to minimize and then appropriately manage waste of all kinds generated some remarkable accomplishments. Some of the most important achievements are chronicled here, along with those figures available at the time of publication.

Building the Stage: Waste Management Achievements of the OCA during the Development/Construction of Infrastructure and Venues

During the seven-year lead-up to the Games, the Olympic Co-ordination Authority guided and managed most Olympics-related remediation, renovation and construction projects. This included the massive Homebush Bay site remediation, construction of dozens of major and minor facilities and service buildings, and development of scores of "public domain" sites, walkways, bridges, etc. Some of the major waste management initiatives and accomplishments during these preparatory years follow.

- Existing buildings were used and refitted wherever feasible. Around one-third of sporting competitions (9 of 28) were held in existing venues, avoiding the impact of new construction.

- Construction materials and wastes were reused and recycled on a large scale, with an average waste recycling rate of 60%.

- Recycled materials — timber, concrete, steel and compostable waste — were used in the construction of venues and facilities and the redevelopment and landscaping of Homebush Bay.

A waste management plan was implemented at all OCA sites, including Homebush Bay in advance of the Olympics. The waste management system focused on separating waste at the source. This three-bin system used separate bins for recyclables (aluminum, cans, glass, etc.), compostables (food, paper, etc.) and residuals (other garbage)

Pre-Olympic waste management results:

Construction and demolition waste recycling rates for key Olympic facilities:

- Sydney Superdome: 98%

- Athletes Village: 94%

- Dunc Grey Velodrome: 94%

- Sydney International Shooting Center: 87%

- Stadium Australia 70%

- NSW Tennis Center 60%

On-site re-use of C&D waste, by type:

- Sydney Superdome: 26,000m^3 of concrete, 106,000m^3 of soil

- Sydney International Shooting Center: 63.5 tonnes of timber, 33.5 tonnes of steel, 667 tonnes of concrete

- Dunc Grey Velodrome: 183 m^3 of timber, 13m^3 of steel, 77 m^3 of concrete,

- Athletes Village: 24,786 m^3 of various materials

Putting on the Show: Achievements of SOCOG's Integrated Waste Management Solution

The Sydney Organizing Committee for the Olympic Games (SOCOG) developed an "integrated waste management solution" that would tackle waste at both ends: reducing the amount of waste being generated by controlling what materials/resources were used; avoiding materials that could not be reused, recycled or composted — particularly hazardous materials; and installing collection and handling system that would maximize diversion from landfill. An Olympic first, four companies signed on as the official Olympic waste management sponsor team, providing a comprehensive set of services.

In most public areas, waste stations included two types of bins: paper, cardboard and food in maroon-colored bins, destined for composting; and plastic, glass and aluminum in yellow bins, destined for sorting and recycling. Caterers and suppliers contributed to six additional streams: clean paper and cardboard, for recycling; glass, for recycling; cooking oil, for reprocessing; medical, veterinary and quarantine waste, for special disposal; reusable materials such as crockery and boxes; and other rubbish, for landfill disposal.

Sydney 2000 set itself the ambitious target of 80% diversion from landfill. In 1996, Atlanta had achieved a 50% diversion rate.

Games-time waste management results:

- Total waste forecast for full 60-day period (2 Sept. — 30 Oct.): 8-10,000 tonnes

- Total waste actually generated: 5010 tonnes

- Percentage of waste diverted from landfill: 68%
- Compostables as percentage of total waste collected: 43%
- Recyclables as percent of total waste collected (glass, tin, plastic): 8%
- Paper/cardboard as percent of total waste collected: 10%
- Paper consumption was reduced from 45 million sheets (Atlanta 1996) to 29 million sheets — a saving of 16 million sheets (approximately 90 tonnes)

(Figures are courtesy of Peter Ottesen, SOCOG and the OCA)

Waste Management Lessons Learned

The Sydney 2000 experience in managing all manner of waste (construction, operations, event-time) over an extended period has generated a series of valuable lessons, from general to highly specific.

- An overarching waste management vision should be translated into an integrated waste management strategy that emphasises waste avoidance and minimisation. All parties in the development project must be active partners in implementing this strategy, requiring a comprehensive campaign of awareness raising and education that targets: administrators, purchasers, designers, builders, tradespeople, suppliers and the general public.
- The most significant gains can be made in reducing and recycling construction and demolition waste. Success depends on:
  - a clear and firm environmental tendering and purchasing process, with objectives carefully communicated to tenderers, designers, suppliers, etc.; and
  - thorough training of site managers and tradespeople in the use of a clear and carefully-monitored waste separation and collection system.
- Recycled materials, often sourced directly from the same site, can be used effectively and economically on-site.
- Materials and supplies (for construction, facilities operation, administration, etc.) with high recycled content can be specified, usually without paying a price in terms of costs or performance of these materials.
- High waste reduction and recycling rates can be achieved during a major multi-venue event and on an ongoing basis. Factors for success include:
  - contractual obligations (for suppliers, caterers, service providers, etc.) stipulating performance requirements;
  - controls over types of materials, packaging, etc. entering the site, to ensure compatibility with recycling/diversion systems;
  - education and motivation of suppliers and the public; and
  - consistent, well-designed, well-located and clearly-signed recycling stations at all venues.
- Markets must exist for each output stream of recycled/composted materials if the whole exercise is to be sustainable. The Olympics can provide a kick-start for new markets and business ventures (i.e. recycled cardboard furniture, vermi-composting).
- During events, each venue requires its own trained waste manager committed to achieving waste goals. This responsibility cannot be left to catering managers and cleaners.
- A clean venue attracts cleaner behavior. The public responds more responsibly to waste management stations that are clean, regularly emptied and attractive.

(Based partially on observations of Colin Dimitroff, Sydney 2000)

Chapter

11

Transportation — Cut the Traffic; Breathe Easier

Nowhere do economic, environmental and social goals intersect more closely than with matters of transportation. The goal of the sustainable sport organization is to reduce the contribution of its activities to environmental threats such as air pollution and carbon dioxide emissions, water and soil pollution, traffic congestion, and noise disturbances. At the same time, it should be aiming to protect its members, users, and facilities from these threats and to reduce the financial cost to itself and to society at large. That being said, the organization must continue to meet its primary transportation obligation: to provide relatively easy access to its events/facilities for all users.

Can all of these goals be met without compromises? Not likely, but none of those compromises need create losers. In fact, the majority of solutions create only winners: pollution and energy consumption are reduced, communities are disturbed less and the overall costs to sport organizations, communities and governments are cut.

The principal objectives by which transportation goals can be realized are several:

1. Reduce consumption of non-renewable energy.

2. Reduce emissions of air pollutants and greenhouse gases.

3. Reduce air, water and soil pollution from chemicals used in vehicle operation and maintenance.

4. Limit traffic congestion and demands on infrastructure.

These general objectives can be met by addressing the following issues, some of which are relevant only to major or minor events or to particular types of facilities; others to the sport industry in general.

Protecting Athletes and Spectators

A critical reason for addressing transportation issues is that air pollution from vehicles is one of the primary threats to the health of all sport participants. By keeping vehicles away from sport venues, limiting the numbers and the emissions of those which must operate near such venues and establishing strict guidelines for operation—such as a no-idling policy—events and facilities managers can go a long way toward protecting athletes and spectators.

Transportation for the Sustainable Organization

Employees and managers can reduce the impact of their transportation choices, both on official business and when commuting. The type of transport used (public vs. private), the choice of vehicle (truck, van, car, bicycle), its fuel type (gas, propane, electric) and efficiency, as well as various maintenance and operating practices should all be considered. Policies should also be reviewed: are official vehicles evaluated for their environmental impact? Are drivers instructed in fuel-saving practices? Does the organization encourage or assist car-pooling, the use of public transport or bicycling? Are bus passes subsidized? Is there protected bicycle parking as well as change rooms with showers?

The steps outlined here are designed to address those issues that arise in the daily operation of an office or a sport organization of any size: commuting, choice and maintenance of company vehicles, etc. The Sustainable Transportation Checklist on the following page provides a more detailed list of steps that can be taken in most sport organizations.

The general point to remember about transportation is that there is a hierarchy of energy-efficiency and environmental impact. The ideal mode of transportation is non-motorized—walking, bicycling, and skiing, for example. It is followed by various forms of mass transit, such as trains and buses, for transporting both people and goods. At the lowest end of the hierarchy is the individual passenger vehicle: cars, vans, trucks, which are making a special trip to move only one or two people or a small amount of goods.

Fleet Vehicles: What Kind and How Many?

Any large sport event and virtually every sport facility owns, leases or operates vehicles of some kind. Ownership of vehicles should always be kept to a minimum, to reduce financing and maintenance costs, and leasing arrangements should be explored prior to purchase. Vehicle rental is often an option where most of the demand occurs at a peak period and vehicles sit idle the remainder of the time. Through good scheduling and sharing arrangements, fleet vehicles can be used as fully as possible.

For those vehicles that are considered essential, the key is to buy the right kind for the job, to seek the most fuel-efficient and non-polluting, and to look for the most durable and easily repaired models. No one vehicle will meet all criteria. Choose the one that responds to the most of your needs. Avoid basing your choice on exceptional needs. If a 12-passenger van is required once a month, but generally no more than three people use it at a time, buy an ordinary 4-seat vehicle and rent a van once a month. Too many purchases are based on the rare exceptions.

Sustainable Transportation Checklist

Individual Actions and Policy Changes

❏ Use public transit wherever possible, and encourage others to do the same. If bus service is poor, lobby for route changes. Provide the transit company with a list of people who would use the bus if service were better.

❏ Start a car pool and encourage others to do the same. Post a map or circulate a questionnaire to find out which employees could car pool. Use electronic mail to create an "electronic ride board" where people can post rides offered and sought on a daily basis.

❏ Encourage management to provide an incentive for car pools by providing parking or reducing parking fees for multi-passenger vehicles.

❏ If you must use a vehicle, don't let it idle for more than a minute. Idling uses more fuel than restarting the engine and creates needless fuel emissions. Use a fuel-efficient vehicle and keep it well maintained. Use certified re-refined motor oil.

❏ Walk to work, if possible, and when you go out for lunch. Encourage others to do the same.

❏ Bicycle to work and encourage co-workers to follow suit. Post maps of good bicycle routes.

❏ Use the telephone, fax or mail instead of couriers wherever possible. For short-distance courier deliveries, encourage the use of bicycle courier services.

❏ Encourage policies to favor teleconferencing instead of travel wherever possible.

❏ Encourage taxi sharing for business meetings.

Equipment and Building Modifications

❏ Encourage facilities management to install secure, covered or indoor bicycle parking. Racks should accommodate bicycles of all sizes and be of good quality, so as not to damage bicycles.

❏ Encourage facilities management to provide showers and lockers for staff that walk, run or cycle to work.

Vehicle Fleets

❏ Ensure that all fleet vehicles are well maintained and that a fleet management information system is in place.

❏ Use re-refined oil, recycle batteries and solvents and use retreaded tires (particularly for trucks) if they are not already doing so.

❏ Purchase high-efficiency vehicles and use the most fuel-efficient vehicle available for the job.

❏ Encourage fuel-efficient driving habits, including a no-idling policy.

❏ Convert high-use vehicles to natural gas or propane. Both produce fewer emissions than gasoline.

❏ Create a no-smoking policy for passengers and drivers of all transport vehicles.

(Based on a document by Environment Canada 1992)

Fuel efficiency is critical to reducing both costs and emissions of pollutants and greenhouse gases. But fuel efficiency means more than just liters of gasoline per 100 kilometers (or miles per gallon). It also includes the various alternative fuel options, such as propane, natural gas, electric, ethanol and even hydrogen. Buying cars that run on propane or natural gas, or converting older ones, can reduce fuel consumption and costs while reducing emissions.

Electric vehicles, though still in the early stage of development, should be considered for use in service fleets and for tasks requiring limited speed and distance. The advantage of electric vehicles is their almost silent operation and their lack of emissions. This makes them ideal for use near sporting facilities where clean air and quiet may be valued, and where speed is not essential. The environmental drawback of electric vehicles, however, is that they are only as clean as the source of electricity that they rely on to recharge. A practical drawback is the limited availability of 220-volt recharging hookups. Recent developments by some manufacturers have significantly boosted operating speeds and battery storage capacity (hence longer ranges) while reducing recharging times.

Most major manufacturers are now developing or have already launched alternative fuel cars, vans and buses. The tremendous amount of resources now being devoted to research and development in "hybrid" vehicles (those can use more than one fuel source) and fuel cells will undoubtedly lead to a greater variety of cleaner-burning vehicles coming to market early in the new millennium. While price is always a factor with new technology, the cost of these vehicles should drop significantly once mainstream production begins, a process that has been accelerated by increasingly strict air quality measures in many parts of the world.

Sport events and facilities offer an ideal venue for manufacturers of alternative fuels and vehicles to get publicity. In many cases, these companies are looking for high visibility and will be willing to offer the use of their vehicles at a substantial discount, if not for free. The use of electric vehicles as pace cars and for television crews during events such as the marathon and bike races should be mandatory to protect the athlete from fumes at close range. Both manufacturers and event organizers (small as well as large events) have been turning this idea to their advantage by prominently publicizing the fact that electric cars are being used for environmental reasons at sport events.

Air conditioning is perhaps the hottest topic of debate. The CFCs traditionally used as coolants in car air conditioning are thought to be

Electric Vehicle Sponsor Uses Sydney as Showcase

British high-technology company and small vehicle-maker Frazer-Nash turned a lot of heads in Sydney as the "official provider of solar-assisted vehicles to the Sydney 2000 Olympics." The Games offered Frazer-Nash the opportunity to showcase its wide range of efficient, electric vehicles, many of which can meet the needs of sport and recreation organizations and event organizers.

Frazer-Nash has designed and developed vehicles for a wide range of applications, including city cars, taxis, hotel courtesy cars, special event transportation and as utility vehicles. Some are fitted with Solar Panels, which can increase driving distances and reduce electric recharge times.

Valuable features of the company's vehicles include: quick recharge time, lack of emissions, quiet operation and ease of customization.

one of the worst offenders in depleting the ozone layer. It's ironic: the cooler you keep your car, the more you'll get burned. The single most effective step you can take is to not buy a vehicle with air conditioning. Or, if your vehicle already has it, don't replenish the CFCs, or any of the moderately less-damaging substitutes, if they leak out. The biggest problem with vehicle air conditioning systems is that they are prone to leaking. This makes them a significant contributor to ozone damage. If you can, suffer through the truly hot days. If climate or preference makes this impossible, ensure that your maintenance garage is collecting and recycling the chemicals that remain, when you bring the vehicle in for servicing. The most effective cooling tip is the simplest. Buy only light-colored vehicles; they heat up far less in the sun! Also, try installing a supplementary dashboard fan available from most automotive stores.

Vehicle Maintenance and Refueling

Regular maintenance will help to extend the life of a vehicle. It will also save the owner money by avoiding expensive repairs and maximizing fuel efficiency. Furthermore, a clean-running engine produces fewer emissions.

Anyone doing maintenance or repairs should take steps to prevent fluids such as oil, anti-freeze and transmission fluid from leaking into the soil. These fluids should be properly be disposed of and never poured down the drain. In the case of oil, it can be sent to recyclers for re-refining. More oil is spilled each year worldwide through poor vehicle maintenance than through oil tanker accidents. Any vehicle maintenance should be done on a leak-proof surface, where accidental spills can be mopped up. This is especially important when servicing must be done on fragile terrain. Refueling of snow grooming vehicles at the Canadian national cross-country ski team's Haig Glacier training center, for example, is always done on special tarps to capture accidental spills.

Transportation of Spectators, Competitors and Media

One of the most critical jobs for any event coordinator is to organize transportation for competitors, officials, media and often for spectators as well. The sheer numbers of people who must be moved into and out of a confined area, or between a number of widely-spaced areas in the case of a multi-site event, present a significant logistical challenge. How do you get everybody to the right place on time while also reducing pollution, noise and congestion? Fortunately, the solutions are one and the same: reduce the number of vehicles on the roads. There are a variety of means for doing this.

Selection of sites

Sites should be selected with transportation in mind. How will the users get there? Are public transport or non-motorized modes of transport an option? It is amazing how many sport facilities can be reached only by private vehicle. There is something fundamentally contradictory about driving to a place where you can get some exercise or watch others who are doing sports.

Sydney's "Environmental Guidelines" note that non-polluting and user-friendly public transport is an integral part of sustainable urban planning. Olympic host cities should commit themselves to locating Games facilities near public transport systems, providing satellite car-parking to facilitate use of public transport, and providing cycleways and walkways at Olympic sites.

Reduce the number of private automobiles

Offer incentives to taking public transportation, walking or cycling, while at the same time banning private cars from the immediate vicinity of an event and not providing parking on site. It is critical to take such a comprehensive approach to these problems—simply making parking prohibitively expensive, as some events and facilities do, will only transfer the problem. Those who can afford the high rates will continue to park on site, while those who cannot will try to find alternative parking nearby. Everyone will still be driving. Alternatively, try instituting "reverse" sliding scale parking fees: vehicles with a single passenger pay a high parking rate; two-passenger vehicles pay half; three-passenger vehicles pay one-quarter; and vehicles with four or more passengers park free!

Atlanta's Olympian Transportation Efforts

Although Atlanta Olympic Organizers were much maligned for problems with transportation system (due primarily to the recruitment of drivers unfamiliar with the city), the 1996 Atlanta Olympics successfully implemented a number of transportation initiatives with positive environmental consequences.

♦ Efforts to encourage residents and visitors to ride the public transit system worked so well that an estimated 1.3 million spectators took buses and/or the subway each day – nearly 4 times the daily average prior to the Olympics.

♦ The largest-ever fleet of alternative fuel buses was assembled in Atlanta.

♦ A major car manufacturer demonstrated its electric vehicles, using them as pace cars for the marathon.

♦ The U.S. Environmental Protection Agency recorded a 15 percent dip in air pollution levels for that time of year, the opposite of what was anticipated.

Provide alternative mass transportation

The use of shuttle buses for spectators and competitors can effectively minimize traffic near an event. These might be shuttles paid for by organizers or special additional service provided by the local public transit authority. By working closely with these authorities it may be possible to agree on a cost-sharing arrangement whereby the sport organization contributes to this improved service. Shuttles should run from main public transit transfer stations and from outlying parking areas. Many professional clubs have arrangements of this type for greatly augmented service on game days.

Offer people incentives to use public transit

For example, make tickets to an event valid for free public transit rides on the day of the event, or offer special prices on public transit tickets for the duration of an event to anyone traveling to one of the event's sites. The many possibilities for encouraging use of public transit should be explored by all event organizers.

Transporting competitors, officials and media offers special challenges, since it is critical that they arrive on time. For multi-sport and multi-site events, good scheduling is one of the keys to improving transportation efficiency and reducing congestion and delays. Events may need to be carefully timed so as to allow traffic to clear before another event starts at the same site or one nearby.

The standard procedure is to provide dedicated shuttle buses or cars that have special access to roads and parking areas that have been closed off to the general public. Assuming that the principal routes are not overly congested, this type of system tends to work reasonably well. Unfortunately, routes are all too often blocked as a result of ineffective measures to limit non-official traffic. Frequently, however, the number of official vehicles alone is enough to cause congestion. Several steps can be taken to alleviate this latter problem, but neither will be popular.

Tackling Traffic Congestion

To deal with traffic congestion and disturbances of residents in adjacent communities, the Kaiserslautern professional soccer team in Germany subsidizes a park-and- ride program, whereby spectators leave their cars in outlying parking lots and take special shuttle buses to the stadium.

At the 1994 Commonwealth Games in Victoria, a combination of free admission onto city buses for ticket holders and a well-publicize ban on private vehicles and private parking in the vicinity if the main sites significantly cut traffic congestion, noise and air pollution. Of the 34,000 attendees at the open and closing ceremonies, 50 percent came by bus.

Athletes and media should always be transported in multi-passenger vehicles. By limiting the number of these vehicles, but ensuring that they leave punctually, it is possible to avoid running a large number of half-empty vehicles. Media in Lillehammer found that bus service was less frequent than at similar events, but that it was always punctual. Most journalists, according to one reporter, became accustomed to having limited options but were grateful that buses left and arrived on time. Some media and a number of the more elite athletes have been known to object to being forced into buses whose schedule they do not control. Should such a situation arise, it may be politic to mention the public Green Games commitment to which organizers are bound and should a voluntary code of conduct be in place for athletes, media, coaches and others, which all other participants have been asked to support.

Transporting officials, however, can be an even thornier problem. The combination of protocol and egos presents significant limitations to organizers who are seeking ways to reduce the number of private vehicles. If everyone from sport federation officials to politicians demands his/her own vehicle, as is common at major events, organizers will have little choice but to provide a large fleet of private cars. If, on the other hand, an efficient system for encouraging car pooling among officials can be arranged and publicized beforehand as part of the green games effort, it may well be possible to get most VIPs to agree to depart from the standard and extremely wasteful procedure.

The official vehicle fleet and shuttle bus service are areas where the use of alternative vehicles should be explored. This may be a tremendous opportunity to test and to publicize the use of cleaner fuels, electric vehicles, etc. Organizers should seek sponsors from these sectors.

Public Transportation at Sydney 2000: A Resounding Success

Getting Sydney 2000 Olympic spectators, volunteers and staff out of their cars and onto public transport was identified early on as the key to getting people where they needed to go in an efficient and environmentally sustainable manner. To accomplish this objective, a number of steps were required:

1. Expand the rail and bus infrastructure to accommodate more people.

2. Tightly integrate transportation planning between different agencies.

3. Set up dedicated trains, buses and park-and-ride lots.

4. Ban private parking at Olympic venues.

5. Provide integrated Olympic transit passes as part of event tickets.

6. Educate the traveling public about the above and about the importance of leaving their cars at home.

A dedicated agency, the Olympic Roads and Transit Authority (ORTA) was eventually created to handle and coordinate all transportation-related issues.

New infrastructure built for the Games included:

◆   a new permanent rail link from city to airport; and

◆   new permanent rail infrastructure serving Homebush Bay area, including a dedicated line into the heart of Sydney Olympic Park, served by a new rail station capable of handling up to 50,000 passengers per hour.

Other Olympic transportation intiatives included:

◆   bicycle paths connecting Homebush Bay and Sydney Olympic Park with the neighboring community;

◆   bicycle storage areas at most venues and marked walking routes; and

◆   clean fuel vehicles integrated into the Olympic Bus Fleet (low sulphur diesel), Olympic Village Fleet (compressed natural gas) and Olympic Park official shuttles (electric and solar-powered buggies).

Games-time performance figures available at the time of printing indicate that:

◆   4.47 million people traveled to Sydney Olympic Park by public transit over the 19 days of the Olympics and 1.1 million during the Paralympics (approx. 75% by rail; 25% by bus).

◆   1.5 million people traveled to outlying venues, predominantly by rail or bus.

◆   29.5 million CityRail trips were taken over the 19 days of the Olympics, compared with a "normal" 13.8 million for a similar time period in September/October.

The fact that only a handful of minor difficulties and delays arose throughout the entire Games period is a testament to the effectiveness of the transport plan.

Alternatives to Motorized Vehicles

The option to which far too little thought is devoted is the use of non-motorized vehicles and the encouragement of self-propulsion. Put simply, how can people be encouraged to cycle, walk or roller blade to an event or a site? We have already looked at one of the primary solutions: better siting. The other is intimately connected with the Active Living philosophy — the idea that by taking the active approach to whatever you do, not only will you be fitter for it, your health and that of your environment will also benefit. This type of approach must be encouraged as part of greening sport, and there is no better starting block than transportation.

It is striking how few people ride bicycles to watch, for example, a soccer match. Why not? In addition to a host of sociological reasons that we can't even begin to discuss here, there are several purely logistical obstacles, namely, too much car traffic, dangerous access roads and a lack of secure parking. Steps to address the traffic problems have been explored, but what about better facilities for cyclists? For spectators at a major stadium, better bicycle routes should be designated and ample and secure parking areas provided. Cyclists should be able to park much closer to the stadium, as they take up little space and contribute little to congestion. In the case of more participatory sport clubs and facilities, providing safe parking and good locker rooms are the principal ways to encourage cycling.

Games organizers and facilities managers must make a conscious effort to encourage non-motorized travel. They will benefit from fewer traffic and parking-related expenses and problems; in fact, they might argue that fewer car parking spaces need to be provided if more people are coming by a more active means. For those who are unable to walk or propel their own vehicles, rickshaws and tri-shaws — until recently thought of as quaint artifacts of poor countries are being seen more and more in modern urban areas. Among their advantages: they are quiet, emission-less and require less space than cars.

Athletes, spectators and journalists attending an event in a smaller town or city could easily cycle to many of the venues if bicycles are provided by organizers or made available for an attractive rental price. There is a tremendous opportunity here for the entrepreneurial bicycle rental business. Some cities have free "city bikes" available for public use at prominent locations, such as rail stations. Visitors should be informed when such a service exists, and special arrangements made to have a "city bike" rack installed at convenient locations for sport events and facilities.

What You Can Do

A Summary of Transportation Recommendations

- Limit the number of vehicles in your fleet and the frequency of use.

- Explore options for alternative fuels and vehicles.

- Choose vehicles for durability, reparability, emissions and efficiency.

- Limit pollution from operation, maintenance and repairs.

- Encourage use of public transport and non-motorized vehicles.

- Work with municipal and transit officials to limit congestion and noise around sporting venues and during events.

- Protect participants from adverse effects of vehicle pollution.

- Prohibit smoking in transport vehicles.

What to Use

Helpful publications

Active Living — Go for Green. 1996. *Developing communities for active transportation.*

————. 1996b. *Retrofitting communities for sustainable and healthy active transportation.*

Markowitz, Frank; Estrella, Alex. July 1998. Campus Moves. Planning Magazine: **http://www.planning.org/pubs/july98.htm**

Whitlock, Edward. 1992. *Parking for institutions and special events.*

Useful web sites

American Council for an Energy Efficient Economy: **www.greenercars.com**

Eno Foundation: **www.enotrans.com**

Go for Green: **http://www.goforgreen.ca/active_transportation/index.html**

Second Nature: **www.secondnature.org/resource_center/resource_center_biblio.html**

Sustrans: **www.sustrans.org**

U.S. Environmental Protection Agency: **www.epa.gov/autoemissions**

Chapter

12

Event Planning, Operations, Services and Facilities

Sport events of any size can be planned and managed more sustainably. While the "green games" initiatives of major events like the Olympics may have garnered most of the publicity, there is no reason why a smaller local event or a medium-sized regional event, whether single-sport or multiple sport, cannot implement an environmental program and capture the benefits of doing so.

As previous chapters have indicated, there are many reasons why a sports event should be taking a more sustainable approach to planning, operations, services and facilities construction/preparation. From a purely defensive perspective, event organizers are increasingly being expected to act more sustainably: by the local community, by regulatory authorities, by national and international environmental groups and media, and, more recently, by sponsors who wish to be associated with positive rather than negative stories. The greatest reason for making sustainability a part of your game plan from the very start, however, are the many benefits you stand to realize, ranging from capital and operating cost savings, to reduced risks and its associated costs, to greater sponsorship appeal.

Elements of an Action Plan

Every event being different in size, type, geography and the demographic profile of participants and spectators, there is no universal one-size-fits-all environmental program. Every bidding and organizing committee will have to decide if it needs a Basic Action Plan or a Comprehensive Environmental Action Plan, and tailor its activities to meet the corresponding specific challenges and objectives.

Not all events/organizations will require a comprehensive environmental action plan, nor will they necessarily have the knowledge or resources to implement one. For smaller events, and those new to environmental management, a basic action plan may be sufficient. It is often better to tackle a smaller number of top priority issues, and to do a good job, than to achieve mixed results on an overly ambitious list of issues.

A Basic Action Plan comprising those issues that all event organizers should attempt to deal with is proposed below, followed by an example from the 1999 Canada Games. A more extensive sample Comprehensive Environmental Action Plan follows, to illustrate the scope of issues that might be addressed by a medium-to-large size event. The Sydney 2000 case study at the end of this chapter illustrates just how comprehensive a sustainable event program can be.

A Basic Action Plan

- Develop and approve an environmental policy.

- Define specific objectives and targets (measurable where possible) to deal with each priority issue.

- Adopt "green office" practices in all stages of planning and organizing: reduce the use of materials, re-use wherever possible and, finally, recycle

- Develop a waste reduction strategy for all venues.

- Involve suppliers, donors and sponsors in the "sustainable event" initiative.

- Reduce the amount of private car use by participants and spectators by emphasizing and facilitating the use of public and active transport means.

- Promote healthy conditions for sport (i.e. air and water quality) at venues and in the community.

- Promote conservation of energy and water in facilities and during operations.

- Protect sensitive green spaces and water bodies from development and excessive or inappropriate use.

- Publicize environmental efforts and achievements in the community and to a broader audience through the media.

A Comprehensive Environmental Action Plan

General

- Define sustainability policies, goals and objectives.

- Implement an environmental management system.

- Train and educate staff and volunteers.

- Involve suppliers, donors and sponsors in the "sustainable event" initiative.

Doing Something With Nothing:
1999 Canada Winter Games in Corner Brook

Corner Brook, the smallest community to ever hold the Canada Games proved it was up to the challenge. The Host Society also took on the challenge of producing the most extensive environmental action plan to date at a Canada Games. With little financial resources the environment committee developed several effective initiatives that relied on community partnerships and in-kind donations. The following is the Action Plan that was created by the Host Society.

Objective: To promote environmental responsibility and awareness prior to, during and after the 1999 Canada Winter Games. This will be done by:

- training all games staff in green office practices and green purchasing;
- training all volunteers in the environmental initiatives of the 1999 Games (e.g., direct participants and spectators to recycling bins);
- implementing a recycling program for the Athlete's Village as well as at all sport venues;
- composting all food wastage generated from the cafeteria;
- minimizing waste by purchasing items that may be reused (e.g., water bottles) and/or become a legacy after the Games (e.g., recycling bins);
- encouraging all spectators to use public transportation and/or car pool to decrease traffic congesting, noise pollution and exhaust;
- implementing a no idling policy for all Games vehicles;
- minimizing paper waste through double-side copying, electronic mail and computer faxing;
- minimizing water use through low-flow showerheads and other water-saving devices within the Village; and
- conserving energy through energy-efficient bulbs, timers, etc.

In conjunction with Sport Canada we will be preparing a list of indicators to evaluate our success with environmental initiatives at the Games. This will be added to a report that will also give guidelines/checklists for tackling environmental issues at future events.

Air Quality

- Select location and times for best air quality.
- Work with authorities to improve air quality for event.
- Minimize air pollution from transportation, pesticide applications and facilities operations.
- Take steps to improve indoor air quality through ventilation, smoking bans and careful review of cleaners, paints, solvents, furniture, etc.

Water Quality

- Select location and times for best water quality.
- Work with authorities to improve water quality for event.
- Minimize water pollution from facilities construction and operations, landscaping and turf management, boats, etc.

Land and Water Use

- Carefully select sites for facilities construction and event activities in order to prevent harm to fragile ecosystems and protected spaces.

- Build on and rehabilitate degraded land where possible.

- Clean up and take steps to protect water bodies used for events and facilities.

- Minimize water consumption through conservation.

- Revegetate with natural species wherever possible.

Waste Management

- Reduce waste generation from construction and demolition through purchasing practices, reduction, reuse and recycling.

- Reduce solid waste generation from event activities through purchasing practices, reduction, reuse, recycling, and composting.

Energy Management

- Minimize energy consumption through facility design, conservation and efficient technologies, transportation plans.

- Explore on-site clean energy (renewables such as solar and wind) generation possibilities.

Facility Use

- Reduce energy consumption.

- Reduce water consumption.

- Seek to maintain high indoor air quality.

- Avoid hazardous materials in maintenance and operations.

Transportation Services

- Encourage and facilitate alternatives to private car transportation, including shuttles, public transit and active means (i.e. cycling).

- Provide efficient, clean-fuel vehicles.

Accommodation Services

- Encourage water and energy conservation and waste reduction in all accommodations.

- Promote use of certified "green" hotels, etc.

Facility Design

♦ Promote renovation and reuse.

♦ Promote appropriate design for the long term, including multiple use, adaptability, durability.

♦ Promote sustainable design elements, including energy and water conservation and waste reduction.

♦ Select materials for impact and cost over their full life cycle.

Transportation Design

♦ Design system to encourage alternative modes of transportation including public and active modes.

♦ Include in fleet purchase/lease decisions such environmental attributes as fuel efficiency, emission controls and clean fuels.

Accommodation Design

♦ Promote renovation and reuse.

♦ Promote appropriate design for the long term, including multiple use, adaptability, durability.

♦ Promote sustainable design elements, including energy and water conservation and waste reduction.

♦ Select materials for life cycle attributes and costs.

Construction: Materials and Systems

♦ In selection of materials and mechanical systems, promote such environmental attributes as: durability, recyclability, recycled content, hazardous content, reparability and life cycle impacts and costs.

Accommodations

It is generally only with a major event that accommodation services are provided. Participants tend to be lodged in hotels, school residences or, on rare occasions, a specially-constructed athletes' village. In each of these cases, the opportunity for event organizers to exercise some control differs. An athletes' village can be constructed to meet organizers' demands; a university residence will typically allow and even welcome a certain degree of renovation or retrofitting; a hotel might consider only minor special requests.

When accommodation has been commissioned especially for an event, the organizer has a unique opportunity to build housing that meets as many as possible of the objectives for more sustainable facilities covered in chapters 7 and 8, such as passive solar design, energy and water conservation, aesthetics, natural light, healthy materials.

Two Models of Sustainable Accommodation: Sydney Olympics and Grande Prairie Canada Games

Each event will have different needs in terms of athlete housing, but in all cases some form of sustainable accommodations can be arranged as is illustrated in the following two examples. At the Canada Games in Grande Prairie, Alberta, the organizers realized that the city should not be constructing a permanent athletes' village, as there would be no use for the accommodations after the event. Instead, they rented mobile home bunkhouses from various mining and oil exploration sites and spruced them up by attaching western style heritage storefront entrances to the bunkhouses.

In preparation for the Sydney 2000 Olympic Games, an opportunity was created to build a permanent sustainable urban development that would temporarily serve as the athlete's village during the Games. At the time of the Olympics, the athletes' village was the world's largest solar-powered suburb. After providing accommodation for the athletes and officials during the Olympics and Paralympics, the Village grew to become a new suburb with up to 2000 permanent dwellings and housing an estimated 5,000 people.

Passive solar design, solar powered cells, highly efficient land use and responsible water and waste management were highlights of the Village design. During the Olympics the athletes used 650 of the permanent dwellings and 500 specially designed modular homes. Afterwards, these modular homes were sold and removed from the site.

With a rented residential building, organizers can request that a number of changes be made. Since these changes will generally be paid for by the event organizer, will remain in the building after the event and will almost always save the residence owner additional money down the road, the organizer can demand and will usually receive considerable latitude to renovate and retrofit. Changes might include better-quality and more efficient lighting, installation of low-flow water fixtures, improved air circulation, upgrading of cafeteria facilities and remodeling all of which can improve the sustainability of the facility.

With a commercial hotel or motel, organizers can request changes to various services, such as housekeeping, restaurants and cafeterias, and the types of amenities offered. Organizers who bring good business to a hotel will have a surprising amount of leverage, especially if their requests will ultimately benefit the hotel. They should use the opportunity to emphasize that they are trying to run a sustainable event, and that any efforts on the part of the hotel to contribute to this goal will be both appreciated and publicly recognized.

The provider of accommodations should address these issues:

- **Purchasing.** Materials and supplies should meet green purchasing guidelines. Suppliers should be invited to join as partners in the environmental effort by meeting criteria for environmentally-preferred products, including packaging.

- **Energy efficiency.** All possible steps should be taken to reduce the amount of energy consumed by the facility and to encourage users to do the same.

- **Water conservation.** Water consumption can be greatly cut by retrofitting and better conservation practices.

- **Transportation.** Accommodation should be situated as close as possible to the sport venues in order to reduce transportation demands. Where good public transportation is not available or appropriate, bus shuttles should be provided.

- **Hazardous materials.** Staff, accommodation users and the environment will benefit from efforts to reduce or eliminate hazardous materials and products, especially in areas such as housecleaning chemicals, kitchen products, and transportation and equipment maintenance.

- **Waste reduction.** The amount of waste produced should be addressed by a waste reduction and management plan. Though the emphasis should be on reduction and reuse, facilities for recycling should always be provided.

An area of particular opportunity is the standard, but wasteful, practice of changing sheets, towels and amenities such as soap and shampoo on a daily basis. Many hotels are now rethinking their daily housekeeping routines to reduce waste and work and save money. Visitors who stay more than one night are asked to place a sign on their door handle indicating if a sheet and towel change is required. Bathroom amenities are in refillable rather than disposable containers.

Choosing Green Hotels

Commercial providers of accommodation, whether for athletes or visitors, can be brought into the environmental partnership, if they aren't already. Various bodies within the hotel and tourism industry have developed certification programs for recognizing "green hotels". The International Hotels Environment Initiative and the UNEP Tour Operators Initiative are among many such programs worldwide. Organizing committees can encourage this trend by encouraging all local hotels to work toward such certification, and by rewarding those who achieve it by recognizing them as "preferred" in some way. The Salt Lake City 2002 Organizing Committee (SLOC) is working closely with local hotels and motels to make the local industry more sustainable.

Medical and First Aid Services

Most sport events are required to provide medical or at least emergency first aid services. While safety and hygiene must take precedence, they are not necessarily incompatible with being green. Medical supplies should be ordered in bulk packs, with as little individual wrapping as is necessary for hygiene. Other practices should be reviewed. In some regions, for example, it is law for an ambulance to be present at a sporting event above a certain size. That ambulance is legally obligated to be kept running at all times, as if the split second required to start the engine might make a difference between life and death. This absurd and anachronistic practice may date from a time when a crank was required to start the engine. Surely it is time to change this law before the idling ambulance actually creates more casualties than it saves lives.

Food Services

The single greatest source of solid waste at a sport event or facility is food-related: the mountains of disposable packaging, dinnerware and utensils, not to mention food itself produced by the snack bars, cafeterias and restaurants. The invention of disposable cups, plates and wrappers was a godsend for fast-food sellers and the events that share their profits. Thanks to the speed of service made possible by these throwaway containers, huge numbers of people could be served in a short period of time.

But there's no free lunch. In most cases facilities operators are now required to pay the waste handling costs of the concessionaires who have been contracted to provide food services.

Clearly the fastest and cheapest solution is through reduction. By generating less disposable garbage, food service operations can save a lot of money in packaging never purchased, clean-up costs reduced and waste disposal fees slashed. Although the solutions will differ for each type of facility — restaurant, cafeteria or snack bar — they share the similar goal of finding appropriate, and not prohibitively expensive, ways of reducing, reusing and recycling.

> ### Super Bowl Waste Reduction
>
> The Super Bowl events generate a prodigious amount of waste in a very short period of time. The Super Bowl XXIX Environmental Program in Miami was developed to divert waste away from the local landfills and have it sent to regional recycling facilities and non recyclable materials were processed at waste-to-energy plants. Through the cooperation of event planners, waste haulers, and more than a hundred volunteers supplied by the Tropical Audubon Society, more than 300 tonnes of solid waste were diverted from overcrowded landfills. Recycling during the Super Bowl week left a legacy in South Florida. Officials from the Joe Robbie Stadium were active partners in setting up this project and planned to permanently incorporate recycling into future stadium events.

The first step a facility/event can take is to make the concessionaire responsible for the amount of waste generated by having them share the expense of waste management. There is no quicker way to get a snack bar operator looking for solutions than to contractually oblige them to pay for their garbage. The first place they will look is to their own suppliers—soft drink companies, cup, utensil and condiment sellers—for assistance. In this way, the effect of raising the cost of generating waste can be to send an incentive right up the entire production process. Producers, wholesalers, retailers, marketers and facilities owners will benefit from working together to find solutions.

Summary of Key Waste Reduction Targets for Food Service Operators

- ◆ Eliminate the use of disposable items. For those items that cannot be eliminated entirely, use reusable, washable alternatives.

- ◆ Consider waxed paper instead of plates for fast food (hot dogs, etc.).

- ◆ Eliminate single-serving condiments. Items such as sugar, creamers, ketchup and salad dressing are more expensive to buy in this wasteful form of packaging. Serve them in jugs, bowls or bulk dispensers.

◆ Serve drinks in reusable cups/mugs. Work with suppliers and sponsors to develop and promote the use of a practical and durable cup or mug.

◆ Order food and supplies in bulk wherever possible.

◆ Follow green purchasing guidelines to work with suppliers to reduce packaging and develop environmentally-preferred products.

◆ Refuse excess packaging on all supplies and products.

◆ Serve sealed drinks in recyclable bottles or cans.

◆ Recycle tins, bottles, jars and paper products.

◆ Compost food waste.

What food is served in or on is important, but equally so is the type of food itself. Where does it come from? How was it grown? And what was it treated with? These are all relevant questions, though not traditionally ones that food-service operators have worried about. Certainly in the case of elite athletes eating at a cafeteria, it seems ironic to be serving pesticide-laden produce to people who are obsessed with health and performance. Most athletes try to follow the strictest of diets at home but are forced to eat whatever is available when away. It seems paradoxical that extraordinary measures are taken to protect athletes from intentional food poisoning, while institutionalized poisoning of food through chemical treatment is entirely ignored.

Cafeterias and restaurants for athletes should work to serve organically-grown produce. By doing so they will improve not only the health of the consumer, but the health of the soil, air and water in farming communities. Organic food is inevitably more expensive because the consumer is paying the true cost of its production. By taking a firm stand in favor of organic food, you can make a strong statement in favor of healthier farming practices while at the same time bringing down prices by expanding demand.

The food-service operator should favor local produce. Food produced locally requires less energy to transport and generally stays fresher with less refrigeration and fewer preservatives.

Sustainable Kitchen Practices

◆ Purchase environmentally-preferred products and equipment.

◆ Eliminate energy waste by purchasing more efficient equipment and doing regular cleaning and maintenance.

◆ Review pre-heating practices and implement new schedules or automatic equipment to limit the amount of heat wasted.

◆ Load ovens and dishwashers to capacity to conserve energy.

◆ Review all cooking and cleaning practices to identify areas where heating, cooling and water demands can be reduced.

◆ Identify substitutes for hazardous cleaning chemicals.

◆ Carefully store and dispose of hazardous materials that may be essential.

◆ Reduce water use through improved procedures and equipment.

VIP Services

High-level officials, politicians and other dignitaries are accustomed to receiving special treatment at sport events. Organizers are accustomed to delivering it. The problem with VIP (very important person) treatment is that it is rarely questioned and can become excessive. VIPs are often treated to first-class travel, hotel accommodation and meals, private car transportation, hospitality suites and gifts from the event organizers or host organization. All of this can be a significant added expense for organizers.

There is no reason why dignitaries and officials, however lofty their title, should be excluded from the goals of making sport more sustainable; some, who could easily live without many of these customary trappings, might even welcome it. Of course there may be others who take offence at any such notion. Organizers will have to use their best judgment in greening the VIPs. Three areas where progress might be most easily made are:

Transportation

All private vehicles for VIPs should follow the same guidelines as other cars in the fleet: fuel efficiency, maintenance, no idling, etc. In addition, it may be possible (except in cases of extreme security) to arrange for dignitaries to share vehicles, either by riding together or by drawing from a fleet, rather than assigning a separate car to each person.

Food services

The food service guidelines and kitchen practices outlined above should apply equally to the dining areas and catering service for VIPs. While disposable cutlery and crockery is less of an issue, waste may appear in another form: excess food. Efforts should be made to accurately estimate food demands and to collect and compost leftovers.

Gifts

It is standard practice for organizers, host organizations and governments to give gifts to visiting officials. These may range from the token to the outlandish. Organizers should make an effort to seek appropriate gifts that are likely to be used and which do not waste rare resources. They should also consider giving alternative gifts, that is gifts which are a service or a gesture, rather than a material object. These might include planting a tree in the recipients name or making a donation to a local sport group or a charity of the recipient's choice. These may be unusual gestures, but it is precisely this uniqueness that could make alternative gift-giving a popular new approach.

Signs and Banners

A tremendous number of signs, banners, posters and other means of directing people and identifying places are used at events/facilities. In the case of events, these are typically used once and thrown away—an expensive and wasteful practice. Event organizers stand to realize significant savings by developing means to:

- reduce the number of signs required to achieve the desired effect;

- reuse these same signs at subsequent events, give them to other events who can make use of them, or find a recipient who can reuse the materials; and

- recycle those signs that cannot be reused.

Greener Signs and Banners

Various ways exist to reduce the number and size of signs: accurate forecasting of needs, not blanketing the same area with signs which are ultimately lost amid the clutter, and using better graphics and symbols to improve the function and visibility of signs without having to make them large or too numerous.

Signs, banners and posters can all be reused if produced in a generic format that does not contain information which will be obsolete by the time they are required again. Spaces can be left for adding information such as the date, names of sponsors, etc. Specific measures might include:

- banners to identify the start, finish, registration, and first aid sites which do not have the date and name of sponsors. This can be attached if need be by velcro, tape or other means;

- posters for a regular or annual event with a strong graphic image or logo, to which additional information can be attached each year;

- signs for guiding people which have movable arrows and word directions that can be stuck on and peeled off. Computer-generated graphics and directions can be printed onto material that can be stuck onto a standard backing;

- durable posts and backing material which can be used many times; and

- brackets for holding signs and banners might be left in place on lamps or posts with the permission and cooperation of appropriate officials.

These are just some of the possible solutions that imaginative event organizers might come up with to deal with this solid waste problem. Ultimately, all materials that have outlived their usefulness will need to be disposed of. By ensuring that only recyclable materials have been used, it is a simple step to divert such signs and banners to the appropriate recycling facility.

Technology Services

Facilities and event organizers are regularly called upon to provide a range of technical support: computing equipment, electronic information systems, video and audio facilities, darkrooms and much more. In each of these cases, there are probably steps that can be taken to make these services more environmentally sustainable. Computing systems were discussed in Chapter 6. Similarly, applying sustainable thinking to other technologies can help to reduce energy consumption, avoid hazardous materials and reduce, reuse and recycle. The darkroom, for example, is an area where a lot of work has gone into developing less harmful materials and to capturing and reusing chemicals so as to limit water pollution. This is just the tip of the iceberg. Organizers and facilities managers, in partnership with suppliers and users of these services, can surely go even further in implementing more sustainable technological services.

Ceremonies and Cultural Events: Make a Splash, not Trash

Sport events tend to feature three types of ceremony apart from the principal sporting attraction: ceremonies to mark the opening and closing of an event; entertainment during breaks in the action, such as pre-game and half-time shows; and ceremonies for the purpose of presenting awards. Several decades of unabashed excess have made many Olympic games ceremonies notorious displays of over-commercialism. In organizing the Lillehammer games, the Norwegians seemed to be delivering a message to the world: be genuine about who you are, have some fun, and the rest will follow. So let's look at how the various ceremonies in sport might be made saner and sustainable.

Opening and Closing Ceremonies

In sport, it is the start of an event that is most frequently celebrated, although some major events also hold a closing ceremony. At its very simplest, the ceremony might include the singing of an anthem, the raising of a flag, and some ritual greetings or handshakes. At its most extravagant, there might be marching bands, parading athletes, choreographed spectacles of dance, fireworks and laser shows. These are the sorts of rituals that help to make an occasion memorable. Such ceremonies can be noisy and wasteful, but this does not have to be the case.

As a manager working with game organizers, you can take steps to control the volume of sound produced and the way in which it is directed, even the most music-filled ceremony need not become a disturbance. You can make yourself knowledgeable about levels of decibel tolerance and health, and you can work with capable sound technicians who share your views. Good sound production can make use of the acoustics of a venue to ensure that all spectators receive a high quality of sound. Announcements should be kept to a minimum, emphasizing clarity and conveying information rather than trying to fill dead air time.

Fireworks add more than a visual display: they are a common source of loud noise. Rare indeed is a ceremony these days without fireworks. If a sport event is to match the typical national-day display that most people see, organizers will have to spend a lot of money and create a lot of noise and smoke. But if ceremonies organizers wish to get the best bang for their buck, they should limit their use of fireworks to several impressive volleys carefully incorporated into the program. They should seek color and light in place of noise.

Pollution is another potential byproduct of ceremonies, from the smoke produced by fireworks to the tens of thousands of "flash cards" which are given to spectators to hold up at a given moment. To work toward reducing waste that is exclusive to ceremonies, you can get together with event designers and props people to examine the materials needed to stage the production. These might include costumes, props, stages, sets and other single-use items. It is hard to stage a good performance without many of these, and there is no reason not to. What you can do as a manager is to carefully review the potential post-ceremony use to which many of these materials can be put. Will props and sets be sold or donated so that they can be reused? Will costumes be kept and worn by performers or donated to a theatrical company? Have efforts been made to use environmentally preferred materials to make costumes, props and sets?

Local Event Organizers Can Make a Difference: The Winterlude Triathlon

For practical and financial reasons, rather than explicitly environmental, organizers of Ottawa's Winterlude triathlon in the late 80s and early 90s, took the approach of minimizing waste, maximizing resource efficiency and guaranteeing optimal health conditions for participants. The result was a remarkably "green" event. Organizer Glenda Jones was matter of fact about their approach: "If we don't protect the environment, we can't hold the event." The triathlon is held primarily on public parkland where rules regarding litter, damage to natural habitat and the disturbance of wildlife all apply.

Steps taken for environmental and economic reasons, as well as to protect the health of the participants, included:

- mapping out courses to avoid sensitive spots;
- conducting a thorough clean-up after the event;
- keeping the size of the participants' race kit small;
- using recycled paper;
- advising out-of-town competitors to use a toll-free number for hotel/tourism information in place of mailing large packages of brochures;
- arranging start times to avoid bus fumes along the running course;
- banning the idling of vehicles;
- forbidding smoking at the start/finish line;
- producing T-shirts for racers the night before to assure the right number;
- purchasing local products (less transportation), in bulk (less packaging);
- doing without an "unnecessary" start/finish banner;
- producing signs on reusable corrugated plastic backing; and
- handing out small medals and "useful" gifts and prizes.

Most ceremonies have souvenir programs. Organizers should review the demand for this type of item. An accurate estimate of the true demand might save in printing costs and keep a lid on waste. The sustainable printing practices found in Chapter Eight cover the principal means of limiting waste and ensuring that more sustainable materials are used.

Travel and Tourism Information

Tourism information is a principal example of where modern technology and good common sense can be married to reduce waste and costs. Out-of-town registrants for an event, and sometimes even local ones, are often automatically sent accommodation and tourism brochures. Recipients promptly throw out most of these. This cost and waste can be avoided by having people specifically request such information on their registration forms. Or, best of all, by providing them with the toll-free telephone number or web site address of the local tourism authority, organizers can avoid having to handle such material entirely.

What You Can Do

See Basic Action Plan and Comprehensive Action Plan above.

What to Use

Helpful publications

Olympic Environment Forum. 2001. *Sydney 2000 Olympic and Paralympic Games environmental benchmarks.*

Earth Council. 2001. E*nvironmental performance of the Olympic Co-ordination Authority: Fourth and final review.*

Sydney 2000. September 2000. *The environmental games: Environmental achievements of the Sydney 2000 Olympic Games* (color brochure and CD).

Greenpeace. September 2000. *Greenpeace Olympic environmental guidelines: a guide to sustainable events.*

Greenpeace. September 2000. *How green the games? Greenpeace's environmental assessment of the Sydney 2000 Olympics.*

Olympic Co-ordination Authority. 1999. *Compendium of ESD initiatives and outcomes. Edition 2.*

Salt Lake Olympic Organizing Committee. 2000. *Environmental annual report 2000.*

Sydney Organizing Committee for the Olympic Games. 1999. *Environment Report: Turning Green into Gold – making an environmental vision a reality*

Sport Canada. 1999. *Environmental management and monitoring for sports events — A practical toolkit for managers.*

Stubbs, D. 2001. *Sydney Olympic Games 2000: The environmental games — A review of the environmental achievements of the "Best Olympic Games ever."*

Stubbs, D., and D. Chernushenko. 1999. *Environmental guidelines for golf events.*

Useful web sites and resources

Committed to Green Foundation: **www.committedtogreen.org**

Global Responsibility Communications Platform: **www.global-responsibility.com**

The Sustainable Sport Source: **www.greengold.on.ca**

Greenpeace Australia: **www.greenpeace.org.au**

Hotel Asociation of Canada's Green Leaf Eco-Rating Program: **www.terrachoice.homestead.com/Background.html**

International Hotel Environment Initiative (IHEI), 15-16 Cornwall Terrace, Regent's Park, London NW1 4QP U.K. Tel +44 (0) 171 467 3620 Fax +44 (0) 171 467 3610

Olympic Coordination Authority: **www.oca.nsw.gov.au/**

Olympic Coordination Authority Ecology Programs: **www.oca.nsw.gov.au/ecology**

Salt Lake Organizing Committee: **www.saltlake2002.com**

Tour Operators Initiative for Sustainable Tourism Development: **www.toinitiative.org/**

UNEP Tourism Links: **www.unepie.org/tourism/wwwlinks.html**

World Tourism Organization: **www.world-tourism.org/frameset/frame_sustainable.html**

Case Study

Sydney 2000: A Pioneer in Integrating Sustainable Development

Never before have the principles of sustainable development been put into practice on such a large scale as by the organizers of the Sydney 2000 Summer Olympic Games. This pioneering effort, though by no means perfect, was nonetheless successful in many ways, and offers a number of useful lessons.

How did it happen? A brief history.

In 1992, the Sydney bid committee was persuaded by environmental groups, spearheaded by Greenpeace, to develop a "Green Games" bid, using the environment as a unique selling point to IOC voters. The bid featured innovative facility designs, notably an Athletes Village that was solar-powered, conserved resources, used non-toxic and recycled materials, used land wisely, and profiled leading environmental technologies.

A set of "Environmental Guidelines for the Summer Olympic Games" was developed by a team of experts including Greenpeace, alternative power and waste experts, sustainable building designers, academics and government regulators. The Guidelines were submitted as part of the bid, with Sydney committing to implement them, if it won.

Sydney won, by a mere two votes, over notoriously polluted Beijing. IOC President Juan Antonio Samaranch later observed, "The Olympic Games in the year 2000 were awarded to the city of Sydney, Australia, partly because of the consideration they gave to environmental matters."

Translating Commitment into Action

Upon being awarded the Games, Sydney 2000 organisers were faced with the daunting challenge of turning the general commitments contained in the Environmental Guidelines into concrete action.

Appropriate structures and processes had to be developed to ensure that sustainable development practices were integrated into all planning and decision making.

Vision

While the Guidelines provided vision, inspiration and a checklist of ideas, they were not an action plan. Never on such a scale, had any organization attempted to integrate

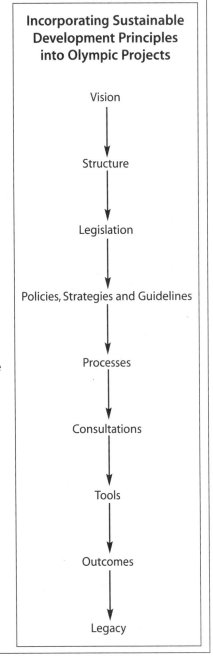

Incorporating Sustainable Development Principles into Olympic Projects

Vision → Structure → Legislation → Policies, Strategies and Guidelines → Processes → Consultations → Tools → Outcomes → Legacy

the principles of sustainable development into all of its decisions and activities. Sydney 2000 would be charting new territory, and doing so with the eyes of citizens, environmental groups, the media and, indeed, the world following their successes, and failures.

Structure

Sydney 2000 consisted of three main bodies. These included two New South Wales (NSW) government bodies — the Olympic Co-ordination Authority (OCA), and the Olympic Roads and Transport Authority (ORTA) — and the Sydney Organizing Committee for the Olympic Games (SOCOG).

Their respective roles can be simplified in this way:

- ◆ OCA had primary responsibility for "building the stage": designing, developing and managing Games venues and facilities.
- ◆ ORTA delivered the transportation solutions, including new infrastructure.
- ◆ SOCOG "put on the show": planning and staging the Games.

Legislation

Sydney 2000 was subject to a host of existing laws and regulations, governing development and construction. Several new laws were also passed, establishing the integration of sustainable development as a fundamental "outcome" for Olympic developments.

Policies, Strategies and Guidelines

Both OCA and SOCOG developed their own Environment Policies, based around the original Guidelines but reflecting their particular concerns (See Chapter 4). These Policies were communicated to the public and to other stakeholders, who were expected to respect, if not actively support, them. The OCA was most successful in this regard, exercising greater contractual leverage over developers and builders than SOCOG was willing or able to with its suppliers and sponsors. SOCOG's "softer" approach did, however, elicit support for its initiatives from a number of corporate partners (See Chapter 6).

Early in the planning process, the OCA produced the Homebush Bay Development Guidelines, to assist developers, designers, planners and managers in the implementation of more sustainable development. These Guidelines, prepared through broad consultation, established principles for implementing sustainable development under three key performance areas:

- ◆ **Conservation of Species** — flora, fauna, people and their environment
- ◆ **Conservation of Resources** — water, energy, materials, open space and soil
- ◆ **Pollution control** — air, noise, light, water, soil and waste management

A Transport Strategy, Structure Plan and Landscape Strategy were also prepared to integrate all elements of land use, movement of people and design and management of the natural and built environment at Homebush Bay.

Processes

All OCA projects were obliged to follow a procedure that included both externally governed environmental compliance processes, and processes or systems created by the OCA to ensure statutory compliance and a high level of environmental performance, in line with high public expectations.

- ◆ The OCA, to ensure that Olympic venues and facilities were developed in accordance with its commitments, developed an Environmental Management System (EMS) that complies with the international standard ISO 14001.

- The OCA's Environmental Tender Specification (ETS) required all tenderers (bidders on individual projects) to demonstrate how they would comply with OCA's environmental commitments. Rather than prescribing specific environmental measures, technologies or materials, the ETS encouraged all tenderers to strive for environmental innovation as part of their bid to win the contract. SOCOG used a similar process in selecting and contracting with its suppliers.

Consultation

No single organization was responsible for the successes (or failures) of the Sydney 2000 environmental programme. The "green team" included a wide range of partners, including government bodies, interest groups, local citizens, industry associations and sponsors. It was essential that the principal organizing bodies — OCA, SOCOG and ORTA — consult and communicate on a regular basis, in order to coordinate and collaborate on their various initiatives. Government bodies — federal, state and local — were also involved in planning, approvals and enforcement roles.

- External consultation was a valuable — though not always smooth — part of the process. OCA initially convened a series of advisory committees, including a general environment group and a series of expert groups on issues such as energy and waste.

- In 1997, the Olympic Environment Forum (OEF) was created as a consultative forum convened jointly by OCA and SOCOG, with a diverse membership, including environment and local community groups.

- As a mechanism for consulting with the neighboring community on the long-term remediation strategy for Homebush Bay, OCA established the Homebush Bay Environment Reference Group (HomBERG).

- Green Games Watch 2000, a coalition of environmental groups funded by the NSW and Federal governments was established in 1995 to provide input and independent monitoring/reporting on the implementation of the Environmental Guidelines. It participated in the OEF and HomBERG.

- Greenpeace Australia maintained an active Olympics campaign to monitor, encourage action, provide expert contributions and criticize OCA and SOCOG.

Tools

A number of tools were developed by OCA to facilitate and evaluate its progress in meeting environmental commitments:

- Environmental Management Plans were required for all venues and facilities, and for all stages of their development: design, construction, project management and operations.

- Regular and occasional reviews and audits were also conducted, each with specific objectives.

- External reviews were conducted by Green Games Watch 2000 and Greenpeace, and OCA commissioned independent reviews from the international environmental body, the Earth Council.

Outcomes

OCA produced and published a number of reports on its environmental objectives, practices and achievements. These included Annual Environment Reports and Quarterly Environmental Reports. A Compendium of Environmentally Sustainable Development Initiatives and Outcomes, was also produced to provide detailed environmental information on the development of Olympic venues and facilities.

SOCOG produced a comprehensive overview of its environmental activities and initiatives in its 1999 Environment Report — a first for an Olympic organizing committee. SOCOG also prepared a series of environmental information publications for the media and a general publication in advance of the Games. In its final report to the IOC, SOCOG provided an environmental report, containing recommendations for future organizers.

Building the Stage

The Environmental Guidelines contain 80 commitments in five general performance areas: Energy conservation; Water conservation; Waste avoidance and minimization; Pollution avoidance; and Protection of significant natural and cultural environments

Significant achievements were recorded in each of these performance areas, and in all of the different aspects and stages of planning and staging the Sydney 2000 Games: design, clean-up, monitoring, land management, construction of venues, transport, catering and waste management.

More sustainable practices were adopted and performance standards raised in all areas. Some of these general achievements are presented here. A number of detailed examples from Sydney 2000 venues can also be found in earlier chapters. Waste management initiatives are covered in detail in Chapter 11.

Energy Conservation

Leading energy conservation practices were commonly adopted, while less polluting and sometimes renewable energy sources were selected at a number of venues.

- Comprehensive efforts were made to use energy-efficient lighting, appliances and mechanical systems in all facilities.
- The majority of buildings are naturally ventilated and have significant natural lighting features.
- Energy efficient features in facilities will save approximately 10,000 tonnes of greenhouse gases per year.
- Air conditioning systems at the Aquatic Centre, SuperDome and Dome stadiums are designed to cool the air around the spectators, reducing the overall energy demand significantly.

Water Conservation

- All Olympic venues conserve water to some degree, through efficient appliances and fixtures, roof-fed rainwater tanks and drip irrigation systems.
- A dual water system at Sydney Olympic Park supplies drinkable water from the mains water supply through one set of pipes, and recycled water for flushing and irrigation from a parallel system of pipes, which has stormwater and treated "gray water" as its source.
- Landscaping favors native, drought-tolerant trees, shrubs and grass, to reduce water and mulching needs.

Pollution Avoidance

Steps to avoid pollution of air, water and soil took a variety of forms:

- extensive avoidance of PVC through the use of substitute materials for piping, cabling, stadium seating, furnishing, building finishes, etc.;

- strong emphasis on reducing off-gassing from building materials, finishes, etc. through selection of alternatives;

- reduction of pesticide risk to the aquatic environment by avoidance of broad-spectrum, high toxicity insecticides and selection of low-toxicity alternatives; and

- on-site generation of energy from renewable sources, as well as use of thermal hot water heaters (reducing the emission of greenhouse gases and a range of other air pollutants) and significant purchases of "green power" by many OCA facilities

Protection of the Natural and Cultural Environment

The Homebush Bay area lands were the subject of a major reclamation and regeneration scheme, encompassing woodlands, grasslands and water bodies. A new park — Millennium Park — was a key feature of the long-term Homebush Bay development and management plan:

- Significant areas of open space were preserved and sometimes expanded at many venues, with existing trees and bushes protected and many more planted.

- Efforts were made to protect various culturally significant features: i.e. Homebush Bay (Abattoir and brick pit) and North Newington (Armaments Depot).

- Careful consideration was given to Aboriginal concerns including significant sites and protection granted to natural features and artifacts.

Homebush Bay Remediation and Regeneration

A keystone of the Olympic commitment to more sustainable development was the choice of Homebush Bay as the site of the Sydney 2000 Olympic Park, with more than half of the Games venues to be located there. This 760-hectare site in the geographic and demographic center of Sydney has, over the past century, been used for a wide range of industrial purposes, including a brick pit, abattoir and a landfill for household, commercial and sometimes toxic waste.

The Big Clean-up

The OCA set out to turn the Homebush Bay precinct into an asset by bringing together the partners and the funding that would make a clean-up possible. Since 1994, A$137 million has been invested in clean up programs.

The OCA developed a remediation program to rejuvenate the natural environment and reduce risk to users, neighbouring residents and native plants and animals. Key issues included groundwater contamination, estuarine water quality, air quality, protection of habitat and native flora and fauna, and the safety of workers on site.

The approach was to relocate the non-toxic wastes to on-site mounds, which would be capped and closely monitored. A decision was made early on not to relocate waste, but to safely contain it and, where possible, treat it on site. Leachate, or liquid waste flowing from the landfills through drains, is now captured and pumped to nearby evaporation ponds, where it is decontaminated by natural processes, preventing it from reaching wetlands and waterways. Where necessary, more hazardous leachate is treated at a dedicated facility.

"Scheduled chemical waste," such as the dioxin- contaminated soils found on site, have been treated using an innovative soil cleaning process, which breaks down the contaminants into their relatively benign constituent parts. It has demonstrated how toxic waste can be safely treated without incineration.

Reviving Haslams Creek

Efforts to protect and enhance saltwater mangroves at Haslams Creek are an example of a commitment to protecting habitat and biodiversity, and to the reintroduction of indigenous flora and fauna at many of the Olympic sites.

Steps to revive Haslams Creek were integrated with the overall site regeneration and management plan. They included:

- redesigning the shorelines to include more natural curves and slopes;
- reintroducing tidal flushing by removing chokes, silt and walls;
- preventing leachate and litter from reaching the creek; and
- recreating ponds, wetlands and other habitat and replanting shorelines and wetlands with native species, to increase biodiversity.

Water Reclamation and Management Scheme

The Olympic Park at Homebush Bay is serviced by an ambitious site-wide water recycling plant called the Water Reclamation and Management Scheme or WRAMS. WRAMS sources sewage and storm water from within Homebush Bay and treats it for non-potable reuse at Homebush Bay venues. The $1.3 million system produces an estimated 800 million litres of treated water each year (the equivalent of 258 Olympic pools). This water is used for toilet flushing and irrigation and can provide 50% of the water needs for Homebush Bay and save $640,000 of potable mains water per year. It will also reduce the amount of sewage being discharged into local sewage systems and water bodies.

Millennium Parklands

Sydney's newest park, the 450 hectare Millennium Parklands, has been developed by linking existing parks and reserves (Bicentennial Park and Silverwater Nature Reserve), regenerating and protecting degraded remnant green spaces, and creating new green spaces, wetlands and water features in place of contaminated land and polluted water bodies.

The Parklands, to be Sydney's largest when complete, will showcase a diverse range of parkland, open space and natural habitat areas, integrating all of the public open space areas at Homebush Bay. Local residents and visitors will have full access to a variety of recreational facilities and spaces.

The Parklands include areas of natural significance (wetlands and woodlands) and cultural heritage significance, for which a long-term Conservation Management Plan has been developed. Creation of the Millennium Parklands is a 10-15 year process. The local community, as well as technical experts, have been closely involved in the development process, and will be in the management of the area.

Putting on the Show

Initiatives to "put on the show" — the Olympic and Paralympic Games — in a sustainable fashion fell into several major categories: transport, waste minimisation and management, energy conservation and management, pollution prevention, protection of the natural environment and education and awareness-raising activities. SOCOG's environmental staff took the lead role, in collaboration with OCA. Sponsors and suppliers and Games-time volunteers also played an important part.

Transport

Getting Olympic spectators, volunteers and staff out of their cars and onto public transport was identified early on as the key to moving people in an efficient and sustainable manner.

To accomplish this objective, six steps were required:

1. Expand the rail and bus infrastructure to accommodate more people.
2. Tightly integrate transportation planning between different agencies.
3. Set up dedicated trains, buses and park-and-ride lots.
4. Ban private parking at Olympic venues.
5. Provide integrated Olympic transit passes as part of event tickets.
6. Educate the traveling public about the above and about the importance of leaving their cars at home.

The fact that only a handful of minor difficulties and delays arose throughout the entire Games period is a testament to the effectiveness of the transport plan.

Other environmental initiatives included:

- bicycle storage areas at most venues and marked walking routes; and
- clean fuel vehicles as part of the Olympic Bus Fleet (low sulphur diesel), Olympic Village Fleet (compressed natural gas) and Olympic Park official shuttles (electric and solar-powered buggies)

Energy

Energy practice during the Games was largely determined by steps taken at the building stage: efficient design; use of natural lighting and ventilation; efficient mechanical systems and appliances; and integration of on-site renewable energy systems (photovoltaic panels and hot water heaters).

A significant Games-time step, however, was the commitment to source all electricity for competition venues from sponsor Energy Australia's "PureEnergy" — a product sourced from a combination of solar, wind and hydroelectric plants and landfill gas.

Showcase examples of renewable energy included a large array of solar panels at the SuperDome and on the "Towers of Power" lighting towers along the Olympic Boulevard. Especially visible to the athletes, were the rooftop solar panels providing electricity and hot water to the Athletes Village.

Probably the greatest contribution to energy efficiency, not to mention avoidance of air pollution, was the strong emphasis on public transit, as opposed to use of private vehicles.

Pollution Prevention

Initiatives to prevent pollution of air, water and soil during the Games included:

- limiting the use of products and materials that could pose a risk, either in their normal use, through accidents or in their eventual disposal;
- careful planning and handling and storage regimes to minimise the likelihood of spills or emissions, and the impact of such accidents, should one occur;
- reducing emissions of airborne pollutants through the use of renewable energy, cleaner fuels, public transit, etc.; and
- preventing pollution of water bodies and wastewater emissions through the comprehensive Water Reclamation and Management Scheme across the Homebush Bay site.

Protection of Natural Environment

Steps taken to protect the natural environment during the Games included:

- controlling or banning access of vehicles and people to areas deemed to be sensitive;
- constructing physical barriers to protect sensitive ecosystems, trees, water bodies, etc.;

- constructing durable surfaces where large groups of spectators would sit, stand or walk, and erecting barriers to keep spectators within these areas; and
- directing crowds to stay away from sensitive areas.

Education and Awareness

A series of education and awareness initiatives were implemented in advance of and during the Olympics targeted at various groups:

- The general public was targeted through environmental publicity initiatives via the media, web sites, brochures, programs, etc. Major messages included advance notice about using public transit, recycling and efforts to restore the Homebush Bay site.
- National and international media were provided with background materials and briefings, and an information center operated in the Main Press Center at Sydney Olympic Park throughout the Games.
- Athletes and officials received information about environmental aspects of the Games, and an IOC publication was produced specifically for athletes.
- All staff received environmental briefings upon joining SOCOG, the level of detail determined by their specific roles. Volunteers received a brief overview of the environmental initiatives and ways in which they could improve their own practices and direct spectators to do so.
- A Youth Camp was held during the Olympics for 500 representatives of Olympic nations, where the environment was a key theme.

Sponsors and Suppliers

SOCOG worked to involve sponsors and suppliers as positive contributors to the Games' environmental objectives. These efforts included:

- Creating an Olympic Sponsors Environment Network to encourage sharing of ideas, initiatives and challenges in a non-competitive atmosphere. A series of Network forums were held, where participants received presentations from environmental experts, environment groups, SOCOG staff and other Network members.
- Developing partnership initiatives and special environmental projects along with sponsors. These included: a major Olympic Landcare tree planting initiative and a Greener Sydney 2000 programme with support from sponsors; public awareness features during in-flight movies on Ansett flights; life cycle assessment work by sponsor BHP; and energy data collection for the Olympic Greenhouse Challenge by Energy Australia.
- A number of sponsors and suppliers chose to showcase more sustainable products and technology during the Games.

The Green Team

The Olympic "Green Team" had many players, some of them obvious and others less so. Each group/individual had its own unique objectives and its own ways of participating and contributing. All, however, played an important role in the successes and outcomes of the Sydney 2000 sustainable development effort. Key groups included:

- Employees
- Volunteers
- Environment/Sustainable Development Consultants
- Contractors

◆ Regulatory Authorities

◆ Environment Groups

◆ Auditors/Reviewers

◆ Sponsors and Suppliers

Outcomes

Not all of Sydney 2000's sustainable development accomplishments are measurable, but a list of those that can and have been quantified provides valuable performance measurements and "benchmark" data for other projects. These fall into three categories:

1. construction and upgrading of infrastructure, including site remediation and regeneration;

2. construction and renovation or retrofit of sport and other support facilities; and

3. actual achievements of systems and processes during the Olympic and Paralympic Games.

Infrastructure

Transportation

◆ A new permanent rail link built from city to airport and a new permanent rail infrastructure to serve Homebush Bay area.

Water and wastewater

◆ Water reclamation (WRAMS) scheme provides 800 million liters (50% of non-potable water needs) to Olympic Park venues and Newington Village.

Energy

◆ On-site generation of renewable electricity at Olympic Park: 1,350MWh/per year.

Pollution prevention

◆ Alternatives to PVC and hazardous/toxic products and materials successfully integrated into many facilities.

◆ Partial success in using non- or less-ozone-depleting refrigerants in facilities.

Protection of Natural Environment

◆ New parklands and open space created: more than 830 hectares in total, with Millennium Parklands totaling 450 hectares.

Facilities

Energy performance results

◆ Athletes Village — Homes consume 50% less than Australian norm; each home will generate most of its energy needs on an annual basis.

◆ Homebush Bay Hotels — 40% less than industry norm

◆ Sydney Showground — 20 % savings, equal to 1,750 tonnes of CO_2 per year

◆ SuperDome — 65% less than industry norm

Water conservation results

◆ Sydney Showground: 50% reduction

◆ SuperDome: 30% reduction

◆ All facilities have water conserving measures; average reductions approx. 20-40%

Waste management results

Construction and demolition waste recycling rate:

- Sydney Superdome: 98%; Sydney International Shooting Center: 87%; NSW Tennis Center: 60%; Athletes Village: 94%; Showgrounds: 60%; Stadium Australia: 70%.

Protection of Natural Environment

- Shooting Center used 350 cubic meters of recycled and salvaged hardwood (90% of needs), reducing demand for virgin timber.

Games Time

Transportation

- 4.47 million people traveled to Olympic Park by public transit over 19 days of Olympics, 1.1 million during Paralympics (approx. 75% by rail; 25% by bus).
- 1.5 million traveled to outlying venues, predominantly by rail or bus.
- 29.5 million CityRail trips were taken over 19 days, compared with a "normal" 13.8 million on the same dates in previous years.

Energy

- Renewable energy supplied to Olympics: 30GWh (100% of Olympic demand)
- Savings in greenhouse gases: 30,000 tonnes

Waste management

- Total waste generated: 5,010 tonnes
- Waste diversion rate: 68%
- Olympic paper consumption reduced by 40% from 45 million sheets (Atlanta 1996) to 29 million sheets — a saving of 16 million sheets (approximately 90 tonnes)

Pollution Prevention

- Alternatives to PVC were used for: 70,000 training manual binders, 130,000 volunteers' raincoats, 14000 square meters of banners, 60 km of fence fabric, 6.5 km of corrals, 48,000 signs, 10 km of facia panels.
- No significant pollution incidents were recorded, either external incidents that may have harmed participants or internal incidents of potential harm.

The Legacy

Anticipation of a positive "legacy" from hosting an Olympic Games or other major event is often one of the major selling points to the community and the taxpayer who typically ends up paying most of the costs. That legacy may include new facilities, infrastructure improvements and, in the best case, a small profit. But what about the environmental or sustainability legacy? What are the social, economic and environmental benefits? And are they outweighed by social, economic and environmental costs?

Although Sydney 2000's environmental efforts have received mixed reviews from various observers, the "sustainability legacy" of Sydney 2000 is, on balance, a positive one. Many of the more notable features of this legacy are as follows.

Bricks and Mortar

Homebush Bay and several western Sydney sites have undergone significant remediation and regeneration work, rendering them safe while at the same time protecting existing natural features/species and expanding biodiversity.

Sydney now boasts an expanded, modernized and more efficient public transit system, with new rail services between the city and both the airport and Homebush Bay.

Homebush Bay is serviced by the innovative WRAMS site-wide system for collecting and treating rainwater and wastewater and supplying it to commercial and residential users as non-potable water.

More than twenty new buildings incorporate features that use resources more efficiently. The buildings are healthier to users and offer long-term operational cost savings and better performance.

Awareness and Skills

- Staff and volunteers of OCA/SOCOG/ORTA are capable of using planning, system and project management, waste management and transportation management skills on future projects and in future jobs.

- Designers, contractors, tradespeople are capable of using newly acquired sustainable design skills to competitive advantage and offering clients improved performance and long-term savings on buildings.

- Regulatory bodies and public planning agencies are capable of applying the planning tools/lessons of Sydney 2000 to future developments and using flexible regulatory approaches to achieve more sustainable results at less cost.

- Sponsors and suppliers are capable of offering more sustainable products and services to future clients/customers, to gain competitive advantage and to improve public image.

- Environmental groups are capable of offering constructive input to developments of all types, based on the lessons of Sydney 2000.

- The business community and the environment industry are capable of selling to wider domestic and international markets those products and services that contributed to the successes of Sydney 2000.

- Sports federations, clubs, and governing bodies are capable of adapting and adopting the practices and tools used in Sydney to the management of future sports events, the operation of sport/recreation clubs and bidding procedures for future hosts.

- The general public is capable of adopting some of the lessons and products successfully demonstrated by the Olympics for use in both the home and workplace.

Conclusion

While it is still be too early to make definitive conclusions about the success of the Sydney 2000 sustainable development efforts, it is clear that much was achieved and many valuable lessons were learned. Many of the Sydney 2000 lessons, skills and knowledge can be, and indeed already are being, applied to new projects, be they urban development, transportation, events or residential housing.

Chapter

13

Conclusion

The Sustainable Sport Organization: Taking the Initiative

Globalization and the Internet — like them or not — have resulted in an increasingly informed and demanding public. Around the world, in big cities and small towns, the public's level of knowledge about social, environmental and economic issues is growing and will continue to do so. With greater knowledge, come greater expectations. People want to know how public and private institutions in their community, region (and even on their planet!) are responding to concerns about social issues, like working conditions, health conditions and the right to free speech; about environmental issues, both local and global; and about economic issues, like fair wages and disparity in living standards. People want to see a commitment, matched by concrete action, to more responsible behavior and practices. They are demanding greater responsibility and accountability.

Some sport organizations will be more accustomed to this level of expectation and scrutiny than others. And some — mostly the largest organizations, with the greatest public visibility — will feel the spotlight shone on them more frequently and with greater intensity in the future. But all, for the reasons explored in this book, will want to anticipate and prepare for the growing demands and expectations that this new century appears certain to bring.

Your organization can best prepare by adopting the approach we have termed sustainable sport. That will mean monitoring social, economic and environmental trends, and anticipating new demands and expectations. More than that, however, it will mean taking the initiative by adopting and promoting a commitment to the pursuit of greater sustainability, matched by appropriate and effective management systems, practices and results.

Sustainability is a Triathlon

Throughout this book, you will have learned of sport organizations large and small, which have begun this journey towards sustainability. None are where they want to be yet, and some are just taking their first steps. Some are looking first at environmental concerns; others are focusing first on social issues. Most, however, have reached the inevitable conclusion that sustainability is a three-legged stool — if you want the stool to stand up, it is better to build it with all three legs at once. Or, to use a sports metaphor, sustainability is a triathlon. If you want to be a winner, you need to be good at all three disciplines. Even the best runner in the world needs to know how to swim and cycle well to finish strongly in the race. And training done in each discipline will inevitably lead to improvement in the others, as well as overall.

So, the triathlete company, facility or event manager will be working to improve environmental, social and economic practices as a package. In doing so — if the lessons of others we have examined are generally applicable — that manager will find that steps taken to improve environmental performance, when adopted as part of an overall sustainability strategy, will have the additional effect of improving social and economic performance as well.

Will it be easy to adopt and integrate a sustainable sport approach? Not likely, and it would be irresponsible of us to suggest otherwise. You will need to adopt the same approach as that triathlete. Improvements and success will be gradual rather than instant, and the result of persistence and dedication. They may even involve some pain. But you can take the occasional day off to rest and recharge!

Of those organizations that have taken this road, what has been their experience?

Lessons from Sustainable Sport's Forerunners

Sydney 2000 took the boldest possible approach, announcing far-reaching intentions to pursue sustainable development in all aspects of planning, construction and operations — and paid the price: very high public expectations. Subject to the most intense scrutiny imaginable — a sign of public and professional interest, as well as local and international concerns — the legacy for the city, for the region and for the "cause" of promoting sustainable development has been a positive one overall.

That Sydney 2000 achieved or partially achieved most of its goals is remarkable. Notable benefits of the Games include such "bricks and mortar" accomplishments as rehabilitated sites, facilities that use relatively little energy and water, and successful integration of sustainable design features, innovative materials and renewable energy systems. Arguably even more important is the contribution of the Games to the spread of awareness and knowledge among a range of professional and tradespeople, suppliers, regulators and the public. This knowledge has been underscored by a wealth of practical experience gained and retained by many of the hands-on participants in planning, construction and operations.

But Sydney 2000 encountered plenty of challenges and obstacles. Organizers attempting to implement the ambitious commitments had to deal with time constraints, price premiums, regulatory delays, technical challenges, unfamiliarity with new processes and materials, high expectations of interest groups, critical media coverage and more.

General Sustainable Development Lessons from Sydney 2000

- It is possible to use the principles of sustainable development as the guiding force behind a major development project.

- Lack of a full "blueprint" of sustainable development need not stand in the way of taking this approach, or of realising many benefits.

- A commitment to sustainable development should be made publicly, in writing.

- This public commitment should have full political and/or top management support, and, where appropriate, legal status.

- Committing to sustainable development at the earliest possible point in a project encourages lower costs and maximum benefits.

- High-level and consistent consultation is essential from the beginning.

- Commitments should be made in the most clear and definitive terms possible, using best practice as benchmarks.

- "Brownfield" sites can be appropriately and safely redeveloped.

- It is possible to regenerate degraded sites, and to have a net positive effect.

- The competitive process can be harnessed using an environmental tendering system to deliver a very high level of environmental result.

- Resource and material savings can be best achieved early in the design process.

- Suppliers, sponsors, contractors etc. should be encouraged to become active partners.

- Education and awareness initiatives are essential to communicate the purpose, objectives and achievements of any sustainable development initiatives. People within the implementing organization, as well as partners, regulators, critics and the general public should all be targeted by education/awareness programs.

Although few, if any, other organizations will be presented with challenges and opportunities on the scale of an Olympic Games, the lessons and insights Sydney 2000 have provided are remarkably transferable, and reflect the experiences of managers of smaller events, facilities and organizations. What have we concluded from Sydney 2000, recognizing of course that only time will tell the full story? Some of Sydney's more transferable and universally applicable lessons are outlined below.

As useful and transferable as Sydney 2000's lessons may be, much can also be learned from the experiences of some very different types of sport organizations.

Several sports that earned and suffer(ed) from a negative environmental reputation can teach us a great deal about the best and worst ways of facing their challenges. Golf and alpine skiing have been assailed by critics for the generally poor environmental practices of many developers and operators. The industries' first response was to deny or minimize the problem. When this strategy did nothing to alleviate concerns, a more progressive approach was tried. Several golf and ski associations, as well some individual developers, operators and clubs have worked hard to develop relationships with two key groups: government regulators and public interest groups (both community and environmental). Multi-stakeholder partnerships nurtured by both the golf and ski industries in the United States and Europe in the late 1990s have produced voluntary charters and principles/guidelines. In some cases, offshoot organizations such as the Committed to Green Foundation have developed programs incorporating technical guidance, certification, and education. Many other sports and sport organizations would do well to study and adapt such partnership approaches to their own situation.

The very progressive Aspen Skiing Company, a true forerunner in its industry, has learned that dialogue with and input from outside stakeholders is invaluable in avoiding costly delays and bad (read unsustainable) decisions. Even better, input from stakeholder committees can sometimes lead to improved business decisions and profitability.

The experience of smaller organizations, be they event organizers or facility operators is equally informative, and probably the most replicable by thousands of similar groups around the world. Like the organizers of the 1999 Canada Winter Games in Corner Brook, Newfoundland, groups with little or no "environmental" budget are using innovative thinking to accomplish great things. Again partnership is a key concept: working with local authorities, sponsors and suppliers, smaller sport organizations are creating programs and answering needs in ways that benefit all parties involved.

Benefits that Can't be Denied

In this vast and multi-faceted industry we call sport, what can we conclude about the types of benefits you might expect from the pursuit of sustainability? Though each case is unique, and each organization will have its own set of priorities, the list of potential but proven benefits to the sustainable sport organization include:

- lower capital costs through avoiding unnecessary materials and systems;
- fewer regulatory obstacles and faster approvals for construction/renovation;
- lower operating costs through energy and water conservation;
- lower waste management costs by reducing the quantity and types of material inputs and by making outputs a source of revenue;
- increased business opportunities by attracting new users/members/customers;

◆ higher rates of user/member/customer retention;

◆ lower insurance and workers compensation premiums by reducing or eliminating risky products and practices;

◆ fewer accidents, leading to lower staff absenteeism;

◆ higher staff morale as a result of improved working conditions, leading to higher productivity, less absenteeism and improved staff retention;

◆ greater staff/volunteer satisfaction from working in an organization that is progressive and which values their health and encourages their ideas;

◆ valuable and sometimes profitable ideas from stakeholder groups;

◆ a positive public reputation/image leading to better publicity and increased sponsorship opportunities; and

◆ a healthier, more supportive neighboring community.

Trends and Predictions

With so many potential benefits at stake, what signs do we see of a growing trend toward sustainable sports management and what developments might we expect to observe?

The IOC has adopted an Agenda 21 for the Olympic Movement, which sets out a general program to spread the principles and practices of sustainable development, throughout sports organizations and through sports organizations to all member countries.

The Olympic bid process increasingly emphasizes environmental and social concerns. More and more bid cities are responding with urban redevelopment plans that incorporate many aspects of sustainability, going well beyond environmental protection and into site remediation, transportation strategies, air and water quality initiatives, low-income housing and more.

Sports that rely heavily on the natural environment for their appeal are becoming active in multi-stakeholder initiatives to protect and even restore that environment. Examples include golf clubs promoting biodiversity, mountain biking clubs actively organizing trail maintenance and user education programs and ski resorts tackling the range of challenges associated with fragile alpine environments and working to reduce their ecological footprint. More and more sports governing bodies are and should be developing their own sustainability charters and associated guidelines, practices, partnership programs and restoration projects.

High and unpredictable energy costs combined with public commitments to reduce greenhouse gas emissions are putting ever-greater pressure on facility developers and operators to build more resource-efficient facilities. Clever design that maximizes natural light and ventilation and combines efficient technology with computerized controls can be found in a growing number of facilities. In the future, clients will demand expertise in this area from design and construction professionals.

Water scarcity is a growing issue in many regions, and one that will likely become critical in this decade. Some designers are showcasing innovative responses in the design of both large and small sport facilities. Interesting responses showcased in Sydney — including efficient systems, rainwater capture and graywater recycling — are becoming more common and will have to become the norm for a sustainable facility. Those with experience in water conservation will have a competitive advantage, if they don't already.

Comprehensive waste reduction and waste management systems are being put in place by many public events, sport or otherwise. Recognizing a business opportunity, some specialists in this area are actively targeting major events and facilities that regularly host large crowds. Done well, the service provider, the event/facility and the local community can all benefit from such a sustainable business arrangement.

Sporting goods manufacturers and retailers are recognizing the need and opportunity to be more sustainable. That "need" is driven by internal efficiency opportunities, growing regulatory pressures and tougher consumer expectations. Nike is devoting enormous energy to defining and integrating sustainability. Mizuno and Adidas are taking the environmental management systems route, including factory certification under ISO 14001. Patagonia has recognized the unsustainability of a business plan based on perpetual growth and is pioneering a new model of business sustainability. Mountain Equipment Co-op in Canada is enforcing strong social and environmental criteria throughout its supply chain, and is leading by example in the renovation and construction of its stores.

For all sport organizations, accountability and transparency will become increasingly important in the years ahead. The sustainability initiatives of any one organization or of the sport sector as a whole must include a commitment to open and full public reporting if they are to be viewed as genuine by an increasingly-cynical public. Sport may still be viewed as a "good thing" on the whole, but the wider public will be expecting high standards from the industry. Sport organizations have no legitimate excuses for ignoring broader social and environmental issues. A vital challenge is therefore first to adopt sustainability measures and second to ensure that they are effectively communicated to and understood by all stakeholders.

Bodies such as the International Olympic Committee have made a bold start, but they are just beginning to appreciate the magnitude of the challenge ahead. Such a leadership role may be uncomfortable, but it has to be accepted. It's ultimate success will depend on support from key stakeholder groups both within and external to the sport industry.

The list of more responsible and more sustainable sport organizations continues to grow. By doing so, it helps to underscore the already strong argument for and validation of this management approach. With so many benefits for the taking, any progressive sports manager and decision maker should be looking closely at how his or her organization can join that impressive list.

The race to sustainability will be a more a long-distance event than a sprint. If your sport organization is looking to come out on top, you would do well to begin, or continue, developing the skills of the sustainability triathlete — building and integrating your economic, social and environmental strengths as a means to improving your triple bottom line.

Bibliography

Active Living — Go for Green. 1996. Developing communities for active transportation. Ottawa, ON: Health Canada.

Active Living — Go for Green. 1996b. Retrofitting communities for sustainable and healthy active transportation. Ottawa, ON: Health Canada.

Alexander, O. 1973. Social accounting if you please. Canadian Chartered Accountant January 73: 22-33.

Ander, G. 1995. Daylighting performance and design. John Wiley and Sons.

Atkinson, G. 1997. "Air Pollution and Exercise" Sports Exercise and Injury. V 3 : 2 -8

Audubon International. 1996. A guide to environmental stewardship on the golf course — Audubon cooperative sanctuary system. Selkirk, NY: Author.

Auf der Maur, N. 1976. The billion-dollar game — Jean Drapeau and the 1976 Olympics. Toronto: James Lorimer & Company.

Auf der Maur, N. 1990. Quebeckers are still paying for the '76 Olympics. Globe and Mail (June 9): D2.

Australian Golf Union. 1998. Environmental strategy for Australian golf courses. Melbourne.

Balogh, J. and W. Walker, eds. Golf course management and construction: environmental issues.

Bascom R. et al. 1996. "Health Effects of Outdoor Air Pollution" American Journal of Respiratory and Critical Care Medicine. 153 (2). 477 - 498

Bearg, D. Indoor air quality and HVAC systems. Lewis Publishers/CRC Press.

Bryson, L. 1990. Sports, drugs and the development of modern capitalism. Sporting Traditions.

Cable, T. and E. Udd. 1990. Endangered outdoor recreation experiences: Contextual development and lexicon. Liesure Studies 9: 48.

Canadian Parks and Recreation Association. 1992. The benefits of parks and recreation. Ottawa: Author. p 76.

Canadian Parks and Recreation Association. 1997. The benefits catalogue. Ottawa: Author.

Carson, R. 1962. Silent spring. New York: Fawcett Crest.

Centre for Disease Control. 1998. Update: Leptospirosis and Unexplained Acute Fibrile Illnesses Among Athletes Participating in Triathlons — Illinois and Wisconsin, 1998. Taken from CDC Web site (**www.cdc.gov/epo/mmwr/preview/mmwrhtml/0005439**) on 21/01/2001.

Chernushenko, David. 1994. Greening our games: Running sports events and facilities that won't cost the earth. Ottawa: Green & Gold Inc.

Ciambrone; David F., 1995. Waste minimization as a strategic weapon. CRC.

Colborn, T., D. Dumanoski and J. P. Myers. 1996. Our stolen future. New York. Penguin Books.

Commission Internationale pour la Protection des Alpes. 1998. Les grande manifestations de sports d'hiver dans les Alpes. Author.

Creighton, Sarah Hammond.1998. Greening the ivory tower: Improving the environmental track record of universities, colleges and other institutions. Cambridge, Mass: MIT Press.

Crognale, D.,P.E. 1999. Environmental management strategies: The 21st century perspective. Prentice Hall Professional Technical Reference.

Cutter Information Corporation. 1997. 1996 Energy Products Directory: The sourcebook for commercial buildings, 3rd ed. Author.

Digel, H. Dr. 1992. Sports in a risk society. International Review for the Sociology of Sport 27 (3): 261.

Dodson, R. Managing wildlife habitat on golf courses. Chelsea, Michigan: Ann Arbor Press.

Dunlop, R. E. and R. B. Heffernan. 1986. In Jackson, E. L. 1986. Outdoor recreation participation and attitudes to the environment. Leisure Studies (January): 2-3.

Earth Council. 2001. Environmental performance of the Olympic co-ordination authority: Fourth and final review. Sydney: Olympic Co-ordination Authority.

Elkington, J. 1998. Cannibals with forks: The triple bottom line of 21st century business. Gabriola Island: New Society Publishers.

Environment Australia. 2000. Greening the Games: Australia creating sustainable solutions for a new Millennium. Canberra: Author.

Environment Canada. 1992. Working your way to a green office. Ottawa, ON: Author.

European Golf Association Ecology Unit. 1995. Environmental guidelines for golf course development in Europe: Revised edition. European Golf Association.

European Golf Association Ecology Unit. 1996. An environmental management programme for golf courses. Pisces Publications.

European Golf Association Ecology Unit. 1997. The committed to green handbook for golf courses. Pisces Publications.

Fahrenkamp, S. and A. Ferre. 1991. Dirty laundry in the national park: A pollution prevention project. Jackson, WY: S.A.F.E. Consulting for the Earth.

Federation of Canadian Municipalities. 1993. The Packaging Waste Reduction Guide: Minimizing solid waste through efficient procurement practices. Ottawa: Author

Fisheries and Oceans, Department of the Environment, and FRAP. 1996. Greening your B.C. golf course: A guide to environmental management. Author.

Frankel, C. 1998. In Earth's company: Business, environment and the challenge of sustainability. Gabriola Island: New Society Publishers

Friedman, M.S. et al. 2001. "Impact of Changes in Transportation and Commuting Behaviors During the 1996 Summer Olympic Games in Atlanta on Air Quality and Childhood Asthma" Journal of American Medication Association. 285:897 - 905

Global Environmental Management Initiative. 1992. Total quality environmental management primer. Washington: GEMI.

Globe and Mail Editorial. 1992. Employment and the environment create a delicate balance. Globe and Mail (Feb 12): E6.

Goldberger, D., and P. Jessup. eds. 1993. Profitting from energy efficiency! A financing handbook for municipalities. Toronto, ON: International Council for Local Environmental Initiatives.

Gong Jr., H. 1987. Effects of ozone on exercise performance. Journal of Sports Medicine 27: 22.

Gong, H. and S. Krishnareddy. 1995. "How pollution and airborne allergens affect exercise" The Physician and Sports Medicine. 23 (7) July

Green Games Watch 2000. 2000. After the Games: ongoing ecologically sustainable development management at Homebush Bay and other Sydney Olympic venues. Sydney: Author.

Greenpeace. August 2000. Greenpeace Olympics report card: one month to go. Sydney: Author.

Greenpeace. 2000. How green the Games? Greenpeace's environmental assessment of the Sydney 2000 Olympics. Sydney: Author.

Greenpeace. 2000. Greenpeace Olympic environmental guidelines: a guide to sustainable events. Sydney: Author.

Hall, A. and D. Richardson. 1982. Fair ball. In Sport: The way ahead. Ottawa: Minister of Supply and Services Canada.

Harmony Foundation of Canada. 1991. Workplace Guide: Practical action for the environment. Ottawa, ON: Author. p 72.

Hart, Stuart L. 1997. Beyond greening: Strategies for a sustainable world. Harvard Business Review, January-February 1997.

Hastings, S., and International Energy Agency, eds. 1994. Passive solar commercial & institutional buildings: A sourcebook of examples and design insights. John Wiley and Sons.

Haugsjaa, S. and E. B. Stromo. 1993. From challenges to opportunities. Olympic Message 35.

Hawken, P. 1993. The ecology of commerce. New York: HarpersCollins.

Hawken, P., A. Lovins and L. Lovins, 1999. Natural Capitalism: Creating the next industrial revolution. Little Brown and Company.

Haymes, E. and C. Wells. 1986. Environment and human performance. Champaign, IL: Human Kinetics. pp. 99 -115.

Henley, T. 1989. Rediscovery: A guidebook to outdoor education. Vancouver: Western Canadian Wilderness Committee.

Hummel, N. 1998. Improving Playing Fields with Compost. BioCycle April: 62-64.

Immig, J., S. Risch and Brown (1998). Indoor air quality guidelines for Sydney Olympic facilities. BCE Technical Report 97/3. East Melbourne, Australia: CSIRO Publishing.

International Chamber of Commerce (ICC). 1991. The ICC guide to effective environmental auditing. Paris: ICC.

International Institute for Sustainable Development. 1992. Business strategy for sustainable development: Leadership and accountability for the 90's. Winnipeg, MB: Author.

International Olympic Committee. 2000. Agenda 21 for Sport. Lausanne:Author.

International Olympic Committee. 1997. Manual on Sport and the Environment. Lausanne: Author.

Koch, A. 1998. Development of environmental performance indicators for European golf clubs. Thesis for Master of Science in Environmental Management and Policy. International Institute for Industrial Environmental Economics, Lund, Sweden.

Korrick, S. et al. 1998. "Effects of Ozone and Other pollutants on the pulmonary function of Adult Hikers" Environmental Health Perspectives. 106 (2) Feb

Kross, B.C. et al. 1996. "Golf Course Superintendents Face Higher Cancer Rates" American Journal of Industrial Medicine. 29(5): 501-506

Jackson, E.L. 1986. Outdoor recreation participation and attitudes to the environment. Leisure Studies (January): 2-3.

Lawson, B. 1996. Building materials, energy and the environment: Towards ecologically sustainable development. Royal Australian Institute of Architects.

Leuzinger, P. 1998. The 1998 Environmental Stewards Awards. Golf Course Management February: 22-88

Levin, H., ed. Indoor air bulletin: Technology, research and news for indoor environmental quality. Indoor Air Information Service.

Lillehammer Olympic Organizing Committee. 1993. From challenge to opportunities. Unpublished document. Author.

Lobmeyer, Dr. H. and Dr. H. Lutter. 1990. The incorporation of environmental education in school sports. International Journal of Physical Education 27 (3): 20-27.

Lopez Barnett, D. and W. Browning. 1995. A primer on sustainable building. Rocky Mountain Institute.

Louria, D. 1996. Solving the energy dilemma at Seven Bridges Ice Arena. ASHRAE Journal August: 67- 70.

Ludwig, A. 1997. Builder's greywater guide: Installation of greywater systems in new construction and remodelling. Oasis Design.

Lyons, Kevin. 1999. Buying for the future: Contract management and the environmental challenge. London, UK: Pluto Press.

Marcotte and Laroche. 1991. Coaching: A profession in the making. S.P.O.R.T.S. 11 (8).

McDonnell W. et. al. 1995. "Proportion of Moderately exercising individuals responding to low level multi hour ozone exposure" American Journal of Respiratory and Critical Care Medicine. 152: 589 - 596

Miller, N., ed. 1995. The healthy school handbook: Conquering the sick building syndrome and other environmental hazards in and around your school. National Education Association.

Minister's Task Force on Federal Sport Policy. 1992. Sport: The way ahead. Ottawa: Minister of Supply and Services Canada.

Morita, G. 1994. Toxic green — the trouble with golf. Worldwatch 7 (3): 32.

Moxen, John; Strachan, Peter A. (eds.) 1998. Managing green.teams: Environmental change in organizations and networks. Sheffield, UK: Greenleaf Publishing.

Mulligan, W. 1992. Business strategy for sustainable development: Leadership and accountability for the 90's. Winnipeg: International Institute for Sustainable Development.

Mumma, T. 1997. Guide to resource efficient building elements, 6th ed. Center for Resourceful Building Technology.

National Roundtable on Environment and Economics. 1991. Decision making practices for sustainable development. Ottawa: Author.

Nattrass, B. and M. Altomare. 1999. The natural step for business. New Society Publishers.

Nature Conservancy Council. On course conservation — Managing golf's natural heritage. Author.

Noble, Duncan. 2001. Cool business guide: Lower costs, higher productivity and climate change solutions. Drayton Valley: Pembina Institute for Appropriate Development.

Olympic Co-ordination Authority. 1996a. Environmental tender specifications: A guide for specification, brief and contract writers. Sydney, NSW: Author.

Olympic Co-ordination Authority. 1996b. Meeting environmental requirements: Environmental tendering requirements for Olympic Games projects and development at Homebush Bay. Sydney, NSW: Author.

Olympic Co-ordination Authority. 1999. Compendium of ESD initiatives and outcomes for OCA facilities and venues: Edition 2. Sydney, NSW: Author.

Olympic Co-ordination Authority. 2000. Environment Report – 1999. Sydney, NSW: Author.

Olympic Environment Forum. 2001. Sydney 2000 Olympic and Paralympic Games Environmental Benchmarks.

Pennsylvania Dept. of Environmental Protection, Guidelines for Creating High-Performance Green Buildings, 1999

Pierson, W. et al. 1986. Implications of air pollution effects on athletic performance. Medicine and Science in Sport and Exercise 18 (3):323.

Puhalla, Jim et al. 1999. Sports Fields: A manual for design, construction and maintenance of sports fields. Ann Arbor Press.

Romm, Joseph J. 1999. Cool companies: How the best businesses boost profits and productivity by cutting greenhouse gas emissions. Island Press.

Royal and Ancient Golf Club of St. Andrews and the European Golf Association. 1997. A course for all seasons — A guide to course management. Author.

Royal and Ancient Golf Club of St Andrews. 2000. On course for change – tackling the challenges facing golf in the first decade of the new millennium. Conference Report. R&A, St Andrews.

Royal Canadian Golf Association. 1993. Environmentally responsible golf — Environmental guidelines for Canadian golf clubs. Author.

Russel, Trevor. 1998. Greener Purchasing: Opportunities and Innovations. Greenleaf Publishing.

Salt Lake Olympic Organizing Committee. 1997. Environmental Report 1997. Salt Lake City:

Salt Lake Olympic Organizing Committee. 2000. Environmental Annual Report 2000. Salt Lake City:

Scherff, J. 1993. Eco-health: Athletes and pollution. Buzzworm: The Environmental Journal (July/August):24-5.

Scottish Golf Course Wildlife Group. 1997. Golf's natural heritage: An introduction to environmental stewardship on the golf course (revised edition). Scottish Golf Course Wildlife Group.

Scottish Natural Heritage and Scottish Golf Course Wildlife Group. 2000. Nature conservation and golf course development: Best practice advice.

Shea, C.P. 1988. Protecting life on earth: Steps to save the ozone layer (Worldwatch Paper 87). Washington, DC: Worldwatch Institute.

Skiing (November) 1991. Editorial.

Smith, G. 1998. Pool power. Athletic Business. December: 85-88.

Sport Canada. 1999. Environmental management and monitoring for sports events and facilities. Ottawa, ON: Green & Gold Inc.

Steven Winter Associates. 1998. The passive solar design and construction handbook. John Wiley and Sons.

Strain, L. Resourceful specifications: Guideline specifications for environmentally considered building materials and construction methods. Siegel & Strain Architects.

Storms, W. and D. Joyner. 1997. "Update on exercise induced asthma" The Physician and Sport Medicine. 25 (3) March

Stubbs, D. 2001. Sydney Olympic Games 2000: The environmental games — A review of the environmental achievements of the "best Olympic Games ever." Dorking, UK: Committed to Green Foundation.

Stubbs, D. and D. Chernushenko. 1999. Environmental guidelines for golf events. Dorking, UK: European Golf Association Ecology Unit.

Suozzo, M. et al. 1997. Guide to energy-efficient commercial equipment. American Council for an Energy-Efficient Economy.

Sydney Organising Committee for the Olympic Games. 1995. Environmental guidelines. Sydney: Author.

Sydney Organising Committee for the Olympic Games. 1998. The Sydney 2000 Olympic Games Integrated Waste Management Solution. Sydney: Author.

Sydney Organising Committee for the Olympic Games. 1999. Environment report: Turning green into gold – making an environmental vision a reality

Sydney 2000. September 2000. The environmental games: Environmental achievements of the Sydney 2000 Olympic Games (colour brochure and CD).

Thompson, G. and F. Steiner, eds. 1997. Ecological design and planning. John Wiley and Sons.

Tibor, T. and I. Feldman. 1995 ISO14000: A guide to the new environmental management standards. Chicago: Irwin Professional Publishing.

Tiner, T. 1991. Green space or green waste. Seasons: (Summer): 16-37.

Tuluca, A. Energy-efficient design and construction of commercial buildings. McGraw-Hill Publications.

United Nations Environment Programme. 1990. One planet: Volume 2. Author.

United States Golf Association. 1994. Wastewater reuse for golf course irrigation. Lewis Publishers.

United States Golf Association, et. Al. 1996. Environmental principles for golf courses in the United States.

Vickers, A. 1998. Handbook of water use and conservation. Lewis Publishers/CRC Press.

Vuolle, P. 1991. Nature and environments for physical activity. InSport for All edited by P. Oja and R. Telama. Elsevier. p 598.

Weisacker, E. von, A. B. Lovins and L.H. Lovins. 1997. Factor four: Doubling resource wealth — halving resource use: The new report to the Club of Rome. Sydney: Allen & Unwin.

Wilson, A. and N. Malin, eds. Environmental building news: A monthly newsletter on environmentally responsible design and construction. E Build.

World Commission on Environment and Development. 1987. Our common future. Oxford: Oxford University Press. p 43.

World Industry Council for the Environment. 1994. Environmental reporting: A manager's guide. Paris: WICE.

Worldwatch Institute. 1994. Toxic green — the trouble with golf. Worldwatch Magazine 7 (3): 29.

Index

About the Authors

David Chernushenko

David Chernushenko is president of Green & Gold Inc., sustainability advisors to the sport, recreation and tourism industries. He is author of Greening Our Games: Running Sports Events and Facilities That Won't Cost the Earth (1994). Since 1999, David has served as a member of the IOC's Commission on Sport and Environment. From 1996-2001, David steered the Earth Council's series of reviews of the Sydney 2000 Olympic Co-ordination Authority's environmental performance. David advises governing bodies, event organizing committees and bidding groups on environmental management, green building and purchasing issues. He lives in Ottawa, Canada.

David can be contacted at **david@greengold.on.ca**

Anna van der Kamp

Anna van der Kamp is project director for Green & Gold Inc. Anna was a silver medallist at the 1996 Olympics in rowing as a member of Canada's women's eight, and was a member of the National Rowing Team for several years. Anna is a graduate of the University of Victoria in geography and environmental studies. During the Sydney Olympic Games Anna served as a volunteer member of the Venue Environmental Management team. She lives in Ottawa.

Anna can be contacted at **anna@greengold.on.ca**

David Stubbs

David Stubbs is a conservation biologist with over twelve years experience working in the sport sector, specializing in the environmental aspects of golf courses. From 1994-1999 he was Executive Director of the European Golf Association Ecology Unit and in this capacity he was responsible for developing the Committed to Green program. He is currently manager of the Committed to Green Foundation and the sport sector adviser to Global Responsibility. In 2000 he worked for two months as a volunteer Venue Environment Manager at the Sydney Olympic Games. He lives in Surrey, England.

David can be contacted at **david.stubbs@dial.pipex.com**

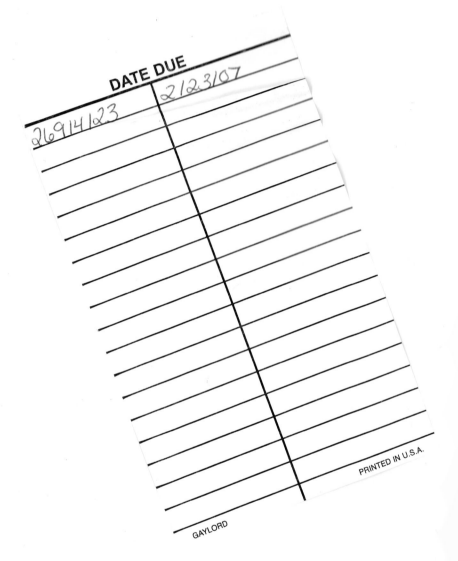

DATE DUE

2/23/07

26914123

GAYLORD   PRINTED IN U.S.A.